Transnational
Organized Crime

Transnational Organized Crime

An Overview from Six Continents

Jay Albanese
Virginia Commonwealth University, USA

Philip Reichel
University of Northern Colorado, USA

Los Angeles | London | New Delhi
Singapore | Washington DC

Los Angeles | London | New Delhi
Singapore | Washington DC

FOR INFORMATION:

SAGE Publications, Inc.
2455 Teller Road
Thousand Oaks, California 91320
E-mail: order@sagepub.com

SAGE Publications Ltd.
1 Oliver's Yard
55 City Road
London EC1Y 1SP
United Kingdom

SAGE Publications India Pvt. Ltd.
B 1/I 1 Mohan Cooperative Industrial Area
Mathura Road, New Delhi 110 044
India

SAGE Publications Asia-Pacific Pte. Ltd.
3 Church Street
#10-04 Samsung Hub
Singapore 049483

Executive Editor: Jerry Westby
Publisher Associate: MaryAnn Vail
Marketing Manager: Terra Schultz
Permissions Editor: Jennifer Barron
Project Editors: Amy Schroller and
          Veronica Stapleton Hooper
Copy Editor: Linda Gray
Typesetter: C&M Digitals (P) Ltd.
Proofreader: Wendy Jo Dymond
Indexer: Jean Casalegno
Cover Designer: Anupama Krishnan

Copyright © 2014 by SAGE Publications, Inc.

Printed in the United States of America

Transnational organized crime : an overview from six continents / [edited by] Jay S. Albanese, Virginia Commonwealth University, USA, Philip L. Reichel, University of Northern Colorado, USA.

pages cm
Includes bibliographical references and index.

ISBN 978-1-4522-9007-2

1. Transnational crime. 2. Organized crime. I. Albanese, Jay S. II. Reichel, Philip L.

HV6252.T7325 2014
364.106—dc23   2013015490

This book is printed on acid-free paper.

13 14 15 16 17 10 9 8 7 6 5 4 3 2 1

Contents

Introduction

Transnational organized crime characterizes the 21st century in the same way that traditional street crimes characterized the 20th century. The provision of illicit goods and services and the infiltration of business and government have become the major problems of the modern age of globalization, technology, international travel and communications, multinational migration and business, and their downsides: smuggling, trafficking, laundering, and corruption.

This book contributes to our understanding of these global trends by examining transnational organized crime from the perspectives of the world's six inhabited continents: North America, Central and South America, Europe, Africa, Asia, and Oceania. It also includes a final chapter that addresses the overlaps between transnational organized crime and terrorism. Each chapter is written by authors who are either native to each world region or who have extensively traveled and worked there. In addition, the contributors to this book possess recognized expertise through their research and writing on organized crime issues and their transnational manifestations.

Therefore, this book provides a unique overview of transnational organized crime in each continental region of the world. It offers students and researchers a perspective that is often lacking in contemporary writing on this issue: a regional perspective by authors having expertise both in the field and also in the region.

Organized crime has been defined through a consensus of scholars as continuing criminal enterprises that rationally work to profit from illicit activities that are often in great public demand. Its continuing existence is maintained through the use of force, threats, monopoly control, and/or the corruption of public officials (Albanese, 2011). But how large a problem is organized crime on a global scale?

Several organizations have attempted define and quantify what the world's largest problems are. The Arlington Institute (2012) identified the five largest world problems as follows:

- Economic collapse: Will a fragile current global economy tip the world into depression?
- Peak oil: Petroleum has powered the world for 100 years; have we reached a peak in oil production?
- Global water crisis: Over the last 50 years, the world population has tripled, but pollution, bad agricultural practices, and poor civic planning have decreased the water supply.
- Species extinction: Certain species that we depend upon for food are going extinct—impacting our own survivability.
- Rapid climate change: Global warming is an empirical fact. Will people from different cultures work together to reduce global warming or will they suffer from it?

In a related way, the U.N. Millennium Development goals identified serious challenges for attention as including ending poverty and hunger, universal education, gender equality, child health, maternal health, combating HIV/AIDS, environmental sustainability, and global partnership (U.N. Office on Drugs and Crime, 2011; U.N. Habitat, 2011).

Two common features are apparent when you consider these serious international issues. First, they are all either entirely manmade, or they have been pushed to a crisis point by decisions of humans. In addition, these decisions appear to be the result of some combination of ignorance, selfishness, criminality, and corruption. To the extent that the problems also reflect opportunities for criminal enterprises to profit from illicit activities linked to those problems, an argument can certainly be made that organized crime and corruption play an important role in their exacerbation.

These largest world problems range from health to environment to social instability to civil conflict—all of which are either created or worsened by organized crime and corruption. The issue addressed in this book is crucial: More effective control of organized crime and corruption would reduce many other significant world problems!

The chapter contributions to this book are noteworthy in several ways. The opening chapter by Jan van Dijk and Toine Spapens examines the global trend away from established organized crime "groups" toward organized crime "networks,'" which are more loosely formed and more difficult to defeat. This chapter also offers a quantitative analysis of the extent of organized crime in different world regions and how its extent is associated with the quality of the institutions responsible for the rule of law in these countries. It provides a useful framework for understanding the local nature of much organized crime and how its reach is enhanced in a globalized world.

Chapter 2 reviews organized crime in North America, including Canada, Mexico, and the United States. This assessment by James O. Finckenauer and Jay S. Albanese describes several major known organized crime threats, which are presented in terms of their nature and extent and the law enforcement response. The economic disparities between Canada and the United States on one hand, and Mexico on the other, create a lucrative supply-and-demand environment, and the land and water access facilitates trafficking routes for illicit goods and services and human smuggling. The influence of the Mexican drug cartels in cross-border trafficking is discussed.

Chapter 3 on transnational organized crime in Latin America by Mary Fran T. Malone and Christine B. Malone-Rowe provides a compelling overview of the organized crime issues and their context in a number of Central and South American countries. Excellent use is made of timely source material to place organized crime in this region in the context of the institutional weakness of countries, the role of political and economic elites, and geography.

Chapter 4 by Klaus von Lampe addresses transnational organized crime in Europe. This review provides an up-to-date summary of transnational organized crime both within and also extending outside Europe. Excellent use of source material explains contemporary research on the issues of transnational organized crimes, the offenders, and their environment. A patchwork of trafficking routes and crime hotspots are found in Europe, involving criminals of different ethnic and national backgrounds, forming networks and groups of varying degrees of sophistication.

Chapter 5 describes organized crime in Africa. Mark Shaw presents a well-documented account of what (little) we know about the African continent in terms of organized crime and how the dramatic changes on the continent are affecting organized crime throughout the region. The overlapping threats of state fragility/failure, organized crime, and corruption are explained clearly, and differences within the continent are noted. Recent data and research are cited throughout this African overview.

In Chapter 6 on transnational organized crime in Asia and the Middle East, Richard H. Ward and Daniel J. Mabrey cover a vast geographic area.

The 21st century has marked both growth in organized crime and a greater emphasis on new forms and new adaptations of technology that foster cross-border and international crime. The emergence of China as a global economic power has also had consequences on a government coping with major changes in crime and corruption. For many of the developing economies of Asia, organized crime continues to be a troubling issue, characterized by corruption, unstable or weak governments, and corruption in the boardrooms and offices of international corporations. In the Middle East, where the so-called Arab Spring has brought down governments, organized crime has flourished as justice systems and law enforcement organizations have been overthrown or handicapped by coping with public disorder. In virtually all cases, organized crime in Asia and the Middle East has been evolutionary, adapting to changing political conditions, warfare, and the development of technology, communications, travel, and the emergence of a global economy.

Chapter 7, by Roderic Broadhurst, Mark Lauchs, and Sally Lohrisch, describes organized crime in Oceania, a large region of 25 countries that includes four geographical regions: Australia (including Norfolk Island) and New Zealand, Melanesia (Fiji, New Caledonia, Papua New Guinea, Solomon Islands, Vanuatu), Micronesia (Guam, Kiribati, Marshall Islands, Federated States of Micronesia, Nauru, Northern Mariana Islands, Palau), and Polynesia (American Samoa, Cook Islands, French Polynesia, Niue, Pitcairn, Samoa, Tokelau, Tonga, Tuvalu, Wallis and Futuna Islands). Drugs, migrant smuggling, human trafficking, weapons smuggling, financial crimes, cybercrime, and illegal fishing are each described in terms of their organized crime linkages.

Chapter 8, by Gus Martin, provides an assessment of how insurgent movements and terrorists have become wealthy customers and entrepreneurs in transnational organized crime. This chapter explains the convergence between illicit enterprise and asymmetrical insurgency in the modern world. It also examines the incentives that link the demand by revolutionary customers for the supply of materials that can be provided by transnational organized crime. A review of the convergence between some terrorist groups and specific organized crime activities is presented.

This book provides a useful supplement for courses on organized crime, transnational crime, and comparative criminal justice to address the global expansion of organized crime in a concise and understandable region-by-region assessment. The contemporary linkage between transnational organized crime and terrorism is also explained in a separate chapter. In this way, students can obtain exposure to both the similarities and differences in manifestations of organized crime around the world. In sum, this short book offers an interesting, unique, and valuable overview of transnational organized crime trends around the world, using the six inhabited continents as a reference point. In this way, readers can appreciate the geographic, cultural, and regional differences that underlie the common threat of transnational organized crime.

⚜ REFERENCES

Albanese, J. S. (2011). *Organized crime in our times* (6th ed.). Burlington, MA: Elsevier.

Arlington Institute. (2012). *The world's biggest problems.* Retrieved from http://www.arlingtoninstitute.org/wbp

U.N. Office on Drugs and Crime and U.N. Habitat. (2011). *Introductory handbook on policing urban space.* Retrieved from http://www.unodc.org/documents/justice-and-prison-reform/crimeprevention/11-80387_ebook.pdf

U.N. Habitat. (2011). *Building urban safety through slum upgrading.* Available at http://www.unhabitat.org/pmss/listItemDetails.aspx?publicationID=3222

1

Transnational Organized Crime Networks Across the World

Jan van Dijk and Toine Spapens

⚶ INTRODUCTION

This chapter discusses the network perspective on transnational organized crime (TOC). A distinct feature of transnational crime networks is
that they complete parts of the "criminal business processes" in different
countries. In the case of ecstasy, for example, the chain may involve
Dutch producers who procure precursor chemicals from China and
Germany, manufacture the pills in the Netherlands and Belgium, export
the product to Australia, and launder the money in the Virgin Islands.
Cross-border illegal activities require coordinated actions by individuals
and groups, sometimes from all over the world, sometimes just from
neighboring countries.

The network perspective on organized crime emerged in the 1990s
(Kleemans, Brienen, & Van de Bunt, 2002; Kleemans, Van den Berg, & Van
de Bunt, 1998; Klerks, 2001; Sparrow, 1991). Its main argument is that
most organized crime groups are loosely knit collectives with constantly

shifting members instead of the well-organized and hierarchically structured "firms" as depicted by, for instance, Donald Cressey (1969). We may therefore view transnational crime networks as collectives of criminals based in different countries who maintain criminal relations.

We first discuss the network perspective on organized crime and present a typology of criminal networks. Then we give an overview of the extent of organized crime in different parts of the world, using a composite index of social indicators of organized crime activities. We use country scores on this index for a quantitative analysis of the impact of institutional controls on the extent of organized crime in individual countries. Next, we elaborate on the concept of transnational crime networks. In the final section, we critically examine the popular notion of Western policymakers that globalization processes allow criminal firms originating from individual countries to expand their criminal activities across the world. The chapter ends with some conclusions regarding the likelihood of such criminal globalization.

◊ CRIMINAL GROUPS AS NETWORKS

Criminologists use the network perspective for mapping crime groups such as narcotics supply networks, youth gangs, and terrorist networks (see McGloin & Nguyen, 2011; Sageman, 2008). Recent network studies on organized crime for example concerned the Hells Angels in Canada (Morselli, 2009), the Italian mafia (Calderoni, 2011; Campana, 2011), and from a historical perspective, the Al Capone organization (Papachristos & Smith, 2011).

The focal point of these studies is predominantly the criminal group because limited availability of data and the lack of suitable analysis software led researchers to focus on relatively small networks. Although a lack of access to primary data, most notably police investigations, continues to be a problem, technical analysis tools have improved considerably. The recent study of the Al Capone organization, for example, included 1,500 persons and 6,000 different connections among them. Social network analysis of crime groups has proved to be a useful tool for describing criminal networks and for understanding the various roles of their members. Police analysts use similar techniques for mapping crime groups under investigation, for instance, by using Analyst Notebook or comparable software.

The term *network organization* usually refers to horizontal organizations with few hierarchical levels and a high degree of flexibility in both internal and external relations. In 2002, the United Nations Office on Drugs and Crime (UNODC) collected data on 40 groups from 16 countries, including the United States, Africa, and Russia. The groups analyzed were seen as representative of their countries by national experts. The researchers distinguished five different types of networks (UNODC, 2002b; van Dijk, Shaw, & Buscaglia, 2002). Their typology includes the following:

- **The criminal network** (defined by the activities of key members, prominence in network determined by position and skills, personal loyalties primarily important, coalescence around criminal projects, low public profile, network reforms after exit of key individuals). A Dutch network of drug smugglers and a Nigerian network involved in different types of crimes were examples of such groups included in the sample.

- **The standard rigid hierarchy** (single leader, clearly defined hierarchy, strong system of internal discipline, often strong social or ethnic identity, violence essential to activities, influence or control over defined territory). Examples of such groups originated from Italy, China, Colombia, and Eastern Europe. They make up a third of the 40 groups.

- **The regional hierarchy** (single leadership structure, line of command from center, degree of autonomy at regional level, geographic/ regional distribution, multiple activities, often strong social or ethnic identity, violence essential to activities). A notable example of such groups are outlaw motorcycle gangs such as the Hells Angels with chapters in different countries.

- **The clustered hierarchy** (number of criminal groups, governing arrangement for the groups present, cluster has stronger identity than constituent groups, degree of autonomy for constituent groups, formation strongly linked to social/historical context, relatively rare). An example of such a group is the "28s prison gang" of South Africa.

- **The core group** (core group surrounded by loose network, limited number of individuals, tightly organized flat structure, small size maintains internal discipline, seldom has social or ethnic identity). An example was a Dutch group involved in the trafficking of persons.

The UNODC researchers have collected further data on the secondary characteristics of the networks/groups (van Dijk et al., 2002). The results showed that most groups operate across borders. Of the groups, 70% carried out criminal activities in three or more different countries. Many even operated in five or more. Most are involved in multiple criminal activities. Of the 40 groups analyzed, 30 used corruption and 33 routinely employed violence. Of the 40 cases, 30 showed evidence of the investment of profits from illegitimate activities in legitimate business activity. These results suggest that organized crime groups in most parts of the world are indeed operating in more than one country.

The results also show that only a minority of these groups is structured as the rigid hierarchy described by Cressey in his early assessment of the mafia in the United States (Cressey, 1969). Cressey claimed that organized crime in the United States consisted mainly of a nationwide alliance of 24 tightly knit criminal mafia "families" led by *capos* (bosses) who commanded "soldiers," "buffers," and "button men" and were advised by *consiglieres.*

An important question is what determines the structure of a criminal network; criminologists assume that the (political) context in which criminal networks operate is an important factor. Mafia-type syndicates, which are large and often structured as standard or clustered hierarchies, seem to have developed, and may still thrive, in countries where state authority is weak, corruption levels are high, and consequently, enforcement is lax (cf. Paoli, 2011; Paoli, Greenfield, & Reuter, 2009). In such circumstances, dominant criminal groups may even develop into an alternative for the state, by offering protection to citizens (Gambetta, 1993; Varese, 2001). According to Paoli (2011), Italian government authorities came to terms with the representatives of mafia power until at least up to the mid-20th century. They delegated to the latter the maintenance of public order over wide areas of western Sicily and southern Calabria, where the authority of the central government was scarce and even the personal safety of state officials was in danger. Mafia-type organizations also prevail in Russia and Mexico (Fijnaut & Paoli, 2004; Gonzalez-Ruiz, 2001). In Eastern Europe (e.g., Bulgaria and Albania), a limited number of major criminal groups seem to monopolize criminal activities in certain areas (Bezlov, 2005). The main criminal organizations in these countries are fairly stable, and their territories are known to the public.

In most other parts of the world, the organized crime scene seems to be in a state of flux. Crime networks tend to be relatively small and decentralized to cope better with the risk of apprehension and prosecution. Most notably in Colombia the notoriously powerful Cali and Medellín cartels have since long been disbanded and superseded by hundreds of smaller, more flexible, and more sophisticated cocaine-trafficking organizations. We can see this transformation at least partly as an adaptation to the gradual improvement of law enforcement and adjudication by the courts. Much of the organized crime, including smuggling of migrants, in mainland China seems also in the hands of small to medium-sized, locally active groups that do not fit the traditional concept of the highly organized 'triad" (Zhang, 2001; Zhang & Chin, 2001). According to the researchers, the use of violence against customers during transportation or in countries of destination is rare because this could hamper future activities in their geographically limited recruitment areas back home. Nigerian organized crime is highly improvised and has therefore even been characterized as "disorganized organized crime" (Shaw, 2002).

⧫ ANALYZING ORGANIZED CRIME AND ITS DETERMINANTS WITH THE USE OF STATISTICAL INDICATORS

The U.N. 2000 Convention against Transnational Organized Crime urges member states to collect and share information on trends in organized crime. Around the turn of the last century, various attempts were made by international organizations such as Europol and Interpol to quantify the number of groups involved in organized crime per country. This counting of the most prominent organized crime groups was predicated on the notion that organized crime is mainly the work of stable and hierarchically structured groups known to law enforcement agencies. As explained earlier, this notion now seems dubious in most parts of the world where small and constantly changing networks seem to be dominant. The diversity and flexibility of criminal networks complicate attempts at counting their numbers as a way of measuring their prevalence. In one Europol study in the 1990s, for example, the Italian authorities listed only 4 criminal groups in the country whereas the Netherlands counted 600 different groups. This was a clear indication of methodological and definition problems, and the counting exercise was subsequently abolished.

An alternative approach, more in line with the social network perspective, is the construction of social indicators of organized crime *activities* rather than of groups. In an explorative study on organized crime indicators—or "mafia markers"—van Dijk has collected statistics on each of the main defining elements of organized crime (van Dijk, 2008). Although definitions in national legislation show great variation, criminologists as well as the international law enforcement community describe organized crime as criminal activities for material benefit by groups that engage in extreme violence, corruption of public officials, including law enforcement and judicial officers, penetration of the legitimate economy (e.g., through racketeering and money laundering), and interference in the political process.

One of the most common activities of organized crime is racketeering, including the collection of protection money from businesses. Since 1997, the World Economic Forum (WEF) has carried out annual surveys among business executives of larger companies to identify obstacles to businesses, which includes a question on the prevalence in the country of organized crime defined as "mafia-oriented racketeering, extortion" (WEF, 2004).

Another source of cross-national data on perceived organized crime is risk assessments made by international business consultancy companies. The London-based consultancy company Merchant International Group (MIG) assesses investment risks in over 150 countries, including the prevalence of different types of organized crime (MIG, 2004). The risk assessments concerning organized crime from MIG were found to be strongly correlated to the perceptions of business executives of the WEF surveys. To facilitate further statistical exploration, a composite index was constructed based on the averaged rankings of countries on the WEF surveys of 1997 to 2003 (WEF, 2004) and the assessments of organized crime prevalence of MIG. The resulting index refers to the level of different types of organized crime activities, such as extortion and drugs, arms, and people trafficking, as perceived by potential victim groups and/or independent experts.

As mentioned earlier, instrumental violence, corruption of public officials, and money laundering are regarded as other defining characteristics of organized crime. It is indeed hard to imagine a country where organized crime is rampant without significant amounts of these mafia-related phenomena. Statistical indicators were selected for the prevalence of each of these three defining characteristics of organized crime as well. Police-recorded homicides divide roughly into emotional attacks on intimates and cool-blooded killings executed by organized crime. The perpetrators of the first category are in most cases arrested. The perpetrators of the second category are not. To develop a proxy measure of "mob-related violence," rates of unsolved homicides were calculated by deducting numbers of convictions for homicide from the numbers of police-recorded homicides. The resulting country rates of unsolved murders per 100,000 population were found to be fairly strongly correlated to the perceptions of organized crime, just mentioned. Similarly, a proxy indicator of "high-level corruption" was derived from studies of the World Bank Institute and indicators of money laundering and the extent of the black economy were taken from the WEF surveys among business executives. All three indicators proved to be strongly correlated to the others. These findings support the construction of a composite organized crime index combining the five interrelated proxy indicators: perceived prevalence of organized crime, especially racketeering; unsolved homicides; grand corruption; money laundering; and the extent of the black economy.

Table 1.1 depicts the mean scores on the Composite Organized Crime Index (COCI) of world regions. To allow a more detailed diagnosis of regional problems with organized crime, the table presents both the absolute scores of regions on the composite index as well as the rank numbers on the five source indicators used.

As can be seen in Table 1.1, organized crime was least prevalent in Oceania (mainly Australia and New Zealand) and most prevalent in Central Asia and the Caribbean. The ranking of regions according to the composite index and those according to the five constituting indicators show a high degree of consistency. Outliers are the relatively high rank numbers on informal sector and money laundering of Central America. Among the high-crime regions, South Africa shows surprisingly low rank numbers on homicides. The latter result could reflect that organized crime groups in the region, which tend to be highly flexible and fluent, are less prone to the use of extreme violence than groups in, for example, Eastern Europe.

The combination of data from different sources allows the calculation of scores for a large number of individual countries. In Asia, rates are the worst in parts of South Asia (Pakistan, Bangladesh), but China and India are also rated unfavorably (even more than Italy with its notorious problems in the southern part of the country). In the international literature on organized crime, India is rarely the focus of attention. Research on Chinese organized crime mainly focuses on Chinese expatriates. Limited available research findings on homeland China point to collusion between corrupt communist party members and local gangs in remote areas (Zhang, 2001).

In Africa, Nigeria, Angola, and Mozambique stand out with the highest scores. Nigerian organized crime activity in both the country and the region has been well documented (UNODC, 2005). Gastrow (2003) gives a detailed account of how organized crime threatens to penetrate state and businesses in Southern Africa, notably in Mozambique. In Latin America, Haiti, Paraguay, Guatemala, Venezuela, and Colombia show the highest scores. High scores are also observed in Jamaica. Within Europe, organized crime prevalence increases diagonally from the Northwest to the Southeast, with levels being low in England and Germany, higher in Spain and Italy, and by far the highest in Russia, Albania, and Ukraine.

The surveys of the World Economic Forum from 2003 to 2010 on one hand indicate incremental improvements in some of the new member states of the European Union such as Poland, Hungary, and Bulgaria, as well as in Russia and Georgia (World Economic Forum, 2012). On the other, the situation in Central America, most notably in Mexico, is worsening. It is also in Central America that statistics on homicides have been on the rise, in contrast to most other world regions (Alvazzi del Frate & Mugellini, 2012). The latter finding confirms the close link between trends in organized crime and lethal violence.

Organized Crime and Institutional Controls

The metrics on organized crime prevalence across regions and countries presented previously allow us to put to the test the hypothesis of criminologists that high levels of organized crime controlled by large-scale pyramid-type criminal groups tend to flourish in countries where state institutions are weak. Statistical analyses have confirmed the link between institutional failure and organized crime. The results revealed a strong link between a composite measure of police performance and the index of organized crime (van Dijk, 2008). Where police forces operate more professionally, levels of organized crime tend to remain relatively modest. A telling example is the near total elimination of organized crime in Georgia after the enactment of new legislation and the establishment of an antimafia department in the national police around 2008 (van Dijk & Chanturia, 2012). Case histories have revealed the crucial role of independent and competent prosecution services and judiciaries in tackling organized crime and corruption (Joly, 2003).

Table 1.1 Regional mean scores on composite organized crime index (COCI) for 2002 and rank numbers on the indicators (perceived organized crime prevalence, high-level corruption, money-laundering, extent of shadow economy, and the rates of unsolved murders per 100,000 population)

	Average of the Composite Organized Crime Index	Organized Crime Perception (Rank)	Informal Sector (Rank)	Unsolved Homicides (Rank)	High Level Corruption (Rank)	Money Laundering (Rank)
Oceania	33	1	1	1	2	1
West and Central Europe	35	2	2	2	4	3
North America	44	4	4	4	6	4
East and South East Asia	45	5	3	7	3	6
Central America	50	4	13	3	8	13
Near and Middle East	50	7	6	11	1	2
World	54					
South Asia	54	13	8	8	7	11
North Africa	55	6	5	6		5
East Africa	55	11	9		11	9
Southern Africa	56	9	12	5	12	10
South America	58	10	14	10	13	12
Southeast Europe	58	14	10	12	9	14
West & Central Africa	60	12	11	15	5	8
East Europe	70	16	16	14	14	16
Central Asia and Transcaucasian	70	15		13	15	
Caribbean	70	8	15		16	15

SOURCE: World Economic Forum, Global Competitiveness Reports, 1997–1998 to 2003–2004 (see WEF, 2004); Merchant International Group (2004); World Bank and European Bank for Reconstruction and Development (1996); UNODC (2002a); Buscaglia and van Dijk (2003).

The relationship between the rule of law, including perceived independence of the judiciary, and the level of organized crime therefore also deserves attention. For this purpose, we used a composite measure of the rule of law developed by the World Bank Institute (Kaufmann, Kraay, & Mastruzzi, 2003). Figure 1.1 shows the relationship between country values on this index of the rule of law and our composite index indicating country levels of organized crime. The two variables were found to be strongly correlated ($r = 0.79$). Multivariate analyses confirmed the relationship between the measure of judicial independence and levels of organized crime (Buscaglia & van Dijk, 2003; Sung, 2004). The critical factor determining the extent of organized crime is the quality of institutions

Figure 1.1 Quality of Rule of Law (including independence of the judiciary) and Prevalence of Organized Crime (Composite Organized Crime Index) Per Country

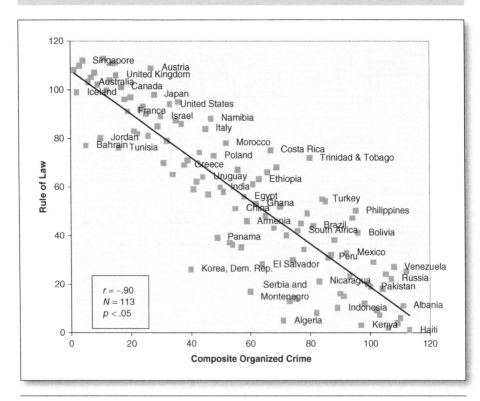

SOURCE: van Dijk (2008); Kaufmann, Kraay, and Mastruzzi (2003); see www.worldbank.org/wbi/governance/govdata.

responsible for the rule of law, including competent police services and independent courts complying with standards of professional integrity. These results signify that weak criminal justice systems promote levels of organized crime at the country level. We rarely observe high levels of organized crime in countries with strong policing and effective maintenance of the rule of law.

Conceptualizing Transnational Organized Crime Networks

As mentioned earlier, scholars usually apply the network perspective to study individual crime groups ("micro networks"). However, we must not forget that such groups do not appear from out of the blue but crop up from a larger network of actors who are willing and able to contribute to one or more illegal activities. "Criminally exploitable ties" that enable them to exchange information on future illegal activities connect these individuals. Similar to social media communities such as Facebook, this network of criminal relations is theoretically a global "macro network," because there are no regulations that prevent (potential) criminals from establishing connections (Spapens, 2006, 2010). In practice, however, it is clustered locally.

Starting from the concept of the macro network, a TOC group, or micro network, may be considered, on one hand, as a group of actors moving from one country to another to execute illegal activities. The notorious "Pink Panther gang," a network originating from Serbia suspected to have conducted more than 100 robberies of jewelry stores in more than 20 countries, is a noteworthy example. On the other, we may view a TOC network as a (temporary) collective, or micro network, composed of a small number of members of the global macro network who live in different countries. A central leader may coordinate such a micro network from a base in one country, but it may also be a fluid-project organization where business relations instead of hierarchical ties prevail. The sections have indicated that loosely knit collectives of the latter type are more dominant than are rigidly controlled hierarchical groups. It is therefore an important question whether it has become easier to establish and maintain criminal relations across borders and to set up actual criminal business processes.

The criminal macro network comprises entrepreneurs, investors, workers, and different categories of facilitators, including technicians, accountants, and legal counselors. Crime groups consist of a mix of actors who possess the necessary qualities to complete a specific illegal activity. Afterward, the criminal relationship usually stays intact and can be used to plan new crimes.

Only rarely do individuals join criminal groups (or terrorist groups for that matter) as complete outsiders. Rather, they typically first join the macro network by establishing criminal relations with persons who are already involved in criminal acts. Prisons are very important places for (transnational) criminal networking. Detainees obviously have the proper "credentials" and track record in crime. Moreover, given the circumstances, there is ample time to develop a relationship of mutual trust. In one case, a Dutch and a German drug courier developed a friendly relation in a Spanish prison where both served a sentence. Upon release they quickly brought their former bosses into contact—a Berlin wholesale drug dealer and a Dutch importer of cocaine—which just as quickly resulted in regular shipments from the Netherlands to Germany.

The micro networks that execute an actual criminal "business process"—for example, the trafficking of 100 kilos of heroin from Turkey to the United Kingdom—may exist for only one operation. They may also develop into more stable and longer lasting organizations, particularly when cooperation remains fruitful and law enforcement does not interfere. Of course, members of micro networks usually also maintain criminal relations with other members of the macro network, with whom they are at the time not actively in business. An analysis of 48 crime groups involved in ecstasy production in the south of the Netherlands, for example, revealed many connections between the members of different groups. Although the composition of the project organizations changed constantly, the names of key indigenous criminals and their extended families stayed very much the same (Spapens, 2006).

Although the macro network is theoretically global, it is of course impossible for all actors to be in direct contact with each other. Instead, comparable to other social networks, the criminal macro network divides into geographical clusters. A first explanation for this is that business processes of organized crime mostly require unskilled labor, which is readily available nearby. Maintaining an international network for the recruitment of such coworkers serves no purpose. In most cases, international relations are of use only for criminal "entrepreneurs" looking for business partners in other countries.

A second explanation is that criminals must conceal their illegal activities, and this includes discussions of future criminal projects. For this reason, the preferred mode of communication are face-to-face meetings, either at people's homes or at places such as shady bars and brothels; the use of telecommunication is avoided to prevent the police from listening in. Such personal meetings are, on average, less easily organized when geographical and social distances increase. Of course, upper level criminal entrepreneurs will readily travel to another continent to discuss a concrete business deal, but flying all over the world just for networking is another matter. In addition, international criminal networking requires language skills, which not all criminal entrepreneurs possess. Language barriers and cultural differences further complicate the required establishment of trust between potential criminal partners from different countries.

Consequently, density of criminal relations is higher locally than at the international level. As mentioned previously, in the ecstasy production scene in the south of the Netherlands, many actors know each other at the local level, but only a relatively small number have the ties that enable them to engage in large international business deals (Spapens, 2006). The result of this is that most TOC that involves the trafficking of goods and persons is "glocal." It concerns entrepreneurs striking international deals who usually depend on local accomplices to execute parts of the criminal business processes.

Following from our assumption that most TOC starts with establishing an international criminal relation, ongoing globalization has obviously made it easier to form and maintain such ties than it was two or three decades ago. For example, international hubs for lawbreakers developed. Many Dutch criminals, for example, bought a house or an apartment in a sunny place, such as a Spanish *costa*, one of the islands in the Dutch Antilles, or, more recently, in Dubai and Thailand, and fly there every few months to relax. Some towns, such as Marbella in the 1990s, thus developed into meeting places for criminals from different countries with many opportunities for networking.

Globalization also made it easier to execute cross-border illegal business processes. This first applies to the trafficking of illegal goods and contraband. The growth of international trade has increased opportunities to conceal such goods. A container filled with used tires that ships from Rotterdam to Accra, for instance, will not attract special attention, and criminals may use it to also transport some stolen car parts. It has also become less complex and cheaper for traffickers to move across the world. There is little in the way of drug couriers who travel by air from South America to Europe, for example, to take extensive detours on their way in order to hide where their journey started. Furthermore, increasing mobility also made it easier for itinerary crime groups to move around and expand their hunting grounds. We already mentioned the Serbian Pink Panther gang. A few years ago the Amsterdam police, for example, apprehended a group of Brazilians who had come over to the Netherlands solely for committing burglaries.

The Internet has opened up new opportunities for organized crime networks to operate across borders without physically crossing them—for instance, by offering illegal services or by committing fraud and theft (Aas, 2007). One example is an illegal sports betting ring in the United States, run by the Gambino "family" in which the group had partly replaced the traditional street bookmakers with websites that gamblers could enter with a password in order to place their bets ("Gambino Captain," 2008). Online gambling also globalized match fixing. Gamblers may now wager on practically every sports event in the world, even amateur matches, and the risk that someone may find it favorable to manipulate the outcome of a game has grown accordingly. Other examples of new opportunities created by the Internet are the theft of identities and the stealing of credit card information.

Although criminals have always succeeded in operating across borders, increased globalization has unmistakably influenced TOC. In sum, more crimes now have an international dimension, even common crimes; more crime groups are operating across borders; the diversity of transnational crime networks has increased; and new transnational crimes have emerged whereas others were "modernized" because of improvements in information and communication technology. The question remains whether such developments imply that TOC groups originating from one country are introducing new types of crime and (violent) modes of operation to countries that did not have a substantial organized crime problem before.

Do TOC Networks Spread Across the World?

The most important perceived threat of TOC networks is the risk of organized crime syndicates spreading their wings across the globe and turning into crime multinationals (see Castells, 1998; Strange, 1996; United Nations, 2004; Williams, 2003; Woodiwiss, 2003). Criminal conglomerates operating globally from safe havens where controls are weak are often presented as destabilizing factors, a threat to the national security of Western nations, and a worry for authorities (Godson, 2003; UNODC, 2010). These notions of an "alien conspiracy" have powerful policy implications, engendering a discourse on the need not just of international cooperation in criminal justice but of a harsh, warfare-like approach similar and linked to the "war on terrorism" (Findlay, 2008; van Dijk, 2012). We examine the validity of these notions and the resulting political concerns from the perspective of social network theory.

Theoretically, foreign crime groups could undermine other societies in three basic ways: by moving to another country to provide additional illegal goods and services or take over the markets of existing providers; by setting up shop abroad for the purpose of committing predatory crimes, including extortion; and by investing "black" money (i.e., money from crime that has not yet been laundered) in legitimate economic activities in other countries. Each of these threats involves the movement of activities of existing criminal networks to other countries. To what extent such export of criminal activity actually takes place is difficult to assess. The mere presence of foreign criminals, however, is by itself no evidence of expansion into other countries.

The police, for example, may establish that the leader of a group of Chinese criminals operating in Europe regularly flies to Hong Kong. Does this mean that he is going there to talk with his Triad bosses to receive "orders," or is he independently running his illegal activities and traveling there just to meet his business partners? The police will usually be inclined to assume the first, but of course, it is impossible to establish whether that is correct.

In practical cases not involving itinerary gangs, we always observe connections with the local underworld when foreign criminals appear on the scene. An example is the Chinese "businessman" Zheyun Ye (probably an alias), who appeared out of the blue in Belgium in 2004, posing as a trader in fur clothing who sought to sponsor football clubs to market the product. His real aim, in which he was partially successful, was to fix matches in the Belgian soccer competition, so that he, and presumably others, could place large bets on the scores. Importantly, Ye immediately teamed up with a Belgian named Pietro Allatta who had served a 4-year prison term for illegal labor brokering. Allatta was connected to Carmelo Bongiorno, a notorious criminal who had been convicted for the murder of a journalist in 1994. The Belgian police arrested Zheyun Ye in 2005 after he had harassed a girl and her mother in the Brussels Hilton hotel but let him go after interrogation. He immediately fled, presumably to China and has not appeared in public since. Hence, it is also impossible to answer the question whether Ye had been working on his own or had been part of a more or less orchestrated cross-border criminal operation (Spapens, 2012). Soudijn (2006) made similar observations with regard to the "Snakeheads'" who were smuggling Chinese nationals to Europe in the 1990s and the first half of the millennium. The police often believed that these operations were masterminded from China, but actual proof of this was lacking. On their turn, the Chinese police were convinced that the main organizers were operating from other countries instead!

From a theoretical perspective, it appears to be highly challenging to a criminal network to move into another country to engage in illegal markets already controlled by local crime groups. To begin with, they can expect fierce resistance because the established providers will not go "bankrupt" without a fight. Next, in countries with homogeneous populations, foreign criminals stand out, and their illegal activities may more readily attract the attention of law enforcement. Newly arrived foreigners usually lack the network relations that enable them to enter into corrupt relationships with law enforcement officers or judges.

In countries where institutions are weak and law enforcement constitutes less of a problem, the opportunities of foreign groups are not favorable either. Here, the absence of functioning institutions is often more than offset by the presence of powerful, hierarchically structured criminal networks used to defend their monopolies with the use of violence. Finally, we may view the investment of illegally acquired assets abroad, either in legal businesses or in illegal activities, as a specific threat. Although there is little information from a scholarly perspective, examples show that knowledge of the local situation and good contacts on the ground seem to be prerequisites when criminals invest in legal businesses or property abroad. When it comes to investment in illegal activities, we may once again assume that criminal relations are the key to success. In practice, foreign groups providing illegal goods or services almost always enter into mutually profitable partnerships with local criminals and use their network for executing illegal activities abroad.

With regard to predatory crimes, however, the situation may sometimes be different, for these do not require local partners and do not necessarily threaten the business of the existing local networks. Examples of this are the extortion of Chinese shopkeepers in the Netherlands by a Chinese group and of Italian nationals in, for instance, Australia and Canada by the 'Ndrangheta, a criminal organization in Italy (Forgione, 2009; Gratteri & Nicasso, 2007). However, if such groups expand their activities to other markets, they establish criminal relations with local lawbreakers. Albanian crime networks that started to appear in Belgium in the mid-1990s are an example. At first, these groups focused on committing predatory crimes, such as theft and burglary (Farcy, 2002). Within a few years after their arrival, they also started to traffic narcotic drugs and smuggle Eastern European immigrants in cooperation with local crime groups. The aforementioned group that extorted Chinese nationals living in the Netherlands also smuggled immigrants and was involved in ecstasy production and trafficking, in which cases they cooperated closely with Dutch criminals. The establishment of new criminal relations also implied that ethnic homogeneity of both the Albanian and Chinese networks soon decreased.

☀ CONCLUSION

In conclusion, globalization of both economical and social relations, through migration, increasing mobility, and the revolution in information and communication technology, has offered unprecedented opportunities for TOC. It is now definitely easier to establish and maintain cross-border criminal relations, to commit predatory crimes over larger distances and to carry out certain illegal activities on the Internet, such as fraud and illegal gambling. However, we must not overrate the effects of globalization on the criminal world. It is not sensible for a crime organization from another country to try to put established local criminal "communities" out of business. In practice, cooperation with local criminals and joint ventures instead of competing with them remains to be an essential ingredient for success. Organized crime seems to have become more transnational under the influence of globalization but not to have lost its strong social roots in local settings (Hobbs, 1998). In the fight against TOC, international cooperation is most certainly required, but the fight should continue to be framed primarily as a domestic law enforcement concern that requires a coordinated response rather than as an external or global threat to national security.

☀ REFERENCES

Aas, K. F. (2007). *Globalization and crime.* Thousand Oaks, CA: Sage.
Alvazzi del Frate, A., & Mugellini, D. G. (2012). The crime drop in non-Western countries: A review of homicide data. In J. van Dijk, A. Tseloni, & G. Farrell (Eds.), *The international crime drop: New directions in research* (pp. 134–159). Basingstoke, Hampshire, England: Palgrave/Macmillan.

Bezlov, T. (2005). *Crime trends in Bulgaria: Police statistics and victimization surveys.* Sofia, Bulgaria: Center for the Study of Democracy.

Buscaglia, E., & Van Dijk, J. (2003). Controlling organized crime and corruption in the public sector. *Forum on Crime and Society, 3*(1&2), 3–34.

Calderoni, F. (2011, October). *Strategic positioning in mafia networks.* Paper presented at the Third Annual Illicit Networks Workshop, Montreal. Available at http://erdr.org/

Campana, P. (2011). Eavesdropping on the mob: The functional diversification of mafia activities across territories. *European Journal of Criminology, 8*(3), 213–228.

Castells, M. (1998). *End of millennium: Vol. 3. The information age: Economy, society and culture.* Oxford, England: Blackwell.

Cressey, D. (1969). *Theft of the nation.* New York, NY: Harper & Row.

Farcy F. (2002). *How is the Albanian mafia setting up? Locally, nationally and in Europe.* Paris, France: Departement de Recherche sur les Menaces Criminelles Contemporaines.

Fijnaut, C., & Paoli. L. (2004). *Organised crime in Europe. Concepts, patterns and control policies in the European Union and beyond.* Dordrecht, the Netherlands: Springer.

Findlay, M. (2008). *Governing through crime: Futures for international criminal justice.* Cullompton, Devon, England: Willan.

Forgione, F. (2009). *Mafia export.* Milan, Italy: B. C. Dalai Editore.

Gambetta, D. (1993). *The Sicilian mafia: The business of private protection.* Cambridge, England: Harvard University Press.

Gambino captain, others busted for sports gambling. (2008, February 2). *North Country Gazette.* Available from http://www.northcountrygazette.org (Subscription necessary)

Gastrow, P. (2003). *Penetrating state and business: Organized crime in Southern Africa* (Vol. 1). Pretoria, South Africa: Institute for Security Studies.

Godson, R. (2003). *Menace to society: Political criminal cooperation around the world.* New Brunswick, NJ: Transaction.

Gonzalez-Ruiz, S. (2001). Fighting drug cartels on the Mexico-United States border. *Forum on Crime and Society, 1,* 19–31.

Gratteri, N., & Nicasso, A. (2007). *Fratelli di Sangue* [Blood brothers]. Cosenza, Italy: Luigi Pellegrini Editore.

Hobbs, D. (1998). Going down the glocal: The local context of organized crime. *Howard Journal, 37*(4), 407–422.

Joly, E. (2003). *Est-ce dans ce monde-là que nous voulons vivre?* [Is this the world we want to live in?]. Paris, France: Editions des Arènes.

Kaufmann, D., Kraay, A., & Mastruzzi, M. (2003). *Governance Matters III: Governance indicators for 1996–2002* (Policy Research Working Paper 3106). Washington, DC: World Bank. Retrieved from http://www.worldbank.org/wbi/governance/pubs/govmatters3.html

Kleemans E., Brienen, M., & Van de Bunt, H. (2002). *Georganiseerde criminaliteit in Nederland, Tweede rapportage op basis van de WODC-monitor.*

[Organized crime in the Netherlands. Second report based on the WODC-monitor]. The Hague, Netherlands: Research and Documentation Centre of the Ministry of Security and Justice.

Kleemans E., Van den Berg, E., & Van de Bunt, H. (1998). *Georganiseerde criminaliteit in Nederland* [Organized crime in the Netherlands]. The Hague, Netherlands: Research and Documentation Centre of the Ministry of Security and Justice.

Klerks, P. (2001). The network paradigm applied to criminal organisations: Theoretical nitpicking or a relevant doctrine for investigators? Recent developments in the Netherlands. *Connections, 24*(3), 53–65.

McGloin, J., & Nguyen, H. (2011, October). *The importance of studying co-offending networks for criminological theory and policy.* Paper presented at the Third Annual Illicit Networks Workshop, Montreal. Available at http://erdr.org/

McIllwain, J. (1999). Organized crime: A social network approach. *Crime, Law and Social Change, 32,* 301–323.

Merchant International Group Ltd. (2004). *Grey area dynamics, organised crime figures 2004.* Special analysis commissioned by J. van Dijk at Turin, Italy. U.N. Interregional Crime and Justice Research Institute.

Morselli, C. (2009). *Inside criminal networks.* New York, NY: Springer.

Paoli, L. (2011). Searching for the determinants of OC: Some initial reflections. In T. Spapens, M. Groenhuijsen, & T. Kooijmans (Eds.), *Universalis, liber amicorum Cyrille Fijnaut* [Universalis, Festschrift for Cyrille Fijnaut] (pp. 735–747). Antwerp, Belgium/Cambridge, England: Intersentia.

Paoli, L., Greenfield, V., & Reuter, P. (2009). *The world heroin market: Can supply be cut?* New York, NY: Oxford University Press.

Papachristos, A., & Smith, C. (2011, October). *The small world of Al Capone. The embedded nature of criminal and legitimate social networks.* Paper presented at the Third Annual Illicit Networks Workshop, Montreal. Available at http://erdr.org/

Rauch, J. E. (2001). Business and social networks in international trade. *Journal of Economic Literature, 39*(4), 1177–1203.

Sageman, M. (2008). *Understanding terror networks.* Philadelphia: University of Pennsylvania Press.

Shaw, M. (2002). *Crime and policing in post-apartheid South Africa. Transforming under fire.* London, England: Hurst.

Soudijn, M. (2006). *Chinese human smuggling in transit.* The Hague, the Netherlands: Boom Legal.

Spapens, T. (2006). *Interactie tussen criminaliteit en opsporing* [Interaction between criminals and law enforcement]. Antwerp, Belgium/Oxford, England: Intersentia.

Spapens, T. (2010). Macro networks, collectives and business processes: An integrated approach to organized crime. *European Journal of Crime, Criminal Law and Criminal Justice, 18*(2), 185–215.

Spapens, T. (2011). Interaction between criminal groups and law enforcement: The case of ecstasy in the Netherlands. *Global Crime, 12*(1), 19–40.

Spapens, T. (2012). *Prijs! Zwarte lotto's en illegale sportweddenschappen in Nederland en het kansspeldebat in de Europese Unie* [Winning the prize! Illegal numbers games and sports betting rings in the Netherlands and the debate on gambling in the European Union]. The Hague, the Netherlands: Boom Lemma uitgevers.

Sparrow, M. K. (1991). The application of network analysis to criminal intelligence: An assessment of the prospects. *Social Networks, 13*, 251–274.

Strange, S. (1996). *The retreat of the state. The diffusion of power in the world economy.* Cambridge, England: Cambridge University Press.

Sung, H. E. (2004). State failure, economic failure, and predatory organized crime: A comparative analysis. *Journal of Research in Crime and Delinquency, 41*, 111–129.

United Nations. (2004). *Challenges and change, a more secure world: Our shared responsibility* (Report of the Secretary-General's high-level panel on threats). New York, NY: Author.

U.N. Convention against Transnational Organized Crime. (2000). http://www.unodc.org/unodc/en/treaties/CTOC/index.html

U.N. Office on Drugs and Crime. (2002a). The eighth United Nations survey on crime and justice. Retrieved from http://www.unodc.org/unodc/en/data-and-analysis/Eighth-United-Nations-Survey-on-Crime-Trends-and-the-Operations-of-Criminal-Justice-Systems.html

U.N. Office on Drugs and Crime. (2002b). *Results of a pilot study of forty selected organized criminal groups in sixteen countries.* Vienna, Austria: Author. Retrieved from http://www.unodc.org/pdf/crime/publications/Pilot_survey.pdf

U.N. Office on Drugs and Crime. (2005). *Why fighting crime can assist development in Africa. Rule of law and protection of the most vulnerable.* Vienna, Austria: Author. Retrieved from http://www.unodc.org/pdf/ART_publication.pdf

U.N. Office on Drugs and Crime. (2010). *Crime and instability: Case studies of transnational threats.* Vienna, Austria: Author. Retrieved from http://www.unodc.org/documents/frontpage/Crime_and_instability_2010_final_low_res.pdf

van Dijk, J. J. M. (2008). *World of crime: Breaking the silence on problems of crime, justice and development across the world.* Thousand Oaks, CA: Sage.

van Dijk, J. J. M (2012). Transnational organized crime, civil society, and civil empowerment. In R. Letschert & J. van Dijk (Eds.), *The new faces of victimhood: Globalization, transnational crimes and victim rights.* Dordrecht, the Netherlands: Springer.

van Dijk, J. J. M., & Chanturia, T. (2012). *The remarkable case of Georgia.* Tbilisi, Georgia: Ministry of Justice.

van Dijk, J. J. M., Shaw, M., & Buscaglia, E. (2002). The TOC convention and the need for comparative research: Some illustrations from the work of the UN Centre for International Crime Prevention. In H.-J. Albrecht & C. Fijnaut (Eds.), *The containment of transnational organized crime: Comments on the UN convention of December 2000* (pp. 31–54). Freiburg, Germany: Max Planck Institut für auslandisches und internationals Strafrecht.

Van Schendel, W., & Abraham, I. (2005). *Illicit flows and criminal things.* Bloomington: Indiana University Press.

Varese, F. (2001). *The Russian mafia: Private protection in a new market economy.* Oxford, England: Oxford University Press.

Williams, P. (2003). Transnational organized crime and the state. In R. Hall & T. Biersteker (Eds.), *The emergence of private authority in global governance* (pp. 161–182). Cambridge, England: Cambridge University Press.

Woodiwiss, M. (2003). Transnational organised crime: The global reach of an American concept. In A. Edwards & P. Gill (Eds.), *Transnational organized crime: Perspectives on global security* (pp. 13–27). New York, NY: Routledge.

World Bank and European Bank for Reconstruction and Development. (1996). Business environment and enterprise performance survey. Retrieved from http://data.worldbank.org/data-catalog/BEEPS

World Economic Forum. (2004). *The global competitiveness report 2003–2004.* New York, NY: Oxford University Press.

World Economic Forum. (2012). *The global competitveness report 2012–13.* Geneva: World Economic Forum. www.weforum.org/gcr

Zhang, S. (2001). The emergence of "black society" crime in China. *Forum on Crime and Society, 1*, 53–73.

Zhang, S., & Chin, K. (2001). Chinese human smuggling in the United States of America. *Forum on Crime and Society, 1*, 31–52.

2

Transnational Organized Crime in North America

James O. Finckenauer and Jay Albanese

*T*he Godfather, The Sopranos, Goodfellas, Scarface, The Gangs of New York, and *American Gangster* are a few of the hundreds of films, television shows, and books that depict organized crime in North America. But few can separate which of these are fact and which are fiction (in fact, most are fiction). The blurring of fiction and reality makes it difficult to have an accurate understanding of organized crime, but greater accuracy is crucial if public opinion, legislation, and the criminal justice system are to properly respond to the actual threat of organized crime in North America.

North America includes the countries of Canada, the United States, and Mexico. Each is a large country sharing long land borders and massive coastlines that provide access to both the Atlantic and Pacific Oceans. Therefore, the three countries of North America are very accessible not only to each other but also from many locations around the world. Mexico, in particular, is strategically positioned, linking South and Central America to the United States and up into Canada as well. The long Mexican land and water borders provide ideal launching points for smuggling people and products to both the United States and Canada, which have large consumer populations that enjoy a high standard of living and income. As a result, North America's geographic location, land and water border access, links to Central and South America, and high standard of living combine to create an attractive environment for organized crime. The requirements for both supply and demand are met in spades.

\\\ HIJTORICAL CONTEXT

Organized crime in North America is not a singular phenomenon. It has always been composed of a variety of groups, both large and small, that emerged to exploit particular criminal opportunities. If the terminology of organized crime had been in use 200 years ago, early European settlers in North America might have been accused of involvement in organized crime activity for avoiding European taxes, engaging in planned thefts from public transport, and bribing government officials to secure favors. Organized crime, indeed, is characterized by planned illegal acts involving multiple offenders who engage in ongoing or recurrent criminal activities.

Traditional crimes associated with organized crime include illegal gambling, prostitution, loan-sharking, drug trafficking, selling stolen property, and extortion. But this list is expanding dramatically with changes in the global economy, technology, and communication. For example, arrests in Long Island, New York, revealed a modest home being used to produce 10,000 bootlegged CDs each week and homeowners connected to known organized crime groups who allegedly helped in the illegal distribution of these CD copies (Holloway, 2002). In another case, it was found that criminal groups in Canada (and Malaysia and Europe) had tapped into data cables from department stores to copy credit card information and transmit it overseas; it was then used to produce fake cards that were imported back into Australia (Nicholson, 2003). In a third instance, seizures of 150 website domains occurred after U.S. undercover agents made purchases of counterfeit professional sports jerseys, golf equipment, handbags, sunglasses, and shoes that were shipped to the United States from suppliers in other countries (U.S. Department of Justice, 2011). These cases demonstrate that the types of offenses associated with organized crime change as opportunities for crime change. Wide access to the Internet and ease of international air travel and shipping are as important to the expansion of human trafficking and fraud as was the invention of the automobile 100 years ago in creating new opportunities for smuggling goods by land and for various types of car registration and ownership frauds.

𝕀𝕀 DEJCRIBING ORGANIZED CRIME IN NORTH AMERICA

Organized crime can be described in terms of the activities it engages in or by the groups involved in it. There are advantages and disadvantages to each approach. The offenses usually involve some variation of provision of illicit goods (e.g., stolen property, drugs), provision of illicit services (e.g., prostitution, gambling, loan-sharking), the infiltration of business (e.g., extortion and protection rackets), or some combination of these (Albanese, 2011). The history of criminality in a region, its economic standing, geographic location, national and ethnic customs and beliefs, and political climate are all important factors in shaping the kinds of organized criminal groups that develop in a country or region (Albanese, Das, & Verma, 2003; Centre for International Crime Prevention, 2000). These organized crime groups usually form and change over time in response to the available criminal opportunities.

Of the myriad forms of organized crime in North America, five major categories are selected for examination here. Although other kinds of organized crime can be found in North America, such as outlaw motorcycle gangs, the five classifications chosen here are well documented and have been subject to study by many researchers and criminal justice practitioners. The five types described here are Cosa Nostra groups, Russian groups, Chinese groups, Mexican groups, and Canadian groups.

Cosa Nostra

La Cosa Nostra or LCN—also known as the mafia, the mob, the outfit—is a collection of Italian-American organized crime "families" (which include many members who are not related) that has been operating in the United States and parts of Canada since the 1920s. Beginning during the time of Prohibition and extending into the 1990s, the LCN was clearly the most prominent criminal organization in the United States. Indeed, it was synonymous with organized crime. In recent years, the LCN has been severely crippled by prosecutions, and over the past two decades, it has been challenged in a number of its criminal markets by other organized crime groups (Albanese, 2012). Nevertheless, LCN remains a viable organization. The LCN still has greater capacity to gain monopoly control over criminal markets, to use or threaten violence to maintain that control, and to corrupt law enforcement and the political system than does any of its competitors. As Jacobs and Gouldin have pointed out, "No other criminal organization [in the United States] has controlled labor unions, organized employer cartels, operated as a rationalizing force in major industries, and functioned as a bridge between the upperworld and the underworld" (Jacobs & Gouldin, 1999, p. 128). This capacity to infiltrate and corrupt business and government agencies distinguishes the LCN from all other criminal organizations in the United States.

Each of the so-called families that make up the Cosa Nostra has roughly the same organizational structure. There is a boss who exercises general oversight of the family and makes executive decisions. There is an underboss who is second in command. There is a senior adviser or consigliere. And then there are a number of "capos" (capo-regimes) who supervise crews made up of "soldiers," who are "made members" of Cosa Nostra. There are also many "associates" who are career criminals, but who are not "made members," who conduct illegal activities in conjunction with Cosa Nostra groups. The capos and those above them receive shares of the proceeds from crimes committed by the soldiers and associates. The illicit operations of the soldiers and associates are not run by the bosses or capos, but the latter are paid a percentage of the profits for "protection" services (often by the power of reputation alone) and for their affiliation with the enterprise.

Made members, sometimes called "good fellows" or "wise guys," are all male and all of Italian descent. The estimated made membership of the LCN is somewhere between 1,000 and 3,000 in the United States, with roughly 80% of the members operating in the New York City metropolitan area. Five crime families make up the LCN in New York City: the Bonanno, the Colombo, the Genovese, the Gambino, and the Lucchese families. There is also LCN operational activity in Boston, Chicago, Philadelphia, and the Miami/South Florida area, but much less so than in New York. In other previous strongholds such as Buffalo, Cleveland, Detroit, Kansas City, Las Vegas, Los Angeles, New Orleans, and Pittsburgh, the LCN is now weakened or nonexistent. In addition to the made members, there are as many as 10,000 associate members who work with the families. Until the recent demise of much of its leadership, a commission of the bosses of New York's five LCN families coordinated control of labor unions, construction, trucking, and garbage-hauling companies and resolved disputes between families (FBI, 2010; Schweizer, Nishimotto, Salzano, & Chamberlin, 2003). In Canada, the influence of Cosa Nostra has been felt primarily in the provinces of Ontario and Quebec (Criminal

Intelligence Service Canada, 2002). Some of this is "spillover" influence from U.S. families across the border, but Hamilton, Toronto, and Montreal have a history of separate Cosa Nostra groups that have been known to communicate with groups in the United States.

Violence

Cosa Nostra, over many years, established its reputation for the ruthless use of violence. This violence has occurred mostly in the form of threats, beatings, and killings. Personal violence and, to a lesser degree, violence against property—bombings, arson, explosions—is the typical pattern of the systematic use of violence as a tool of doing business. The business often involved extorting money from legitimate businesses, as well as drug dealers, in addition to collecting payments from the customers of loan shark operations (Griffin & Didonato, 2010; Maas, 1999). Violence, and subsequently just the threat of violence, was the means by which the LCN gained monopoly control over its various criminal enterprises. Violence discouraged and eliminated competitors, and it reinforced the reputation and credibility of the LCN. Violence was also used for internal discipline. Murder, and conspiracy to commit murder, has often appeared as one of the predicate offenses in organized crime prosecutions.

The history of violence and the LCN demonstrates the importance of reputation in this respect. Peter Reuter (1982) has made the point that when there is sufficient credible evidence of the willingness to use violence, *actual* violence is rarely necessary. This is especially true when the targets are not professional criminals. The Cosa Nostra personifies this principle.

Economic Resources

One of the LCN's major assets is its general business acumen in being entrepreneurial, opportunistic, and adaptable. They find ways to exploit market vulnerabilities while at the same time maintaining the necessary stability and predictability that business requires to be profitable. One of the ways they do this is by taking over only a piece of a legitimate business—and providing a service in return—rather than taking over the whole business (Jacobs & Gouldin, 1999). The latter would, of course, require a management responsibility that they do not want to handle.

LCN's illegal activities cover a wide range. Gambling and drugs have traditionally been the biggest moneymakers. Loan-sharking is linked to these activities, because the money loaned is often first obtained through gambling and drug transactions. Extortion of businesses for "protection" from damage (by the extortionist) is an example of how the reputation for violence is important in order to instill the necessary fear in victims so they will pay extortion demands. When the fear is high enough, of course, actual violence is not needed (and sometimes can impair the victim's ability to pay).

The specialties of the five New York LCN families include labor racketeering, various kinds of business racketeering, bid rigging, business frauds, and industry cartels. In these areas, the LCN demonstrates its most effective penetration of the legitimate economy. Labor racketeering involves organized crime control of labor unions. With this control, gained by the threat and use of violence, large sums of money are siphoned from union pension funds, businesses are extorted in return for labor peace and an absence of strikes, and bribes are solicited for sweetheart contracts (Jacobs, 2006; Jacobs & Cooperman, 2011). Another specialty, business racketeering, has occurred in New York City in the construction, music, and garbage industries. The LCN controls unions, bars, strip joints, restaurants, and trucking firms. The five families have also controlled at various times the Fulton Fish Market, the Javits Convention Center, the New York Coliseum, and air cargo operations at JFK International Airport, among other targets. Again the principal tools of control are bribery and extortion (Jacobs, Friel, & Radick, 1999).

Partly in reaction to effective law enforcement and prosecutions in recent years, the Cosa Nostra has diversified its activities and extended its penetration in legal markets by switching to white-collar crimes (Raab, 1997). It has carried out multimillion dollar frauds in three areas in particular: health insurance, prepaid telephone cards, and victimizing small Wall Street brokerage houses. Professional know-how is demonstrated in each of these scams.

LCN's control over various illegal markets, and its diversification into legal markets, has so far not been matched by any other criminal organization in the United States. This is so despite its having been substantially weakened over the last three decades.

Political Resources

In its heyday, the LCN exercised its political influence mostly at the local level, through its connections with the political "machines" in which bribery was the common method of operation, in U.S. cities such as New York, New Orleans, Chicago, Kansas City, and Philadelphia. With the demise of these machines came the advent of political reforms stressing open and ethical government and increasingly effective law enforcement. Many of the avenues for corrupt influence were subsequently closed. Today, the LCN exercises political influence only in certain selected areas, where politicians remain open to bribery and kickback schemes.

With respect to police and judicial corruption, there is much more evidence of this in the past than there is today. In recent years, there have been a handful of corruption cases involving law enforcement and one or two involving judges linked to LCN families.

Responses of Law Enforcement Agencies to LCN

Law enforcement, and particularly U.S. federal law enforcement, has been tremendously successful in combating LCN over the past 20 years. Crime families have been infiltrated by informants and undercover agents, and special investigating grand juries have been employed in state and local jurisdictions. The techniques employed in these cases include electronic surveillance, the use of informants, the witness protection program, and the RICO law (Racketeer Influenced and Corrupt Organizations). The RICO statute has clearly been the single most powerful prosecution tool against the LCN (Jacobs, Panarella, & Worthington, 1996). There are now state RICO statutes (to prosecute state crimes) in many states as well as the federal law. RICO enables law enforcement to attack the organizational structure of organized crime and to levy severe criminal and civil penalties, including forfeitures of illegally obtained assets. The threat of these penalties has convinced many made members of the LCN to become informants or to seek immunity from prosecution in return for becoming cooperating witnesses. If their life is in danger, they are placed in the witness protection program and relocated. Civil remedies have included the court-appointment of monitors and trustees to administer businesses and unions that had been taken over by the LCN, to ensure that these enterprises remain cleansed of corrupt influences (Jacobs, 2006; Jacobs et al., 1999).

Two of the latest weapons against LCN penetration of sectors of the legitimate economy are regulatory initiatives. These are administrative remedies designed to expand a local government's ability to control public services such as waste hauling and school construction (Jacobs & Cooperman, 2011; Jacobs & Hortis, 1998).

"Russian" Organized Crime in the United States

An example of the transborder nature of a kind of organized crime involving Canada, Mexico, and the United States is the human-trafficking case of the Botsvynyuk brothers and their criminal colleagues. This group allegedly lured about 30 victims from Ukraine, between 2000 and 2007, smuggling them to Philadelphia through Mexico. Victims were housed in deplorable conditions and had to work for years until they had paid off smuggling debts of $10,000 to $50,000. By night, the victims cleaned big-box stores and supermarkets, including Target, Kmart, Walmart, and Safeway. They slept five to a bedroom on dirty mattresses or on floors. Some escaped despite numerous threats. Law enforcement authorities accused one of the brothers of raping one of the victims and threatening to force the young daughter of another victim into prostitution back in Ukraine if she fled. During the investigation into the case, two suspects fled to Canada and fought their extradition back to the United States, thus bringing Canadian authorities into the matter (Matza, 2011).

In the manner of this case, Russian organized crime (ROC) is an umbrella label that captures a variety of crime groups and criminal activities. Often, the criminal groups in question are small and loosely structured as in the preceding case and may not actually be Russian. The Botsvynyuks are from Ukraine.

In some instances, the crimes and the forms of criminal organization in the United States differ from those of ROC in Russia or elsewhere in the world. This may be a result of differing external environments and criminal opportunities. Because of the proliferation of groups, there is no specific organizational structure that can be delineated as if it described one criminal organization. And the characterization "Russian" is used generically to refer to a variety of Eurasian crime groups as illustrated by the case cited earlier. For a general discussion of Russian organized crime in the United States see *Russian Mafia in America* (Finckenauer & Waring, 2001), and for a global perspective see *McMafia* (Glenny, 2008).

Among the active criminals in the United States are Armenians, Ukrainians, Lithuanians, and persons from the Caucasus region of the former Soviet Union (Chechens, Dagestanis, and Georgians). The media and law enforcement call these groups various names—Russian mafia, Russian mob, Organizatsya, Bor, or Bratva. Some of the group names refer to geographical locations in Russia—Izmailovskaya, Dagestantsy, Kazanskaya, and Solntsenskaya. The latter are indicative of the local geographically defined roots of some Russian crime groups.

The segment of ROC most similar to traditional forms of Italian-American organized crime—in terms of hierarchy, internal codes of conduct, recruitment, and internal conflict resolution—is what is known as the *vory v zakone* or "thieves-in-law." Other than a belief that certain Russian criminals in the United States have themselves been *vor,* there is little evidence of any organized presence of the *vory v zakone* in North America.

Violence

The threat and use of violence is a defining characteristic of ROC. Violence is used to gain and maintain control of criminal markets, and retributive violence is used within and between criminal groups. The common use of violence is not surprising, because extortion and protection rackets are staples of Russian criminal activity. ROC has engaged extensively in contract murders, kidnapping, and arson against businesses whose owners refuse to pay extortion money.

The Tri-State Joint Soviet-Émigré Organized Crime Project looked specifically at violent crimes in the New York, New Jersey, and Pennsylvania region. Their report indicated that generic Russian criminals were implicated in numerous murders, attempted murders, assaults, and extortion. As evidence of their intimidation effect, witnesses to crimes often cannot be found, or both witnesses and victims refused to cooperate in investigations. Of 70 murders and attempted murders over a 15-year period, all suggested that the victim, the perpetrator, or both were involved in ongoing criminal activity. In some cases, there was evidence to indicate the victim was attacked as a result of a dispute between two individual criminals or gangs or in retaliation for a prior violent act. The homicides in some cases appeared to have been well planned, and assassins or hit men were used. The report concluded that a great deal of the violence attributable to ROC in the United States was a result of the unregulated competition that exists in their criminal ventures (Tri-State Joint Soviet-Émigré Organized Crime Project, 2000; New York State Organized Crime Task Force et al., 1996).

Russian Criminal Business

With the principal exceptions of extortion and money laundering, ROC has had relatively little or no involvement in some of the more traditional crimes of organized crime, such as drug trafficking, gambling, and loan-sharking. On the other hand, these varied criminal groups are extensively engaged in a broad array of frauds and scams, including health care fraud, insurance scams, stock frauds, antiquities swindles, forgery, and gasoline tax evasion schemes. Russians have recently become the principal purveyors of credit card fraud in the United States, supplanting the West African scams.

ROC is very adept at changing criminal activities and diversifying into new criminal markets. For example, financial markets, banks, and various corporate entities have become new targets of criminal opportunity for ROC. A recent case in point is Semion Mogilevich, a Ukrainian "businessman," who was added to the FBI's Ten Most Wanted Fugitives list for his alleged participation in a multimillion-dollar scheme to defraud investors in the stock of YBM Magnex International, a company he controlled that is incorporated in Canada (Federal Bureau of Investigation, 2009). The company was supposed to manufacture magnets but instead bilked investors out of $150 million. Mogilevich has been charged with more than 40 counts of racketeering, wire fraud, mail fraud, money laundering, and other economic crimes carried out in dozens of countries around the world. Other alleged crimes include weapons trafficking, contract murders, extortion, drug trafficking, and prostitution on an international scale. Mogilevich and his criminal enterprises are described in detail by Glenny (2008).

Contrary to its pervasive corrupt political influence in Russia and in the other republics of the former Soviet Union, ROC has had little or no political influence in North America. Although they have the financial capacity to do so, Russian criminals have not cultivated the political and law enforcement contacts necessary to corrupt them. There have been no reported cases of police or judicial corruption. There is no evidence that ROC has attempted to manipulate either politicians or the political process, that they have managed to get criminals elected or appointed to political office, or that they have influenced media coverage of issues. Similarly, there is no evidence of any connections between ROC and political terrorism in North America.

Combating Russian Organized Crime

The U.S. law enforcement strategy for combating ROC (as well as all forms of transnational organized crime) includes expanding the U.S. presence in other countries and building the new relationships needed to attack transnational crime (National Security Council, 2011). That presence includes both law enforcement personnel overseas and attorneys to facilitate requests for mutual legal assistance and extradition, provide substantive legal guidance on international law enforcement and treaty matters, and increase cooperation with foreign police and prosecutors. With respect to ROC and other joint criminal matters, the U.S. Department of Justice has stationed resident legal advisers, who provide training and technical assistance to foreign prosecutors, judges, and police, in a number of countries, including Russia, Ukraine, Latvia, and Georgia.

〉〉〉 CHINEƒE TRANƒNATIONAL ORGANIZED CRIME: THE FUK CHING

The organizational structure of Chinese organized crime in the United States is quite complex. Broadly defined, there is a great variety of Chinese criminal organizations that includes gangs, secret societies, triads, tongs, Taiwanese organized crime groups, and strictly U.S.-based tongs and gangs. (Tongs are part of a Chinese secret society originally created for mutual support and protection, but now its activities are often criminal as a form of organized crime. Triads are branches of a Chinese underground group that consists of decentralized entrepreneurs who engage in organized crime activity for profit. The size and scale of triad membership are unknown because the groups act independently in their illicit activities.) According to Ko-lin Chin, a leading academic expert in the United States on Chinese organized crime, there is no empirical support for the belief that there is a well-organized, monolithic, hierarchical criminal cartel called the "Chinese Mafia." Chin (2000) says, "My findings . . . do not support the notion that a chain of command exists among these various crime groups or that they coordinate with one another routinely in international crimes such as heroin trafficking, money laundering, and the smuggling of aliens" (p. 123). Other analyses have had similar findings (Sein, 2008; Zhang, 2012; Zhang & Chin, 2002).

Chin's analysis concentrated on the Fuk Ching gang, active in New York City, generally regarded as one of the most powerful Chinese organized crime groups in the United States. When the Chinese woman who is regarded as one of the most successful human smugglers of modern times—Cheng Chui Ping, better known as "Sister Ping"—was smuggling thousands of undocumented Chinese into the United States in the 1990s, she hired armed thugs from the Fuk Ching to transport her customers and ensure they paid their smuggling fees (Sein, 2008).

Other gangs in New York City include the Ghost Shadows, Flying Dragons, Tung On, and Born-to-Kill. The New York City gangs, like the Fuk Ching, mainly operate extortion and protection rackets in defined neighborhoods in New York's Chinatown. Their victims are mostly businesses in Chinatown. In California, where there is also a large Chinese community, the Chinese organized crime presence and problem is quite different from that in New York. In California, the dominant groups are the Wo Hop To and the Wah Ching.

One of the structural characteristics that make Chinese organized crime different from other forms is the relationship between some of the street gangs and certain adult organizations, or tongs. The Fuk Ching, for example, is affiliated with the Fukien American Association. The Fukien American Association—as with other tongs and their relationships with gangs—provides the Fuk Ching with a physical place to gather and hang out. It allows the gang to operate on its (the tong's) territory, thus legitimizing it with the community. It also provides criminal opportunities (such as protecting gambling operations), as well as supplying money and guns. The Fuk Ching originally emerged in New York in the mid-1980s, and as with other gangs, its main criminal activity in Chinatown was extortion. It was founded by a collection of young men (youths in their late teens and early 20s) from Fujian province in China—many if not all of whom had criminal records in China. Fuk Ching recruitment today continues to be among Fujianese teenagers (Huston, 2001).

Violence

Use of violence within the group and against other organized crime groups is very prevalent. Disputes over territory and criminal markets among the gangs are typically resolved using *kong so,* a process of peaceful negotiation. When this does not occur, however, the resolution is usually a violent one, in which guns are used against rival gang members. Law enforcement authorities believe that an escalation of gang violence has taken place in recent years, due in part to the advent of the Fuk Ching and to gang involvement in alien smuggling activities. Based on his research, Chin (2000) concludes the following with respect to Chinese gang violence in general:

> The capacity for violence appears to be one of the key defining characteristics of street gang culture. Its employment, however, is shaped and determined by a cluster of constraints related to profit-generating goals. Violence between and among gangs is regulated through an agent or ah kung who attempts to channel aggressive behavior in ways that effectively maintain gang coherence. Gang coherence in turn supports the gang's involvement in extortion activities and in the provision of protection services to organized vice industries in the community. (p. 138)

The Fuk Ching are violent, but their use of violence has not been very sophisticated or specialized. It is not the systematic use of violence (including threats) to protect and gain monopoly control of criminal markets associated with more mature forms of organized crime. Instead, the Fuk Ching violence is more likely to be random street-level violence, with guns, employed by anyone in the gang. Sometimes this violence is sanctioned by superiors, and sometimes not.

Criminal Activities

Alien smuggling is the illegal movement of migrants across national borders, and human trafficking is migrant smuggling that includes coercion and exploitation. As exemplified by the Sister Ping case, the Fuk Ching have been extensively involved in both types of activities. Indeed, these criminal activities, along with kidnapping, are the main transnational crimes of the Fuk Ching. Their dominance is related to Fujian Province being the principal source of Chinese people smuggled and trafficked into North America. On the domestic scene, their main criminal activities in New York City's Chinatown are extortion and gambling. Each Chinese gang dominates these crimes in their particular Chinatown neighborhoods. This includes the Fuk Ching.

The professionalism and sophistication of the Fuk Ching have been quite low, again compared with more traditional forms of organized crime. The same has been true of other Chinese criminal gangs operating in the United States. This may be due to their generally being much younger than LCN or ROC figures. Also, their criminal activities have not been particularly sophisticated, although the Fuk Ching may be becoming more complex in their organizational structure as they become more heavily engaged in human trafficking, which requires a greater degree of planning and organization.

That this characteristic may be changing somewhat is illustrated in two major cases involving other Chinese criminal groups in recent years—Operation Royal Charm in New Jersey and Operation Smoking Dragon in Los Angeles. The investigations into these cases uncovered a criminal organization that was smuggling numerous forms of contraband. The investigations resulted in the indictment of 87 individuals who were involved in smuggling goods into the ports of Newark, New Jersey, and Los Angeles and Long Beach, California, by using shipping containers with bills of lading that falsely identified the contents as toys and furniture from China. Instead, the smugglers brought in high-quality counterfeit U.S. currency that had reportedly been produced in North Korea, as well as contraband from China. The contraband included counterfeit cigarettes, ecstasy, methamphetamine, and counterfeit pharmaceuticals. In addition, two of the defendants had entered into a deal to provide various weapons, including silenced pistols, rocket launchers, silenced submachine guns, and automatic rifles (U.S. Department of Justice, 2005).

Political Connections

The expert consensus is that the Fuk Ching, like other Chinese gangs, does not have the connections and stature to make it capable of corrupting U.S. police and judges. There have been only one or two cases of police corruption (none in recent years) and no cases of judicial corruption involving Fuk Ching.

Law Enforcement Response

The New York City Police Department (NYPD), which polices the neighborhood in which the Fuk Ching are active, uses all the standard law enforcement practices commonly used to combat organized crime.

These include informants, undercover investigators, and electronic surveillance. In addition, both the police and the FBI support and encourage extortion victims to use telephone hot lines to report their victimization. The NYPD has also created an Asian Gang Intelligence Unit that employs street patrols to monitor street gangs.

On the international level, U.S. law enforcement has undertaken a number of initiatives to improve international cooperation against Chinese organized crime groups. These include the creation of the International Law Enforcement Academy (ILEA) in Bangkok, Thailand, and sponsorship of numerous international meetings on Asian organized crime. Annual meetings of the International Asian Organized Crime Conference attract more than 1,000 law enforcement officials from dozens of countries. Both the ILEA and the conferences promote interaction among officials of affected countries and lead to better cooperation and more reliable information (King & Ray, 2000).

Many crimes in Chinese-American communities—especially drug trafficking, money laundering, and human trafficking—are linked to China. Chinese gang members flee to China when sought by American law enforcement. Ko-lin Chin (2000) recommends that "deportation, extradition, joint operations, and intelligence sharing among law enforcement authorities from various countries . . . be carried out routinely, . . . extradition treaties . . . be [instituted] . . . [and that] U.S. authorities . . . be more culturally sensitive in dealing with foreign law enforcement agencies" (p. 187).

Because of the compartmentalized nature of Chinese organized crime in the United States, the public at large is little aware of and little concerned about what is going on in Chinatowns in U.S. cities. National media pay relatively little attention to these problems. Chinese involvement in human smuggling, however, may be the exception to this rule, because Chinese human smuggling has received considerable attention. Human-trafficking activities by Chinese gangs such as the Fuk Ching are contributing to this higher profile.

MEXICAN DRUG CARTELS

For years, the border between Mexico and the United States has been crossed by millions of Mexican nationals going north in search of work. Most are hardworking, law-abiding citizens looking for legitimate opportunities to better socioeconomic circumstances for themselves and their families. But some are criminals. And during the decade of the 1990s especially, those criminals became more organized, more sophisticated, and more violent, as they sought and gained considerable control over the lucrative drug business in North America.

In Mexico, the violence generated by drug-trafficking organizations in recent years has been unprecedented. It is estimated that some 50,000 lives have been lost in Mexico's drug wars since 2006. Violence has long been an inherent feature of the trade in illicit drugs, but the character of the drug-trafficking-related violence in Mexico has changed over the past half-dozen years—exhibiting increasing brutality. For example, a number of public servants, including mayors and a gubernatorial candidate, have been killed. According to a U.S. Congressional Research Service report,

> The massacres of young people and migrants, the killing and disappearance of Mexican journalists, the use of torture, and the phenomena of car bombs have received wide media coverage and have led some analysts to question if the violence has been transformed into something new, beyond the typical violence that has characterized the trade. For instance, some observers have raised the concern that the Mexican DTOs [drug-trafficking organizations] may be acting more like domestic terrorists. Others maintain that the DTOs are transnational organized crime organizations at times using terrorist tactics. Still others believe the DTOs may be similar to insurgents attempting to infiltrate the Mexican state by penetrating the government and police. (Beittel, 2011)

That the transnational direction of this crime wave is not all one way is evident in the inputs from the United States that fuel the violence in Mexico—namely, high-powered guns and illicit profits. For example, the Mexican government reported that over a 4-year period between 2006 and 2010, approximately 80,000 illegal firearms were seized. The U.S. Department of Justice's Bureau of Alcohol, Tobacco, Firearms, and Explosives determined that approximately 80% (62,800 firearms) came from the United States (Beittel, 2011). This lends considerable credence to Mexican complaints that the United States is not justified in simply pointing the finger at Mexico as the sole source of the crime problems affecting both countries.

In the recent past, it was criminal groups with names like the Juarez cartel, and the Cardenas-Guillen, Valencia-Cornelio, and Caro-Quintero organizations that operated in and from Mexico. Now, the two most dangerous of the Mexican cartels are the Sinaloa Federation and a group known as Los Zetas (both highlighted in the following).

Although drug-trafficking groups have operated in Mexico for more than a century, the size and scope of their operations (along with the violence) have increased dramatically in recent years. Today, they are the major wholesalers of illegal drugs in the United States, and have increasingly gained control of U.S. retail-level distribution through alliances with local U.S. gangs. According to the U.S. government, more than 95% of cocaine destined for the U.S. market now flows through Mexico. Mexican-related drug operations are said to be present in some 230 U.S. cities as well as in Canada (see U.S. Department of Justice, National Drug Intelligence Center, 2009).

The various criminal groups operating in and from Mexico have largely become both polydrug (dealing in heroin, methamphetamine, and marijuana as well as cocaine), and poly-criminal (engaging in kidnapping, assassination for hire, auto theft, prostitution, extortion, money laundering, and human smuggling and trafficking). The major groups in Mexico itself are said by U.S. law enforcement to be fairly centrally organized. The distribution networks in the United States and Canada, on the other hand, are more fragmented. The core criminal organizations and their extended networks are composed of Mexican nationals living in Mexico, Mexican Americans, and Mexican immigrants living in the United States. The vast majority (estimated at about 85%) is male. To get a sense of the size of these criminal operations, it is estimated that in Ciudad Juárez alone [bordering El Paso, Texas] there are some 500 gangs with a combined membership of between 15,000 to 25,000 persons (Gutiérrez, 2010).

The drug cartels in Mexico should not be confused with the Mexican mafia, which is the oldest prison gang in the United States. It consisted originally of young Mexican-American gang members who organized in a California prison in 1957. Its name was chosen to imitate Italian-American Cosa Nostra groups. Also called EME (Spanish for the letter *M*), members of the Mexican mafia come from the barrios of East Los Angeles, expanding from a self-protection racket to the control of drug trafficking and extortionate debt collection. The threat posed by the Mexican mafia is high in Southern California, the southwestern United States, and in areas where local drug trafficking is controlled by Hispanic gangs. In some of these areas, the Mexican mafia controls the illegal activity from behind the scenes by collecting a percentage of the profits of drug-trafficking activities (Albanese, 2009; Rafael, 2009). But the activities of the Mexican mafia, based in the United States, are distinct from the drug-trafficking groups based on Mexico.

The main drug customers are, not surprisingly, in the United States and, to a lesser extent, in Canada. But the transnational nature of Mexican organized crime is not limited to North America in that, for example, their cocaine comes from Colombia, the precursor chemicals for producing methamphetamine come from various countries, and they launder money in the Caribbean and certain Latin American countries.

As suggested earlier, the criminal activities in which these Mexican criminal organizations are involved have expanded beyond drugs and drug-related crimes. That extended list includes armed robbery, extortion, and illegal dealing in firearms. Money laundering of the illegal proceeds from drug trafficking is a dominant criminal activity. For the most part, any other criminal activities in which the Mexicans become engaged are for purposes of furthering their drug business. Their annual average income from all these illicit activities is estimated to be in the billions of dollars (Mazzetti, Thompson, Schmitt, & Walsh, 2011).

The extensive use of violence—more so in Mexico itself than in the United States—is said to be the result of a desire to avoid attracting undue attention. Violence is employed both internally—for discipline and to quell power struggles—and externally against other organized crime groups. The increasing level of violence in Mexico has been linked to the current government attempts to take on the drug cartels more forcefully. There has been some success in this effort, but obviously many murders have occurred, as the cartels have challenged the institutional capacity of the state to respond effectively (Cordoba, 2012; Drug Enforcement Administration, 2009; Schatz, 2011).

With respect to cocaine, the Mexican drug traffickers have business arrangements with the Colombians who grant the Mexicans a portion of the cocaine shipments they transport. This means they both traffic for the Colombians and also deal on their own. With heroin, it is estimated that Mexico is now the second largest source of the heroin used in the United States. The cartels are the predominant foreign source of marijuana in the United States, and their labs in Mexico and California are estimated to produce about 85% of the methamphetamine distributed in the United States (*Black-tar heroin*, 2000).

The various Mexican criminal organizations also make extensive use of corruption in Mexico. The targets of this widespread corruption range all the way from poorly paid local police officers to high-ranking elected and appointed officials. The combination of violence and intimidation and the vast sums of money have effectively undermined efforts by Mexican law enforcement to combat these criminals and have also made collaborative efforts between Mexican and U.S. law enforcement very problematic (*Updating U.S. Policy*, 2011).

The Sinaloa Federation. Sinaloa, which is actually a network of smaller organizations including the aforementioned Juarez cartel, has clearly become the dominant drug cartel operating in Mexico today. It is estimated that they control 45% of the drug trade in Mexico (Beittel, 2011). In addition to its operations in North America, Sinaloa reportedly has a substantial international presence in South America, Europe, and West Africa as well. Its earnings are estimated to be on the order of USD 3 billion per year. Some claim that given its longevity, profitability, and scope, Sinaloa may be "the most successful criminal enterprise in history," and its head, Joaquin Guzman, known as El Chapo, may well be "the world's most powerful drug trafficker" (Keefe, 2012).

Sinaloa uses many of the traditional modes for moving its drugs north but has raised its use to new levels of sophistication and has added wrinkles of its own. For example, Sinaloa Federation drugs come into the United States and some eventually to Canada, by means of cars, dune buggies, trucks, trains, buses, underground trolleys (via tunnels under the U.S./Mexico border), fishing boats, and ultralight airplanes.

Los Zetas. This group was originally composed of former elite airborne special force members of the Mexican Army who first defected to the Gulf cartel and became its hired assassins. Since going into business for themselves, the Zetas have expanded their operations to Central America to collaborate with their Guatemalan equivalent, Los Kaibiles, and with Central American gangs in an effort to take control of cocaine shipments from Guatemala to Mexico (Beittel, 2011). It is considered to be among the most violent, if indeed not the most violent, of the organized crime groups operating in Mexico today. In addition to drugs, the Zetas are also engaged in kidnapping, extortion, and human trafficking.

According to a report by The National Consortium for the Study of Terrorism and Responses to Terrorism (START),

The military skill and spirit, the brutal tactics used to enforce agreements, their sophisticated layered network, and their rapid expansion throughout Mexico, Central and South America, some

U.S cities and Europe, has led to the Zetas Organization being labeled as one of the most dangerous criminal organizations in the world. . . . three common denominators for the members of the Zetas Organization, which reflect its uniqueness [are]: a) reckless violence as a means to enlarge profits for them and the organization, b) no long-term expectations for their future and c) military training. (Mercado et al., 2011)

The following were cited as "common denominators" of the Zetas by different law enforcement experts interviewed for the START study:

Violence and money is the common denominator among Zetas. They are very pragmatic since they are willing to use as much violence as necessary to enlarge money and profits.

The common denominator is the absolute loss of values. Zetas perform their criminal activities for the profit, without caring for anything or anyone.

The organization attracts young people who see themselves without a future (going to school to become an engineer or forming a family) who are living day-to-day and willing to engage in any activity.

The common denominator among Zetas is that many members were originally military personnel. This makes it that much harder for law enforcement agencies to combat them since the Zetas members know what actions to expect. Furthermore, because they once were part of the government military structure, they know how it works and what its capabilities are. It then becomes a doubly difficult task for the authorities, since the Zetas know where the major weaknesses of the state are and plan accordingly as if planning for military engagement. (see Mercacdo et al., 2011)

ॐ CANADIAN ORGANIZED CRIME

Canada also has a long history of organized crime activity over many years, although at not nearly the level of that in the United States and Mexico. The primary organized crime groups in Canada have been identified as four types: Asian groups, East European groups, Italian groups, and outlaw motorcycle gangs. Like the United States and Mexico,

Canada is a large country, so there is tremendous variation within its borders—from a number of very large metropolitan areas to expanses of rural areas that are hundreds of miles across.

Asian organized crime groups have been identified in British Columbia, Ontario, and Quebec, the provinces that contain Canada's largest cities: Vancouver, Toronto, and Montreal. Some of the Asian groups are actually street gangs that engage in drug trafficking or perform criminal activities for more sophisticated organized crime groups. Asian groups on Canada's west coast have been found to be involved in trafficking drugs, firearms, and human beings. The primary drugs trafficked are heroin, cocaine, and ecstasy. Some of these drugs have been found to have been smuggled by individuals of Chinese descent. Vietnamese-based groups have also been found to be extensively involved in large-scale cultivation of marijuana across Canada. In one operation, organized crime members of Chinese descent bought marijuana from Vietnamese-based drug-trafficking gangs to transport in the United States (Criminal Intelligence Service of Canada, 2002; Organized Crime Agency, 2003). In another case, two Chinese-Canadian citizens were caught trying to smuggle four Chinese nationals across the Niagara River into the United States. The Chinese nationals had arrived in Canada through Vancouver airport ("Immigrant Smugglers," 2002).

More recently, multiethnic criminal groups are being detected by Canadian law enforcement. These groups are not hierarchical but, rather, loosely structured networks with changing linkages among members and associates as criminal enterprises come and go. The number of known groups/networks in Canada has fluctuated between 600 to 900. Canadian law enforcement undertakes an annual survey of criminal organizations, finding 800 in 2006, approximately 950 in 2007, about 900 in 2008, and about 750 in 2009 (Criminal Intelligence Service of Canada, 2006, 2007, 2008, 2009). The changes in these numbers over time are said to reflect a degree of fluidity in the criminal marketplace, disruptions by law enforcement, changes in intelligence collection practices, or a combination of these factors (Criminal Intelligence Service of Canada, 2010; Tusikov, 2009).

A study interviewed 50 high-level drug traffickers in Canada who were serving prison sentences. These offenders represented a number of different racial and ethnic categories and, surprisingly, 60% had operated small, legal businesses prior to becoming drug dealers (Desroches, 2000, 2005). This suggests that market demand and opportunities, as well as entrepreneurial skills, are factors in the expansion and contraction of the illicit drug industry. Drug monies fuel a variety of activities, possibly including terrorism. According to a report by the Royal Canadian Mounted Police, heroin arriving through Montreal and Toronto comes from Pakistan and Afghanistan, and about $20 million annually finds its way back to those source countries, helping to fund terrorism (Moore, 2002).

Significant law enforcement efforts have been made in Canada. One of them was the Anti-Smuggling Initiative that focused on alcohol and tobacco smuggling and on the profits from it that are used to fund other illegal activities. An evaluation of that program concluded that a substantial reduction was achieved in the contraband tobacco market, but it is unclear whether a simultaneous reduction in Canadian cigarette taxes also played a role in this decline. There was evidence as well that the law enforcement effort had the effect of displacing smuggling groups to use other locations and methods (Schneider, 2000, 2009). This experience indicates the need for continued and varied enforcement efforts combined with demand-reduction efforts to offset the adaptability of criminal organizations to changes in risk.

Similar to other countries, Canada has witnessed organized crime involvement in new kinds of activities involving the exploitation of technology, identity fraud, and money laundering. Examples of these activities include mortgage frauds, securities fraud, counterfeit goods, and street gangs engaging in crimes as ongoing organized crime activity—all of which have occurred in Canada in recent years (Criminal Intelligence Service of Canada, 2010; Tusikov, 2008).

The Royal Canadian Mounted Police have linked the leaders of telemarketing fraud rings operating out of so-called boiler rooms with traditional organized crime groups in Canada. Estimates are that 500 to 1,000 criminal telemarketing boiler room operations are conducted on any given day in Canada, grossing about $1 billion a year. For example, one Montreal-based telemarketing ring, broken up in a U.S.-Canadian joint operation in December 2006, victimized as many as 500 people per week, many of them U.S. citizens. The criminals used two different telemarketing schemes to swindle unsuspecting victims, netting $8 to $13 million annually. In the first, a lottery scheme, victims were persuaded they had won the lottery, but needed to send check payments ranging from $1,500 to $60,000 to cover various costs. Approximately 90 percent of the victims in this case were older than 60 years old. The second scheme, a mass telemarketing fraud, used several approaches, including telling victims they were eligible to receive a $7,000 grant, selling victims health care kits, or billing victims for services never rendered. In each instance, victims were told to send money via certified check or money order. These examples illustrate both the expansion and increasing sophistication of organized crime activities and the ease with which advanced communication technology facilitates transnational organized crime.

⁂ CONCLUSION

Organized crime in North America is shaped by the presence of three geographically large countries that share very long land borders as well as extensive coastlines along both the Atlantic and Pacific Oceans. The economic disparities between Canada and the United States, on one hand, and Mexico, on the other, create a lucrative supply-and-demand environment, and the land and water access facilitates trafficking routes for illicit goods, services, and human smuggling/trafficking.

Organized crime historically has been shaped by the presence of Cosa Nostra groups, composed primarily of Italian Americans whose influence was concentrated in major eastern U.S. cities. An unprecedented massive prosecution effort beginning during the 1980s severely reduced the strength of the Cosa Nostra groups. These prosecutions in the United States corresponded with global political changes that included the fall of the Soviet Union, the emergence of the newly independent states of Eastern Europe, and a growing ease of international travel and communication.

What might have been localized organized crime problems just a generation ago have become manifestations of transnational organized crime as criminal groups from Eastern Europe and Asia have also found North America to be a desirable market for the provision of illicit goods and services that support organized crime enterprises. Criminal groups within North America also have exploited new opportunities for crime. The growing recognition of the size and importance of organized crime operations that emanate from a variety of foreign countries distinguishes concern about organized crime today from the more local concerns about Cosa Nostra groups and other city-based gangs in years past.

It remains to be seen whether North America can reduce its high demand for illicit products and services (especially drugs), secure its borders from outsiders interested in exploiting the region, and prosecute those individuals and organized crime groups already in Canada, Mexico, and/or the United States. The long-term solution to organized crime is a reduction in the demand for the products and services that support it, but in the short-term, greater collaborative efforts at detection and prosecution will be necessary to disrupt more effectively both foreign and North American organized crime groups.

≋ REFERENCEſ

Albanese, J. S. (2009, January). The Mexican mafia: Linking prison gangs to organized crime. *Jane's Intelligence Review, 21* 8–15.

Albanese, J. S. (2011). *Organized crime in our times* (6th ed.). Burlington, MA: Elsevier.

Albanese, J. S. (2012). The Cosa Nostra in the U.S.: Adapting to changes in the social, economic, and political environment after a 25-year prosecution effort. In D. Siegel & H. van de Bunt (Eds.), *Traditional organized crime in the modern world* (pp. 93–108). New York, NY: Springer.

Albanese, J. S., Das, D., & Verma, A. (Eds.). (2003). *Organized crime: World perspectives.* Upper Saddle River, NJ: Prentice Hall.

Beittel, J. S. (2011, January 7). *Mexico's drug trafficking organizations: Source and scope of the rising violence.* Congressional Research Service. Washington, DC: Library of Congress. Retrieved from http://cnsnews.com/sites/default/files/docu ments/MEXICO%27S%20DRUG%20TRAFFICKING% 20ORGANIZATIONS-CRS-2011.pdf

Black-tar heroin, meth, cocaine continue to flood the U.S. from Mexico: Hearing before U.S. House of Representatives, Subcommittee on Criminal Justice, Drug Policy and Human Resources, 106th Cong. (2000, June 30) (testimony of Joseph D. Keefe).

Centre for International Crime Prevention. (2000). Appendix: Overview of the 40 criminal groups surveyed. *Trends in Organized Crime, 6*(2), 93–140.

Chin, K. (2000). *Chinatown gangs: Extortion, enterprise, ethnicity.* New York, NY: Oxford University Press.

Cordoba, J. (2012, May 14). Mexican drug war yields a grisly toll. *Wall Street Journal,* p. A11.

Criminal Intelligence Service of Canada. (2002). *Annual report on organized crime in Canada 2001.* Ottawa: Author.

Criminal Intelligence Service of Canada. (2006). *2006 Annual Report on Organized Crime in Canada.* Ottawa: Author. http://www.cisc.gc.ca/products_services/ products_services_e.html

Criminal Intelligence Service of Canada. (2007). *2007 Annual Report on Organized Crime in Canada.* Ottawa: Author. http://www.cisc.gc.ca/products_services/ products_services_e.html

Criminal Intelligence Service of Canada. (2008). *2008 Annual Report on Organized Crime in Canada.* Ottawa: Author. http://www.cisc.gc.ca/products_services/ products_services_et.html

Criminal Intelligence Service of Canada. (2009). *2009 Annual Report on Organized Crime in Canada.* Ottawa: Author. http://www.cisc.gc.ca/products_ services/products_services_e.html

Criminal Intelligence Service of Canada. (2010). *2010 Annual Report on Organized Crime in Canada.* Ottawa: Author. Retrieved from http://www.cisc.gc.ca/annual_ reports/annual_report_2010/document/report_oc_2010_e.pdf

Desroches, F. J. (2000, Fall). Drug trafficking and organized crime in Canada: A study of high level drug networks. *Nathanson Centre Newsletter,* p. 26.

Desroches, F. J. (2005). *The crime that pays: Drug trafficking and organized crime in Canada.* Toronto, Ontario, Canada: Canadian Scholars' Press.

Drug Enforcement Administration. *Statement of Joseph M. Arabit Special Agent in Charge, El Paso Division,* Regarding "Violence Along the Southwest Border" Before the House Appropriations Committee, Subcommittee on Commerce, Justice, Science and Related Agencies, March 24. Retrieved from http://www .justice.gov/dea/pr/speeches-testimony/2012-2009/s032409.pdf

Federal Bureau of Investigation. (2009). FBI ten most wanted fugitive: Semion Moglilevich. U.S. Department of Justice Federal Bureau of Investigaton. Washington, D.C.: Author. http://www.fbi.gov/wanted/topten/semion-mogilevich

Federal Bureau of Investigation. (2010). *Italian organized crime.* Washington, DC: U.S. Department of Justice. Retrieved from http://www.fbi.gov/about-us/ investigate/organizedcrime/italian_mafia

Finckenauer, J. O., & Waring, E. J. (2001). *Russian mafia in America.* Boston, MA: Northeastern University Press.

Glenny, M. (2008). *McMafia.* New York, NY: Alfred A. Knopf.

Griffin, D. N., & DiDonato, A. (2010). *Surviving the mob: A street soldier's life in the Gambino crime family.* Las Vegas, NV: Huntington Press.

Gutiérrez, E. G. (2010, November 3). Cómo reducir la violencia en México [How to reduce violence in Mexico] *Nexos en Línea* (Nexus Online). Retrieved from http://www.nexos.com.mx/?P=leerarticulo&Article=1197808

Holloway, L. (2002, December 2). Arrests illustrate a growing concern over boot-legged recordings. *New York Times,* p. C10.

Huston, J. (2001). *Tongs, gangs, and triads: Chinese crime groups in North America.* New York, NY: Writer's Club Press.

Immigrant smugglers caught in broad daylight. (2002, May 6). *Edmonton Journal,* p. 1.

Jacobs, J. B. (2006). *Mobsters, unions, and feds: The mafia and the American labor movement.* New York, NY: New York University Press.

Jacobs, J. B., & Cooperman, K. T. (2011). *Breaking the devil's pact: The battle to free the teamsters from the mob.* New York, NY: New York University Press.

Jacobs, J. B., Friel, C., & Radick, R. (1999). *Gotham unbound: How New York City was liberated from the grip of organized crime.* New York, NY: New York University Press.

Jacobs, J. B., & Gouldin, L. P. (1999). Cosa Nostra: The final chapter? In M. Tonry & N. Morris (Eds.), *Crime and justice* (Vol. 25, pp. 129–190). Chicago, IL: University of Chicago Press.

Jacobs, J. B., & Hortis, A. (1998). New York City as organized crime fighter. *New York Law School Law Review, 42*(3 & 4), 1069–1092.

Jacobs, J. B., Panarella, C., & Worthington, J. (1996). *Busting the mob: United States v. Cosa Nostra.* New York, NY: New York University Press.

Keefe, P.R. (2012, June 17). The snow kings of Mexico. *New York Times Magazine,* pp. 37 ff.

King, L. E., & Ray, J. M. (2000). Developing transnational law enforcement cooperation: The FBI training initiatives. *Journal of Contemporary Criminal Justice, 16,* 386–408.

Maas, Peter. 1999. *Underboss: Sammy the Bull Gravano's story of life in the mafia.* New York: Harper.

Matza, M. (2011, September 13). Trial set to begin for Botsvynyuk brothers in human-trafficking case. *Philadelphia Inquirer.* Retrieved from http://articles .philly.com/2011-09-13/news/30149728_1_t- visa-program-human-trafficking-immigrant-rights-groups

Mazzetti, M., Thompson, G., Schmitt, E., & Walsh, B. (2011, August 26). U.S. widens role in Mexican fight. *New York Times,* p. 1.

Mercado, G. V. del Devia, L., Porth, M., Jacome, M., O'Brien, M., & Sanchez, G. (2011). *Group and country organized crime case studies.* College Park, MD: START.

Moore, D. (2002, July 15). Canadian drug trade aids terrorism. *Ottawa Citizen,* p. A2.

National Security Council. (2011, July). *Strategy to combat transnational organized crime.* Washington, DC: Author.

New York State Organized Crime Task Force et al. (1996). An analysis of Russian émigré crime. *Transnational Organized Crime, 2*(2–3), 1–25.

Nicholson, B. (2003, July 20). Cyber gangs skim millions in Australia. *Sunday Age* (Melbourne), p. 4.

Organized Crime Agency of British Columbia. (2003). *Annual Report 2001.* Westminster, BC: Author. Retrieved from www.ocabc.org/publications/OCA_Annual_Report_2001.pdf

Raab, S. (1997, February 10). Officials say mob is shifting crimes to new industries. *New York Times,* p. A-1.

Rafael, T. (2009). *The Mexican mafia.* New York, NY: Encounter Books.

Reuter, P. (1982). *The value of a bad reputation: Criminals, cartels, and barriers to entry.* Santa Monica, CA: RAND.

Schatz, S. (2011). The Mexican judiciary & the prosecution of organized crime: The long road ahead. *Trends in Organized Crime, 14,* 347–360.

Schneider, S. (2000). Organized contraband smuggling and its enforcement in Canada: An assessment of the anti-smuggling initiative. *Trends in Organized Crime, 6*(2), 3–31.

Schneider, S. R. (2009). *Iced: The story of organized crime in Canada.* New York, NY: John Wiley.

Schweizer, H. O., Nishimotto, C., Salzano, J., & Chamberlin, M. T. (2003). Organized crime: A U.S. perspective. In J. Albanese, D. Das, & A. Verma (Eds.), *Organized crime: World perspectives* (pp. 22–45). Upper Saddle River, NJ: Prentice Hall.

Sein, A. (2008). The prosecution of Chinese organized crime groups: The Sister Ping case and its lessons. *Trends in Organized Crime, 11,* 157–182.

Tri-State Joint Soviet-Émigré Organized Crime Project. (2000). New Jersey State Commission of Investigation. http://www.state.nj.us/sci/pdf/russian.pdf

Tusikov, N. (2008). Mortgage fraud and organized crime in Canada: Strategic intelligence brief. *Trends in Organized Crime, 11,* 301–308.

Tusikov, N. (2009, February). *Toward a risk-based analysis of organized crime: The experience of Canada.* Paper presented at the annual meeting of the International Study Association's 50th Annual Convention, Exploring the Past, Anticipating the Future, New York, NY.

U.S. Department of Justice. (2005, August 22). Federal racketeering indictments target international smuggling, counterfeit currency operation [Press release]. Washington, DC: U.S. Department of Justice, Office of Public Affairs.

U.S. Department of Justice. (2011, November 28). Federal court order seizure of 150 website domains involved in selling counterfeit goods [Press release]. Washington, DC: U.S. Department of Justice, Office of Public Affairs.

U.S. Department of Justice, National Drug Intelligence Center. (2009). *National drug threat assessment 2009.* Johnston, PA: Author. Retrieved from http://www.justice.gov/archive/ndic/pubs31/31379/31379p.pdf

Updating U.S. policy to counter threats of insurgency and narco-terrorism. U.S. House of Representatives, Committee on Foreign Affairs Western Hemisphere Subcommittee. (2011, October 11) (testimony of Rodney G. Benson). Retrieved from http://www.justice.gov/dea/pr/speeches-testimony/2012-2009/111003_testimony.pdf

Zhang, S. (2012). China tongs in America: Continuity and opportunities. In D. Siegel & H. van de Bunt (Eds.), *Traditional organized crime in the modern world* (pp. 109–128). New York, NY: Springer.

Zhang, S., & Chin, K. (2002). Enter the dragon: Inside Chinese human smuggling organizations, *Criminology, 40,* 737–768.

3

Transnational Organized Crime in Latin America

Mary Fran T. Malone and
Christine B. Malone-Rowe

A t the end of the 20th century, observers appraised political developments in Latin America with enthusiasm. The end of the century appeared to close the door on legacies of authoritarian rule, insurgency, and human rights violations. Democratic governance became the rule rather than the exception in the region. Democratization spread throughout South America during the 1980s, and in the 1990s, the end of the Cold War propelled democracy's march across Central America as well. Unfortunately, in many countries the end of authoritarianism opened the door to new challenges, such as rising crime rates. In several cases, transnational organized crime took advantage of the waning power of authoritarian states to entrench themselves in the politics, economy, and society of Latin American countries. Fueled by the international drug trade, organized crime is currently a formidable opponent to democratic states struggling to establish and uphold the rule of law.

⚜ HISTORICAL OVERVIEW OF ORGANIZED CRIME IN LATIN AMERICA

Though organized crime has captured recent headlines, Latin American history is replete with examples of transnational criminal activity, particularly those involved with the trade of illegal goods. During colonial times, piracy was a highly organized enterprise specializing in the transfer of illicit goods, frequently operating with the complicity of European powers. Indeed, the 1670 Treaty of Madrid explicitly addressed the problem of piracy, as Spain made its recognition of British colonies contingent on its ability to reign in its pirates. Throughout colonial times, the Caribbean islands served as bases for contraband trade, as their geographical location facilitated the transfer of illegal and smuggled goods throughout the hemisphere. Ports such as Buenos Aires were also valuable staging grounds for smugglers, and illicit trading typically operated with at least the tacit consent of colonial governments. Such illegal activity did not disappear with the independence movements of the 19th century but, rather, evolved over time to adapt to new political and economic circumstances. For example, when the United States passed the Prohibition amendment to its constitution in 1919, illicit traders in neighboring countries were ready and waiting. The illegality of alcohol made its trade highly lucrative, and smugglers formed a row of ships right off the U.S. coast to facilitate their alcohol sales. So prominent was this contraband activity that the row of ships was dubbed "Rum Row" (Okrent, 2010).

To understand historic patterns as well as contemporary trends in illicit activities in Latin America, it is important to focus on three main factors: the institutional power of the state, the role of political and economic elites, and geography. When state institutions are weak, they are unable to control social and economic relationships within their borders; consequently, organized crime views such states as ideal candidates for hosting illegal activities such as drug trafficking and money laundering (Pérez, 2000). Economic elites can also take advantage of weak state institutions by using corruption to grease the wheels of their economic transactions (both legal and illegal) rather than relying on the rule of law. If public officials seek to enrich themselves through illegal activities, they discard their roles as impartial actors in order to use their positions to shield criminal activity (Pérez, 2000). In some cases, corrupt officials go even further than shielding illegal activity, and agree to tailor state policy (e.g., extradition, banking regulations, and tax codes) to meet the needs of illicit actors. Finally, basic geography can make some weak states with corrupt elites particularly valuable, depending on their ability to facilitate the transfer of illegal goods or to hide the activities of illicit actors.

Latin American countries vary tremendously in terms of the degree to which transnational organized crime has operated within their borders. Countries such as Chile have had very low levels of such activity, whereas states such as Guatemala have been havens for transnational organized crime. Pérez (2000) refers to such extreme cases, whereby political and economic elites monopolize control of government to maintain their grip on illicit activities (particularly through the use of repression and fraud), as "mafiacracies" (p. 138).

Pérez (2000) traces the legacy of organized crime in Panama to illustrate how a mafiacracy operates. Throughout Panamanian history, transnational organized crime has specialized in the trade of illicit goods and has adapted and evolved to meet changing economic and political circumstances. Given its geographic location, Panama has long served as a hub facilitating the transfer of legal and illegal goods and services. During the colonial era, many elites built their power base around the control of illicit activities such as the slave trade, which offered numerous opportunities for enrichment and served to stimulate further investments in local real estate and business ventures (Pérez, 2000, p. 150). In the postcolonial period, the economy continued to revolve around the transfer of goods, and the merchants eventually became the most powerful economic and political class. To protect their interests, the commercial elite monopolized control of government and excluded average citizens from power, allowing elites to protect their economic stake in illicit and/or licit commerce. The military soon challenged merchants' grip on power, however, given the potential for power in government to lead to personal enrichment. The military increased its involvement in politics and trade throughout the mid-20th century, relying on "repression, manipulation of elections, and general corruption, including heavy involvement in drug trafficking and other illicit enterprises" (Perez, 2000, p. 138). In 1968, General Omar Torrijos led a coup and solidified the military's control over the government and its accompanying trade; his successor, General Manuel Noriega, increased the military's role in illicit activities. By 1982, Noriega was collaborating extensively with the Medellín Cartel "smuggling drugs, protecting traffickers, guarding cocaine-processing plants in Panama, and laundering money" (Perez, 2000, p. 152). Panama's strong international banking center, its use of the U.S. dollar, and its lax foreign exchange regulations also made it an appealing site for money laundering.

Noriega's lucrative career in the illicit economy was interrupted in 1989 when the United States replaced its war on communism with the war on drugs. The U.S. Department of Justice issued a warrant for Noriega's arrest on several charges, including drug trafficking and collaboration with notorious drug lord Pablo Escobar. The United States invaded Panama on December 20, 1989, destroying the Panamanian army and capturing Noriega. However, even with Noriega behind bars the problems of corruption and illicit trade proved intractable. In the early 1990s, when state institutions underwent tremendous overhaul, drug trafficking actually increased in Panama (Sullivan, 1997). Democratic reforms transformed Panamanian politics throughout the 1990s, but this progress continued to occur under the shadow of a vibrant illicit sector, which thrived with the help of corrupt elites. Throughout its history, Panama offers clear examples of how the proximity to strategically important trade routes, as well as to consumer markets for illicit goods, can attract illicit trade and organized crime.

To determine where mafiacracies will emerge, it is important to assess the ability of the state to control the social and economic relationships within its borders, and to uphold the rule of law. By measuring this power of the state, one can determine whether organized crime will find a hospitable host for its activities. Figure 3.1 depicts the World Bank's rankings of state capacity to uphold the rule of law, scores that help ascertain the ability of state institutions to ensure that social and economic relationships are governed by the law rather than by the interests of governing elites or powerful nonstate actors.[1] These rankings help identify the countries with weaker institutions, which have the potential to be undermined by transnational organized crime. As Figure 3.1 demonstrates, state capacity varies throughout the Americas. For example, Haiti, Honduras, El Salvador, and Guatemala all rank very low on this measure of the rule of law, and all have had serious problems with organized criminal elements. Still, these national averages can mask subnational variations. For example, Brazil scores in the top 50% for the rule of law, yet in cities like Rio de Janeiro, organized criminal groups have operated freely, particularly in neighborhoods of lower socioeconomic status like the favelas.

Colombia also illustrates how state institutions can govern social and economic relationships according to the law in some places, while simultaneously proving unable to control other geographic areas. As Figure 3.1 indicates, Colombia's ranking is below the 50th percentile globally but in the middle of the scores in the Americas. This national average glosses over an ongoing insurgency, which has its roots in the political upheavals of the mid-20th century. Armed insurgencies grew more powerful during the middle of the 20th century and increasingly challenged the state's power and monopoly of force, especially in rural parts of the country.

Figure 3.1 World Bank Rule of Law Rankings (2010)

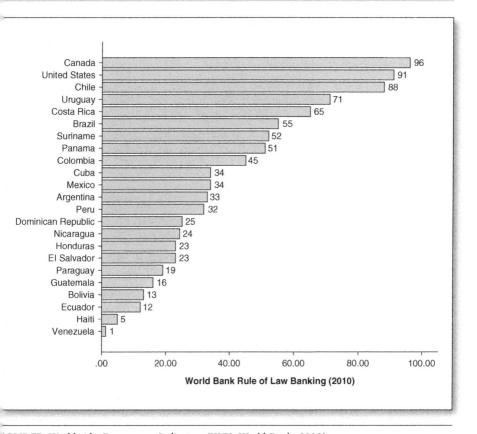

SOURCE: Worldwide Governance Indicators (WGI; World Bank, 2012).

Of these groups, the Revolutionary Armed Forces of Colombia (FARC) emerged as particularly important. At the height of its power in 2006, FARC controlled approximately 30% of Colombia's national territory (Bailey, 2011). FARC is not alone in challenging the power of the Colombian state, however, as drug cartels have also co-opted state institutions and officials, and unleashed waves of violence to further their transnational illicit trade. In the late 1980s and early 1990s, drug-related violence reached its height, endowing Colombia with the infamous distinction as the murder capital of the world (Bailey, 2011).

Colombian insurgent groups like FARC are very different from drug cartels, but ultimately they have pursued similar tactics. To help fund an insurgency that originally aimed to appeal to the rural poor, FARC began guarding and growing cocoa bushes and later expanded its activities to manage its own drug-processing facilities and distribute cocaine (Rubio & Ortiz, 2005). FARC moved up the ranks of this illicit supply chain, eventually moving onto the world stage and serving as a supplier for Brazilian and Mexican drug distributors. Drug cartels have also blurred the line between illegal economic activities and politics. The Cali Cartel has sponsored social projects to gain the support of the lower classes, a practice referred to as competitive nation building. Under Pablo Escobar, the rival Medellín Cartel also provided social services to underserved populations, and Escobar even held political office and offered to pay off Colombia's national debt (Naím, 2005). This mixture of illegal economic activities and political corruption is a practice that has long historical roots—even notorious gangster Al Capone once operated a soup kitchen.

A weak state and corruptible elites set the stage for the rise of organized crime in Colombia, but this rise was also facilitated by basic geography. Throughout the 1980s, Colombian cocaine used the same island-hopping transport routes as the pirates used during colonial times. Cocaine left Colombia, hopscotched across the Caribbean islands, and ultimately landed in south Florida, where it was further distributed throughout the highly lucrative U.S. market (Gootenberg, 2010). A U.S. crackdown in the 1980s disrupted these trade routes, redirecting cocaine traffic through Mexico. The only Caribbean island that remained a viable option for international traffickers was Haiti, "the closest 'failed state' to U.S. borders" (Gootenberg, 2010, p. 8). In 1989, one third of cocaine in the United States came from Mexico; by the turn of the century, this figure rose to approximately 85% (Gootenberg, 2010). The violence associated with this illicit trade has also shifted geographically. Today, drug-related violence has abated in Colombia but has risen in Mexico, particularly following the latter's 2006 militarized government crackdown on organized crime.

※ CONTEMPORARY TRENDS IN TRANSNATIONAL ORGANIZED CRIME

Transnational organized crime has strong historical roots in several Latin American countries, mainly because the constellation of weak states, complicit elites, and geography increases the likelihood of such illegal enterprise. More recently, additional factors have strengthened the power of transnational organized crime. Most important, the consumption of illegal drugs in the United States has promoted the evolution of a highly lucrative market in narco-trafficking, a magnet for organized crime. In addition, the political and economic transitions at the end of the Cold War created a window of opportunity for transnational organized crime to gain a foothold in the socioeconomic and political fabric of several Latin American countries.

When examining the problem of organized crime in contemporary Latin America, observers typically note that there is a great deal of variation in the size, strength, and organization of criminal groups (Bruneau, Dammert, & Skinner, 2011; Jütersonke, Muggah, & Rodgers, 2009). The smallest, weakest, and least organized criminal groups are the *pandillas*, which are local bands of disaffected youth that typically engage in more localized and small-scale crime. These small gangs are territorial in nature and do not have transnational contacts with other organized criminal elements or their corresponding drug activity (Sibaja, Roig, Rajaraman, Bolaños, & Acuña, 2006). Pandillas are very different from the *maras*—larger, more organized street gangs, with a much wider geographic span. Maras have a much stronger, hierarchical organizational structure and engage in more violent and orchestrated crimes, such as extortion rackets (Bruneau et al., 2011). Most of the maras originated in Los Angeles, California, in the 1980s and were later deported to El Salvador, where they established formidable criminal groups like Mara 18 (M18) and Mara Salvatrucha (MS) (Wolf, 2011).[2] These maras are increasingly tied to even larger criminal organizations, such as the Mexican drug cartels. These cartels form the apex of organized crime in Latin America, as they are international in scope and capable of mounting armed assaults against government forces, such as the Mexican and Colombian armies. These three different levels of criminal groups tend to be concentrated geographically. Pandillas are most common in Nicaragua, for example, while maras are concentrated in Honduras and El Salvador. In Guatemala and Mexico, organized crime is the most formidable actor in transnational illicit trade and has the power to co-opt government and respond decisively to government confrontation.

In most cases, these organized criminal elements strengthened their foothold in Latin America during the period of political and economic transformation precipitated by the end of the Cold War. While the widespread transition to democracy was heralded throughout the region, there were some unanticipated consequences. The political transition to democracy, coupled with the economic transition to neoliberalism, fundamentally changed the politics, economies, and societies of most countries.

In several cases, criminal elements capitalized on the upheaval of these transitions and asserted themselves into the new economic, political, and social structures.

When organized crime and gangs have taken advantage of political transitions, rates of violent crime have escalated exponentially, particularly when the transition takes place against a backdrop of civil war, demobilized soldiers, and incomplete disarmament. As Millet (2009) notes,

> The end of civil conflicts frequently leaves thousands of former combatants, drawn from all sides, without jobs, land, or education and accustomed to a violent lifestyle. Efforts to incorporate these individuals into society are often inadequate and not sustained, providing ready recruits for criminal organizations. (p. 252)

U.S. policy further exacerbated postwar problems, as the United States deported record numbers of Salvadoran gang members (particularly from Los Angeles) back to postwar El Salvador, where legitimate job prospects were dim (Wolf, 2011). These trends combined to create a particularly hospitable environment for gangs and organized crime to set up shop. El Salvador is currently a gang stronghold, and the prisons in particular serve as venues for training and recruiting gang members.

Of the Central American countries, Guatemala, El Salvador, and Honduras have been most affected by gangs and organized crime. Together, these three countries compose what is called the "Northern Triangle." Millet (2009) estimates that the total number of gang members in Guatemala, El Salvador, and Honduras is over 60,000. In Guatemala and El Salvador, criminal elements capitalized on the legacy of civil war and political transitions (Call, 2003; Cruz, 2006). Honduras does not have this legacy of civil war but still inherited many of the same problems. Honduras escaped the direct violence of civil war in the 1970s and 1980s, but unfortunately its geographical location doomed it to experience many of the same problems as its war-torn neighbors— Guatemala, El Salvador, and Nicaragua. Due to its proximity to the civil wars of other countries, in the 1980s Honduras faced "tens of thousands of refugees, armed incursions across its borders, and a flood of weapons which became widely available" (Millet, 2009, p. 255). Even after peace accords ended fighting throughout the isthmus in the 1990s, Honduras still found itself home to former combatants from the conflict in Nicaragua, many of whom were unable to assimilate into the workforce and retained access to weapons. Thus, when Honduras transitioned to democracy in the 1990s, it did so against a backdrop of prior militarization, decommissioned combatants, and incomplete disarmament.

Basic geography has continued to make Honduras an appealing location for organized criminal groups. For drug traffickers, its northeastern coast "offers a remote, largely uninhabited rainforest that is perfect for the single-engine planes traffickers use, then hide or burn to destroy the evidence" (Archibold & Cave, 2011, p. A1). Dense jungles and a long Caribbean coastline position Honduras as "the first corner of the triangle, leading into trade routes that eventually reach Mexico and the United States" (Shifter, 2011, p. 51). The situation in Honduras is one of the most dire in the Western Hemisphere, as gangs have opened fire on civilians in terrorist rampages, such as the indiscriminate execution of bus passengers (in 2004) as well as the more recent massacre on a soccer field (Reuters, 2010). The 2009 coup created an additional opportunity for transnational criminal elements to tighten their grip on Honduras, as the temporary power vacuum created an additional space for these illicit actors to intensify their activities. The presence of gangs and organized crime in Honduras, and the accompanying high rates of homicide (among the highest in the world), demonstrate that a legacy of civil war is not the only factor that can turn a democratizing country into a safe haven for crime.

Other regional trends have exacerbated the problems of organized criminal groups in Guatemala, El Salvador, and Honduras. Most important, the increased profit of drug trafficking, coupled with the removal of top leaders in several prominent cartels, fueled violence in Mexico in the mid-2000s. When Mexico responded by launching a militarized effort to crush drug cartels in 2006, the conflict eventually spilled over into Guatemala, El Salvador, and Honduras. In 2006, 23% of cocaine shipments moving north passed through Central America. By 2011, this amount had jumped to 84%, as the Mexican offensive pushed cartel activity south (Archibold & Cave 2011, p. A1). This southern extension of drug activity has even increased violence in Costa Rica, as drug-trafficking boats have increased their activities on its Pacific coast.

Some countries have been able to insulate themselves (at least partially) from transnational organized crime during political and economic transformations, however. Nicaragua provides a particularly interesting example, as past experiences with civil war and chronic poverty did not open the door to organized crime during the transition to democracy in the early 1990s. Despite plenty of demobilized combatants and a disarmament process that generated criticism, organized crime has not penetrated

Nicaraguan society. Small-scale pandillas do exist, but these small gangs are territorial in nature and do not have transnational contacts with other organized criminal elements or their corresponding international drug activity (Sibaja et al., 2006).

Why hasn't transnational organized crime taken up shop in Nicaragua? First, the form of the Sandinista response to the Contra War seems to have impeded the ability of transnational criminal organizations to gain a foothold in Nicaragua in the 1980s, as they did elsewhere in Central America. Former Sandinista soldiers point out that their assignments in the war focused on securing the borders to block Contra attacks launched from Honduras. This emphasis on border security proved disruptive to organized crime, as the same border patrols that were tasked with confronting the Contras simultaneously blocked transnational gangs from entering Nicaragua in the first place (Malone, 2012). The Sandinista response to the Contra War also created neighborhood-level defense organizations, the Committees for the Defense of the Sandinista Revolution, which have evolved into community organizations that have helped civil society to self-police neighborhoods and to keep more dangerous foreign gangs out (Sibaja et al., 2006, pp. 5–6). Second, the police of Nicaragua have evolved quite differently from the other postconflict countries of Central America, making a complete break from their authoritarian and repressive past following the overthrow of the Somoza dynasty in 1979. The new constitution stipulated that the police would not be repressive, focusing instead on the prevention of crime. This has led Nicaragua to emphasize prevention and intervention over repression when designing plans to reduce criminality (Herrera & Espinoza, 2008; Sibaja et al., 2006). Even incarcerated populations have access to some rehabilitative measures, such as activities and job training. This model of crime prevention has blocked the easy recruitment of disaffected youth to work in the maras and the use of prisons as training grounds for new members, although some youth do still join smaller scale neighborhood pandillas. Finally, the economy of Nicaragua has also deterred violent crime by reducing the ability of organized criminal groups to operate (Malone, 2012). While the other postconflict countries are also poor, the Nicaraguan economy lacks basic opportunities for money laundering, an essential need for organized crime. This lack of economic structures makes other Central American countries more appealing bases of operation for sophisticated crime networks.

Legacies of internal conflict, coupled with economic and political transitions, help explain why transnational organized crime has emerged as a powerful force in many Latin American countries. Still, these are not the only factors facilitating the rise of transnational organized crime. In countries that did not face political violence and/or major political and economic transformation at the turn of the century, other factors have strengthened the hand of organized crime. Naím (2005) argues that contemporary trends of trade liberalization and economic integration have rendered borders more porous and provided increased opportunities to illicit entrepreneurs. In addition to the global embrace of neoliberalism, technological advances have also strengthened the hand of business (both legal and illegal) vis-à-vis that of government, dissolving "the sealants that governments traditionally relied on to secure their national borders" and boosting "the incentives to break through these sealants—legal or otherwise" (Naím 2005, p. 4).

⚜ ORGANIZED CRIME AND ITS EFFECTS ON DEMOCRATIC GOVERNANCE TODAY

To understand the political and socioeconomic challenges organized crime poses, it is important to examine the ways in which organized criminal elements interact with state forces. Bailey and Taylor (2009) provide a helpful framework for understanding these relationships, arguing that government and organized criminal groups "co-exist in uneasy equilibrium" (p. 3). Table 3.1 outlines Bailey and Taylor's (2009) model of criminal and state strategies for interaction. As the first column indicates, the state can choose to coexist with criminal elements, disrupt their activities, or try to eliminate them altogether. Mostly, states choose the two strategies with the least potential for confrontation—coexistence and/or disruption. Corrupt elites obviously have a personal incentive for pursuing coexistence, but coexistence with criminal organizations

Table 3.1   State and Criminal Organization Interaction Strategies

State Strategies	Criminal Organization Strategies
Coexistence	Evasion
Disruption	Corruption
Elimination	Confrontation

SOURCE: Bailey and Taylor (2009).

might also be preferable if the activity at hand is not thought to be extremely harmful and the cost of disrupting or eliminating it are high (e.g., Brazilian *jogo do bicho* or gambling rackets) (Bailey & Taylor, 2009). If coexistence is not appealing, states typically prefer to disrupt illegal activities over complete elimination. Under disruption, the state interrupts a particular illicit enterprise or changes its nature or location. Elimination is usually not desirable from a state perspective, because it tends to be costly, to be difficult to achieve, and can usher in unintended consequences.

In a similar vein, criminal organizations also tend to rely on the strategies that are less confrontational—evasion and corruption. Open confrontation with the state is costly in terms of individual security, economic well-being, and overall maintenance of the criminal organization. Criminal organizations tend to prefer to evade capture, or when that is not possible, corrupt the state to turn a blind eye to their operations. Because both the state and criminal organizations have strong incentives to pursue less confrontational strategies, typically their interactions fall into an equilibrium characterized by coexistence/disruption and evasion/corruption (Bailey & Taylor, 2009).

Sometimes this equilibrium is disturbed, however, and the state and/or criminal organizations find reasons to pursue strategies of elimination and confrontation respectively. Bailey and Taylor (2009) apply their model to understand the more violent interactions between the state and criminal organizations in Brazil and Mexico and argue that when criminal organizations decide to openly confront the state, their willingness to incur the high costs of confrontation is an alarming signal that they perceive the state to be a weak provider of security and susceptible to their armed challenge.

Evidence from Brazil provides a sobering illustration of what happens when the equilibrium between the state and criminal organizations falls out of balance. Brazil's major organized criminal group is the Primeiro Comando da Capital (PCC), which originated from gangs within the prison system. Originally the group formed to press for prisoners' rights, but eventually it branched out to become the largest, most powerful organized crime group in the country. It controls activities within dozens of prisons in São Paulo (where two of every five prisoners are housed) as well as around the country (Bailey & Taylor, 2009). It also coordinates illicit activities outside the prison walls. Logan (2006) explains how the PCC controls major sale points and transportation routes for drugs and guns flowing into Brazil from source countries such as Paraguay, Bolivia, Colombia, and Suriname. He also points to evidence that indicates that the PCC formed an alliance with the Red Command, Rio de Janeiro's top criminal organization, to jointly control drug trade in Brazil's two largest cities. Members of these gangs are also reported to conduct weapons-for-cocaine barters with members of FARC (Logan, 2006). Estimates gauge PCC membership at approximately 15,000 members both inside and outside the prisons and the earnings of senior gang members to be nearly USD 2 million per month (Bailey & Taylor, 2009).

Since its inception in the early 1990s, the power of the PCC grew steadily, reaching its height in 2006 when it orchestrated a series of violent attacks that paralyzed the city of São Paulo and challenged the state. São Paulo had largely been considered immune to such violence, as attacks by criminal groups on this scale were typically associated with places like the favelas of Rio de Janeiro. The 2006 attacks included the murders of police officials, attacks against police stations, and the firebombing of buses and banks (Bailey & Taylor, 2009). They were so severe that businesses, transportation, and entire sections of the city were forced to shut down. Multiple attacks even disabled security forces, leaving them unable to help civilians. Prisons were overtaken and thousands of visitors were held hostage (Logan, 2006). Approximately 140 deaths were directly tied to the attacks (Bailey & Taylor, 2009).

The open challenge of the PCC was a clear sign that the group's interactions with the state were in disequilibrium. The fact that the PCC was prepared to unleash such a violent attack against state forces is a clear indication of its perception of its power vis-à-vis that of the state (Bailey & Taylor, 2009). The PCC was willing to confront the state openly and decisively to challenge state disciplinary policy and living conditions in prisons. In addition to addressing these goals, the violent confrontation also strengthened the PCC leadership's power within its organization and in the prisons. In the aftermath of the 2006 attacks, it appears the PCC did increase its bargaining power with the state. Despite official denials, there was evidence of PCC negotiation with the state to end the attacks (Bailey & Taylor, 2009). Even though the state retaliated with police crackdowns on suspects and senior PCC leaders were isolated in a high security prison, many argue that the PCC's ability to orchestrate such violent attacks did increase its future bargaining power. The state's relationship with the PCC may have returned to the equilibrium of disruption/corruption, but the potential for future violent confrontation may enhance the PCC's power. This dynamic is not unique to Brazil. Recent events in El Salvador share many similarities to those of Brazil, as news reports indicate that the state has negotiated with gang members to reduce violence outside the prisons in exchange for better conditions within them (Archibold, 2012).

This was not always the preferred tactic of the Salvadoran government, however. Overall, under democratization, El Salvador has relied extensively on *mano dura*, or iron fist, tactics to confront criminal groups. The goal of mano dura tactics is the elimination of criminal elements, not coexistence or disruption. To be sure, since El Salvador's murder rate of 52 per 100,000 inhabitants makes it one of the most violent countries in the world, it is easy to see why the government would not favor coexistence and disruption strategies when dealing with its criminal groups. By the turn of the century, the state clearly embraced a mano dura strategy, launching Plan Mano Dura in 2003. Included in this plan was the controversial measure that allowed police to arrest suspected gang members on the basis of their physical appearance (Amnesty International, 2003). Plan Mano Dura proved very popular with the public, despite its inability to actually reduce rates of violent crime. Homicide rates in El Salvador dipped from 2000 to 2002, but then continued to climb by the mid 2000s, just like in the other countries of the Northern Triangle (Malone, 2012).

In light of the failure of Plan Mano Dura to curb rising homicide rates, in the late 2000s El Salvador unveiled a new plan to confront the maras—Plan Super Mano Dura (Wolf, 2011). Like its predecessor, Plan Super Mano Dura proved very popular with a public weary of so much crime and violence. Its provisions included increasing the penalties for gang membership to up to 5 years of incarceration and allowing the conviction of minors under the age of 12 (Ribando Seelke, 2011). In one year, Plan Super Mano Dura led to the arrests of approximately 11,000 alleged gang members (Booth, Wade, & Walker, 2010). Also like its predecessor, Plan Super Mano Dura failed to curb violence. The high rates of incarceration proved to be a boon to some gang leaders, as overcrowded prisons served as a fertile ground for recruiting and training new members. Gang members adapted to the new playing field and employed more violent tactics (Wolf, 2011). By 2010, experts considered the gang problem to be intractable. In response, the state announced a "comprehensive crime policy comprising social prevention, law enforcement, rehabilitation, victim support, and institutional and legal reforms" (Wolf, 2011, p. 1). While this response did include some preventive measures and police reforms, lack of funding has put these parts of the program on the back burner, and in some cases the state has even dispatched the military to patrol the streets and curb the power of gangs. Reports that the state was negotiating with gang members in March of 2012 was a break from past trends, and it is unclear whether the corresponding drops in the homicide rates would encourage more of these negotiations in the future. To be sure, there was a great deal of opposition to such negotiations in El Salvador. A spokesperson for an opposition party told newspapers that negotiating with gangs "would be a nefarious precedent. . . . The government would be offering itself to extortionists" (Archibold, 2012).

The case of Guatemala highlights a very unique model of addressing the problems posed by organized crime. High levels of violence, alongside concern that Guatemala was a disintegrating narco-state, raised alarm not just within Guatemala but in the international community as well. The United Nations declared that the Guatemalan government was infiltrated "by criminal clandestine organizations and the operation of violent illegal security forces outside of the control of the Guatemalan state" (Hudson & Taylor, 2010, p. 56). To combat criminal organizations in Guatemala, the United Nations collaborated with domestic reformers to pilot an unusual experiment. On September 4, 2007, Guatemala and the United Nations established the Comisión Internacional Contra la Impunidad en Guatemala (the International Commission Against Impunity in Guatemala), known by its Spanish acronym, CICIG. Funded by voluntary contributions from the international community, CICIG is a unique hybrid organization comprising international and domestic actors but operating solely within the legal framework of Guatemala. CICIG has the power to investigate government abuses of power and the activities of criminal organizations, to make policy recommendations, and to act as a "complimentary prosecutor" when needed (particularly in controversial or sensitive cases) (CICIG, 2009). Since its inception, CICIG has focused particularly on the problem of organized crime, launching several high-profile investigations of drug trafficking and drug-related murders.

After 3 years, CICIG can boast some success. The mere fact that a former president, Alfonso Portillo, was arrested along with several other high-ranking government officials is a sign that CICIG has worked with its domestic partners to change a status quo of impunity. CICIG has also influenced reform efforts and provided valuable technical assistance. This has resulted in the passage of important legislation such as the Law on Arms and Ammunition, as well as the strengthening of the national witness protection program and the national wiretapping system (CICIG, 2009). In addition, CICIG has garnered support from citizens in Guatemala. In 2010, the Latin American Public Opinion Project (LAPOP) survey asked people to indicate how much trust they had in a variety of institutions in Guatemala, including CICIG. Compared to the domestic institutions in Guatemala, respondents viewed CICIG in a significantly more favorable light, earning a level of legitimacy far above that of domestic institutions (Malone, 2012). Still, despite these important successes, CICIG's work has been undermined by corrupt officials, weak institutions, and recalcitrant crime lords. For example, the prosecution of one corrupt national police chief linked to organized crime is a step forward, but not if another corrupt chief takes his or her place. Both domestic and international reformers have become frustrated with the resilience of corruption and impunity. On June 7, 2010, CICIG Commissioner Carlos Castresana resigned to protest the appointment of an attorney general he charged had links to organized crime (Malkin, 2010). The ability to address high-profile cases of official impunity is laudable, and this ability has become a potent symbol of the potential for reform. However, the number of cases investigated by CICIG is a small fraction of the whole. In CICIG's first year, it discarded 49 of the 64 complaints received (Hudson & Taylor, 2010, p. 62).

There are additional international collaboration efforts to curb the power of organized crime in the region. For example, programs such as the Mérida Initiative have attempted to coordinate domestic fights against drug trafficking, organized crime, and the related violence. In June 2008, the Mérida Initiative launched a 3-year partnership among the United States, Mexico, the Dominican Republic, Haiti, and the Central American nations. This program prioritizes several justice reforms, such as the provision of equipment and training for law enforcement and security operations. Such efforts are laudable in that they recognize the regional nature of the problem of organized crime in the region; however, it is not yet clear whether they can mount a decisive response to such a resilient foe.

⁂ NOTEſ

1. These rankings are part of the World Bank's (2012) Worldwide Governance Indicators (WGI 2012), available online at http://data.worldbank.org/data-catalog/worldwide-governance-indicators/.

2. Mara is a diminutive of *marabunta*, the name of "a brutal ant that reproduces like the plague and is capable of destroying everything in its path" (Nowalski, 2006, p. 32).

⁂ REFERENCEſ

Amnesty International. (2003). El Salvador: Open letter on the Anti-Maras Act. Retrieved from http://www.amnesty.org/es/library/assetAMR29/009/2003/es/3fb7905f-d65d-11dd-ab95-a13b602c0642/amr290092003en.pdf

Archibold, R. (2012, March 24). Homicides in El Salvador dip, and questions arise. *New York Times*. Retrieved from http://www.nytimes.com/ 2012/03/25/world/americas/homicides-in-el-salvador-drop-and-questions-arise.html?_r=0

Archibold, R., & Cave, D. (2011, March 23). Drug wars push deeper into Central America. *New York Times*. Retrieved from http://www.nytimes.com/2011/03/24/world/americas/24drugs.html?page wanted=all

Bailey, J. (2011, March 31). Prepared statement for the House Committee on Homeland Security, Subcommittee on Oversight, Investigations, and Management. *Hearing on the U.S. Homeland Security Role in the Mexican War against Drug Cartels*. 112th Cong. 82 (2011).

Bailey, J., & Taylor, M. (2009). Evade, corrupt, or confront? Organized crime and the state in Brazil and Mexico. *Journal of Politics in Latin America, 1*(2), 3–29.

Booth, J., Wade C. J., & Walker T. W. (2010). *Understanding Central America: Global forces, rebellion, and change* (5th ed.). Boulder, CO: Westview Press.

Bruneau, T., Dammert, L., & Skinner, E. (2011). *Maras: Gang violence and security in Central America*. Austin: University of Texas Press.

Call, C. T. (2003). Democratisation, war and state-building: Constructing the rule of law in El Salvador. *Journal of Latin American Studies, 35*(4), 827–862.

Comisión Internacional Contra la Impunidad en Guatemala. (2009). *Two years of work: A commitment to justice* (United Nations report). Retrieved from http://cicig.org/uploads/documents/report_two_years_of_work.pdf

Cruz, J. M. (2006). Violence, citizen insecurity, and elite maneuvering in El Salvador. In J. Bailey & L. Dammert (Eds.), *Public security and police reform in the Americas*, pp. 148–168. Pittsburgh, PA: University of Pittsburgh Press.

Gootenberg, P. (2010). Blowback: The Mexican drug crisis. *NACLA Report on the Americas, 43*(6), 7–12.

Herrera, A., & Espinoza, B. (2008). *La Seguridad ciudadana en el municipio de León, Nicaragua* [Public safety in the city of Leon]. León, Nicaragua: UNAN-Editorial Universitaria.

Hudson, A., & Taylor, A. W. (2010). The International Commission against Impunity in Guatemala: A new model for international criminal justice mechanisms. *Journal of International Criminal Justice, 8*, 53–74.

Jütersonke, O., Muggah, R., & Rodgers, D. (2009). Gangs, urban violence, and security interventions in Central America. *Security Dialogue, 40*(4–5), 373–397.

Logan, S. (2006, May 24). Brazil s P.C.C.: True power behind the violence. *Power and Interest News Report*. Retrieved from http://www.samuellogan.com/articles/brazils-pcc-true-power-behind-the-violence.html

Malkin, E. (2010, July 4). Strains in Guatemala's experimental justice system. *New York Times*. Retrieved from http://www.nytimes.com/2010/07/04/world/americas/04guatemala.html?pagewanted=all

Malone, M. F. (2012). *The rule of law in Central America: Citizens' reactions to crime and punishment*. New York, NY: Continuum.

Millet, R. L. (2009). Crime and citizen security: Democracy's Achilles heel. In R. L. Millet, J. S. Holmes, & O. J. Pérez (Eds.), *Latin American democracy: Emerging reality or endangered species* (pp. 252–264). New York, NY: Routledge.

Naím, M. (2005). *Illicit: How smugglers, traffickers and copycats are hijacking the global economy*. New York, NY: Anchor Books.

Nowalski, J. (2006). Human security and sustainable livelihoods in Central America: The case of the maras. In S. Pattnayak & L. Gustafson (Eds.), *National and human security issues in Latin America: Democracies at risk* (pp. 25–34). Lewiston, NY: Edwin Mellen Press.

Okrent, D. (2010). *Last call: The rise and fall of prohibition.* New York, NY: Scribner.

Pérez, O. (2000). Drugs and post-intervention political economy in Haiti and Panama. In I. L. Griffith (Ed.), *The political economy of drugs in the Caribbean* (pp. 138–161). New York, NY: Palgrave.

Reuters. (2010, October 30). 14 killed on sports field in Honduras. *New York Times.* Retrieved from http://www.nytimes.com/2010/10/31/world/americas/31honduras.html

Ribando Seelke, C. (2011). *Gangs in Central America (updated).* Congressional Research Service (CRS), Washington, DC: Library of Congress. Retrieved from http://www.fas.org/sgp/crs/row/RL34112.pdf

Rubio, M., & Ortiz, R. (2005). Organized crime in Latin America. In P. Reichel (Ed.), *Handbook of transnational crime and justice* (pp. 425–437). Thousand Oaks, CA: Sage.

Shifter, M. (2011). Central America's security predicament. *Current History, 110*(733), 49–53.

Sibaja, H., Roig, E., Rajaraman, A., Bolaños, A., & Acuña, A. (2006). *Central America and Mexico gang assessment, Annex 5: Nicaragua profile.* Washington, DC: U.S. Agency for International Development. Retrieved from http://transition.usaid.gov/locations/latin_america_caribbean/democracy/nicaragua_profile.pdf

Sullivan, M. P. (1997). *Panama-U.S. Relations: Continuing policy concerns.* Congressional Research Service (CRS), Foreign Affairs and National Defense Division. Retrieved from http://www.fas.org/man/crs/92-088.htm

Wolf, S. (2011). Mano Dura: Gang suppression in El Salvador. Retrieved from http://sustainable security.org/article/mano-dura-gang-suppression-el-salvador

World Bank. (2012). Worldwide governance indicators. Retrieved from http://data.worldbank.org/data-catalog/worldwide-governance-indicators

4

Transnational Organized Crime in Europe

Klaus von Lampe

░ TRANSNATIONAL ORGANIZED CRIME IN EUROPE

This chapter examines transnational organized crime in the European context. There are two sides to this issue. First of all, transnational organized crime is an internal problem in the form of cross-border crime connecting countries within Europe. At the same time, it is a facet of the global landscape of cross-border crime. Both aspects are considered here.

However, before delving into a discussion of the underlying phenomena, it is necessary to first establish a conceptual framework that is more meaningful and more concise than the concept of "transnational organized crime," which adds the notion of transnationality to the fuzzy and ambiguous concept of "organized crime" (Van Duyne & Nelemans, 2012; von Lampe, 2011; von Lampe, van Dijck, Hornsby, Markina, & Verpoest, 2006).

The concept of organized crime can be broken down into three basic dimensions: criminal activities, offender structures, and illegal governance. According to one view, organized crime is about crime that is organized in contrast to spontaneous, irrational criminal behavior. According to another view, organized crime is about organizations of criminals labeled, for example, "networks," "cartels," or "mafias." A third view, finally, holds that organized crime is about the exercise of power by criminals in those areas that the government is unwilling or unable to regulate—for example, illegal markets or remote parts of a country.

Along these lines, *transnational* organized crime can be conceptualized in terms of three main categories: (1) illegal activities that somehow transcend international borders; (2) transnationally mobile criminal organizations—respectively, criminal organizations with a presence in more than one country; and (3) the extension of illegal governance across international borders.

Although empirically these three categories may overlap, in the interest of clarity it appears preferable to examine each category separately with regard to the situation in Europe.

≋ GLOBAL CRIMEJ

Transnational criminal activities—namely, the smuggling of illegal goods—connect Europe with other parts of the world, and different countries within Europe (Europol, 2011a; U.N. Office on Drugs and Crime [UNODC], 2010). When one looks at the trafficking routes that span the globe, Europe can be found at either end: It is a destination for as well as a source of contraband that is being moved between continents. Most commonly, however, Europe is seen as a major consumer market.

This applies in particular to illegal drugs—namely, cocaine originating in South America and heroin originating in Central Asia. According to the U.N. World Drug Report, Europe is the world's second largest consumer market for cocaine (UNODC, 2011, p. 111) and the main consumer market for heroin (UNODC, 2011, pp. 71–73).

Both cocaine and heroin arrive in Europe as finished products. From what is known, there are no laboratories within Europe that manufacture heroin and few if any laboratories that manufacture cocaine from raw materials or intermediate products. What have been found in Spain and Greece are installations for repackaging heroin and for the secondary extraction of smuggled cocaine from substances used to prevent detection during overseas transport (UNODC, 2011, pp. 61, 104, 105).

A somewhat different picture presents itself with regard to cannabis. Although Europe is an important market for cannabis from Africa, in particular Morocco, it appears that European consumers are increasingly supplied with cannabis produced in indoor plantations within Europe (European Monitoring Centre for Drugs and Drug Addiction [EMCDDA], 2011, p. 41; UNODC, 2011, p. 190). Interestingly, indoor cannabis plantations in a number of European countries—namely, the United Kingdom, have been prominently linked to Vietnamese immigrants (Larsson, 2009; Nozina, 2010; Silverstone & Savage, 2010).

In the case of synthetic drugs, likewise, the European market is primarily supplied by producers within Europe. At the same time, Europe is the world's main producer of amphetamine (EMCDDA & Europol, 2011) and it has in the past also been an important source for ecstasy (MDMA) marketed overseas. However, as a result of successful law enforcement intervention, Europe's role as a supplier of ecstasy has declined sharply in recent years (UNODC, 2011, pp. 38–39; U.S President, 2008, p. 21).

Besides illegal drugs, Europe is an important destination for other illegal goods such as protected cultural artifacts (Lane, Bromley, Hicks, & Mahoney, 2008), protected wildlife (Liddick, 2011), and counterfeit brand products, including medicine (World Health Organization [WHO], 2010), software (Nill & Shultz, 2009) and cigarettes (von Lampe, Kurti, Shen, & Antonopoulos, 2012).

Human trafficking for sexual exploitation and labor exploitation, since the fall of the Iron Curtain, appears to have been primarily a phenomenon within Europe. But there are also trafficking routes into Europe—for example, from China and Nigeria (Dowling, Moreton, & Wright, 2007; Europol, 2011a; Lebov, 2010; Smit, 2011; UNODC, 2009). However, the main illegal movement of people into Europe involves alien smuggling rather than human trafficking. All European countries are believed to be affected to some degree by illegal migration, facilitated in part by commercially operating alien smugglers (Antonopoulos & Winterdyk, 2006; Coluccello & Massey, 2007; Düvell, 2008; Kaizen & Nonneman, 2007; UNODC, 2010, pp. 67–77).

There are also illegal cross-border movements in the opposite direction, out of Europe to other parts of the world. Europe's role as an exporter of ecstasy and amphetamine has already been noted. Two other areas of transnational crime are also noteworthy: the trafficking in stolen motor vehicles and the trafficking in illegal waste. Main trafficking routes for stolen cars extend from Western Europe to Asia and to Africa (Europol, 2004). Likewise, in the case of illegal waste disposal—namely, second-hand electric and electronic equipment—main target countries are located in Asia and Africa (Europol, 2011b; Interpol, 2009).

Europe is an important global center for the theft and sale of credit card data and similarly valuable information over the Internet. This pertains in particular to the Russian-speaking parts of Eastern Europe (Chu, Holt, & Ahn, 2010). At the same time, European Internet users are the target of advance fee fraudsters from Africa (Ampratwum, 2009).

In the case of arms trafficking, smuggling routes lead into and out of Europe, and they also connect countries within Europe (Sagramoso, 2001; Spapens, 2007; UNODC, 2010, pp. 129–146).

The global illegal trade in human organs is a special case. There is a strong European component here as well, both in terms of organ donors from poor countries such as Moldova and in terms of wealthy Europeans receiving trafficked organs, with the transplantations typically, it seems, taking place outside Europe (Lundin, 2012; Scheper-Hughes, 2004).

The common pattern these global crime connections follow for the most part, with the notable exception of synthetic drugs, is the transfer of wealth (e.g., in the case of agricultural drugs from Latin America, Africa, and Asia being sold in Europe) or of costs (e.g., in the case of electronic waste trafficked from Europe to Africa and Asia) from richer to poorer countries. A similar pattern can be observed within Europe.

⟫ TRANSNATIONAL CRIMES WITHIN EUROPE

Transnational organized crime within Europe is mostly framed as an expression of the socioeconomic contrast between Western Europe on one hand and the former Soviet Bloc and Balkan countries on the other. There are indeed certain transnational crimes that to some extent are defined by an East-West axis. For example, the trafficking in stolen motor vehicles typically goes from Western Europe to Eastern Europe (Antonopoulos & Papanicolaou, 2009; Gounev & Bezlov, 2008), similar to other forms of predatory crimes such as cross-border serial burglary where Eastern European criminal groups operate in Western Europe (Weenink, Huisman, & van der Laan, 2004). In contrast, the trafficking in women for sexual exploitation (Surtees, 2008; Viuhko & Jokinen, 2009) and the smuggling of cigarettes (Europol, 2011a, pp. 32–33) goes primarily in the opposite direction, from Eastern Europe to Western Europe. There are, however, variations. Human-trafficking routes are in part determined by geographical proximity—for example, between Scandinavia and the Baltic states; in part they appear to reflect consumer demands and to connect source countries in Eastern Europe with Western Europe over greater distances. At the same time, trafficking routes also exist between different countries of transition in Eastern and Southeastern Europe (Englund, 2008; Kelly, 2002; Surtees, 2008; Viuhko & Jokinen, 2009).

In the case of cigarette smuggling, particular European countries have at different times stood out as main source and transshipment countries—such as Belgium, Poland, Lithuania, Montenegro, and Ukraine—and main destination countries—such as Italy, Spain, Germany, and the United Kingdom (Hornsby & Hobbs, 2007; Hozic, 2004; Joossens & Raw, 2008; Vander Beken, Janssens, Verpoest, Balcaen, & Vander Laenen, 2008; von Lampe, 2006).

Other transnational crimes fit even less readily into a strict East-West schema. In fact, the European crime landscape can perhaps best be described as a patchwork where trafficking routes and regional crime hotspots are unevenly distributed across space and time (von Lampe, 2008). This is best documented in the case of illegal drugs.

The main point of entry for cocaine and cannabis imports into Europe is the Iberian Peninsula (Spain and Portugal) while heroin enters Europe primarily through the traditional Balkan route involving countries in Southeastern Europe, and the silk route through Russia. The Netherlands and to a limited extent Belgium likewise serve as important points of entry as well as distribution centers within Europe for these agricultural drugs (EMCDDA, 2011; UNODC, 2011).

The Netherlands and Belgium also figure prominently in the production and distribution of synthetic drugs, namely, amphetamine and ecstasy (EMCDDA, 2011). The production of methamphetamine, however, is historically concentrated elsewhere in Europe, namely, in the Czech Republic and Slovakia. Labs have also been found more recently in Lithuania, Germany, and Poland. At the same time, consumption of methamphetamine is most prevalent in Scandinavia and the Baltic region, underscoring the patchwork character of transnational crime in Europe (EMCDDA, 2011, p. 52; Europol, 2011a, p. 16).

Other examples for the uneven distribution of crime patterns across Europe include the concentration of the production of counterfeit Euros in Bulgaria and Italy (Europol, 2011a, p. 34) and the concentration of certain kinds of cybercrime in the Russian-speaking parts of Eastern Europe (Chu et al., 2010).

〰 THE ORGANIZATION OF TRANSNATIONAL OFFENDERS

When one shifts the focus from patterns of criminal activities to the organizational structures that connect the offenders involved in these criminal activities, an even more complex picture emerges. This is true especially when one departs from superficial accounts fixated on the ethnic background of offenders.

Transnational organized crime is often classified along ethnic lines or by the nationality of offenders. This makes sense to some extent since in particular areas of transnational crime there is a disproportionate involvement of offenders of certain ethnic or national backgrounds (Europol, 2011a). This may reflect the strategic importance of certain countries for specific types of transnational crime or particular trafficking routes, and it may reflect links between former colonial powers and their colonies or links between source and destination countries of migration. For example, offenders with personal links to important production and transshipment centers such as Colombia, Venezuela, the Antilles, or West Africa in the case of cocaine trafficking tend to have a competitive advantage over offenders with no such ties (Zaitch, 2002).

Migrant communities are also often highlighted as an important support infrastructure for transnational offenders. They constitute "niches of familiarity" (von Lampe, 2011, p. 6) and provide some level of protection from law enforcement because of the shielding effects of cultural and language differences (Kleemans & van de Bunt, 2002, p. 25; Paoli & Reuter, 2008, p. 24; Williams & Godson, 2002, pp. 330–331).

At the same time, ethnicity and nationality are too broad and too superficial categories for the conceptualization of transnational criminal structures. And they are misleading in the sense that they fail to capture the ethnic diversity of criminal structures in Europe. A more careful analysis needs to take other dimensions into account—namely, the form and function of criminal structures.

A Conceptual Framework for Analyzing Transnational Criminal Structures

Offender structures, generally speaking, serve one or more of three functions: economic, social, and quasi-governmental. Economic criminal structures aim at material gain. This category comprises entrepreneurial structures in a broad sense, including, for example, drug-smuggling rings and burglary gangs. These entrepreneurial structures have to be distinguished, analytically, from criminal structures that serve social functions. These noneconomic, associational structures support their members' illegal economic activities only indirectly. For example, they facilitate contacts, give status, reinforce deviant values, and provide a forum for the exchange of information. Examples for structures serving these social purposes include criminal fraternities such as the Sicilian Mafia (Paoli, 2003) and outwardly legal associations such as so-called outlaw motorcycle gangs (Barker, 2007).

A third type of criminal structures serves quasi-governmental functions. These illegal governance structures support illegal economic activities in a more abstract way by establishing and enforcing rules of conduct and by settling disputes in a given territory or market. A textbook example for this kind of criminal structure is once again the Sicilian Mafia (Gambetta, 1993). This highlights the fact that the three functions (economic, social, and quasi-governmental) may empirically overlap (von Lampe, 2008).

Entrepreneurial, associational, and quasi-governmental structures are not linked to a particular form of organization. Criminal structures may be formal or informal, and the interactions between offenders may vary with the degree to which they are integrated in long-term relationships. Following a threefold typology of markets, networks, and hierarchies, borrowed from economics (Powell, 1990), three basic forms of cooperation between offenders can be distinguished. Interactions may involve *independent actors* engaged in market-based transactions. In other cases, offenders may be integrated in *networks* that provide some level of commitment beyond a single transaction. Finally, in the case of *criminal organizations* in the narrow sense, coordinated action is the result of authoritatively assigned tasks. What form of organization emerges depends on various factors, including the specifics of the criminal activity offenders are involved in and the social environment they operate in.

Criminal structures, irrespective of their form and function, can be transnational in different ways. They may temporarily cross borders, they may establish a permanent presence in two or more countries, or they may migrate from one country to another.

Illegal Entrepreneurial Structures

Fairly complex criminal organizations have been reported in the area of cross-border predatory crime. These organizations operate from bases in Eastern Europe and engage in crimes such as serial burglary or pickpocketing in Western Europe. They typically consist of a management level and an operative level that may comprise several teams charged with separate tasks, such as casing a target, committing a burglary, and disposing of the loot (see, e.g., Europol, 2007; Weenink et al., 2004, p. 186).

One example is the so-called Koszalin gang (also known as "hammer gang" and "Rolex gang"), named after a town in northwestern Poland. The gang comprised about 200 members and existed over a time span of about 10 years until it was dismantled in 2004. It engaged in robberies of jewelry stores in Western European countries, using either stolen cars to gain entry into stores by brute force or entering stores during business hours to then, within minutes, smash showcases with sledgehammers and remove high-value merchandise such as luxury watches. Gang members were typically recruited for the execution of these crimes from among unemployed men in their mid-20s to mid-30s. They operated in teams under the direction of "group leaders" who cooperated with "residents" in the target areas and reported to the gang leadership in Poland (Rieger, 2006).

Predatory crime groups tend to retreat from an area of operation after committing a certain number of crimes. They constitute what may be called 'transnationally mobile criminal organizations." In some cases, however, including the Koszalin gang, they rely on individuals who permanently reside in the country of operation and assist in the selection of targets and provide logistical support (Vander Beken & Van Daele, 2009; von Lampe, 2009). Such residents, who may have been sent or recruited by a criminal group or who may operate as independent entrepreneurs, can also be found in other areas of crime—namely, drug trafficking (Soudijn & Huisman, 2011).

In contrast to transnationally mobile criminal organizations with little or no permanent presence abroad, there are also criminal organizations with branches in two or more countries where similar tasks are completed in each country or a division of labor exists between branches in different countries. In these cases, one may speak of "multinational criminal organizations." For example, in the case of trafficking in stolen motor vehicles it appears to be more common for offender structures to extend across international borders on a more permanent basis. This means that tasks such as the stealing of cars and the changing of the identity of the stolen cars is typically done in one country, while the overall management of the operation, including the selling of the stolen cars, is handled in another country (von der Lage, 2003).

However, Gounev and Bezlov (2008) argue with regard to Bulgarian car traffickers that in recent years there has been a tendency away from complex, multinational illegal enterprises. They found that offenders involved in this type of crime—such as car thieves, mechanics, document forgers, courier drivers, and intermediaries—now tend to flexibly cooperate in changing combinations of individuals and small groups within larger transnational networks of criminally exploitable ties (Gounev & Bezlov, 2008, pp. 419–420).

In fact, such fluid structures, rather than vertically and horizontally integrated organizations, appear to be common for many other transnational criminal activities. Drug trafficking, human trafficking, and alien smuggling, it seems, tend to involve chains of individual offenders, partnerships, and small clusters of criminals linked up by more or less temporary cooperative arrangements (Bruinsma & Bernasco, 2004; Englund, 2008; Kostakos & Antonopoulos, 2010; Leman & Janssens, 2008; Matrix Knowledge Group, 2007; Ruggiero & Khan, 2007; Soudijn & Kleemans, 2009).

Underlying Associational Structures

Illegal entrepreneurial structures are in many cases embedded in underlying social network ties that facilitate both the creation and the maintenance of entrepreneurial structures by providing a basis of trust (von Lampe & Johansen, 2004).

Ethnicity is often mentioned in this respect. In most cases, however, it appears that ethnic homogeneity is a superficial characteristic of criminal networks based on family, friendship, or local community ties (Kleemans & van de Bunt, 2002, p. 23). As a result of migration, these close social ties may span great geographical distances. For example, heroin trafficking from production in Eastern Turkey to sale in Western Europe may be handled by members of the same family (Bruinsma & Bernasco, 2004, p. 87).

Ritual kinship ties can potentially provide a similar support infra-structure for transnational criminal activities. This is true for various criminal fraternities with membership spread across different European countries, such as the Sicilian Mafia (or Cosa Nostra), the Camorra, the Calabrian 'Nrdangheta, the Russian and Georgian Vory v Zakone, and the Chinese triads, as well as outlaw motorcycle gangs such as the Hells Angels and Bandidos (Barker, 2007; Kukhianidze, 2009; Pullat, 2009; Roth, 2009; Schwirtz, 2008; Silverstone, 2011; Soudijn & Kleemans, 2009; Wright, 2006).

How this plays out in practice has been shown by Campana (2011) in his analysis of a Camorra clan that included some members who had relocated to Scotland and the Netherlands. The members residing abroad assisted members in Italy in a number of ways—namely, in the launder-ing of money, by providing refuge, and by sharing investment opportuni-ties in legal and illegal businesses.

Criminal Networks Not Embedded in Associational Structures

While kinship ties and ritual kinship ties provide a basis for illegal entrepreneurial structures, close bonds of that nature are not necessarily a precondition for the emergence of transnational criminal networks. Relatively weak social ties such as childhood acquaintance or contacts established in the context of legitimate business relations can be sufficient grounds for criminal cooperation (Antonopoulos, 2008, p. 277; Kleemans & de Poot, 2008, pp. 90–91; von Lampe, 2009, pp. 26–34; von Lampe & Johansen, 2004).

Prisons are an incubator sui generis of transnational criminal networks. An illustrative case is Ronald Miehling who went from pimp and small-time criminal to one of Germany's major drug traffickers as a result of meeting a cocaine dealer from the Dutch Antilles in a German prison. At a Christmas party in Amsterdam, Miehling was subsequently introduced to a drug trafficker from New York City who eventually brought him in direct contact with cocaine suppliers in Colombia (Miehling & Timmerberg, 2004).

The Christmas party Miehling mentions is an example for convergence settings that bring transnational criminals together without preexisting ties. It also underscores the special role that the city of Amsterdam plays for transnational organized crime in Europe and, in particular, the drug trade. Amsterdam has been identified as an important European meeting place for drug traffickers involved in the trade of cannabis, cocaine, and heroin as well as synthetic drugs (Caulkins, Burnett, & Leslie, 2009, p. 68; Huisman, Huikeshoven, & van de Bunt, 2003; Junninen, 2006, p. 157; Ruggiero & Khan, 2006, p. 479, 2007, p. 170; Zaitch, 2002, p. 106).

A different kind of international offender convergence setting has been pointed out by Kleemans and van de Bunt (2008). They describe a case of financial professionals who regularly met at international tax conferences and under the guise of "tax seminars" and conspired in the commission of large-scale tax fraud. This example underscores the importance of legitimate social network ties and of "routine activities of everyday life" (Decker & Chapman, 2008, p. 108) in the creation of transnational criminal structures. While certain patterns in the organization of transnational offenders exist, reflecting, for example, flows of migration and the direction of trafficking routes, the multiplicity of factors that shape criminal structures almost inevitably results in the diffuse patchwork of activities and actors that characterizes transnational organized crime in Europe.

⬚ ILLEGAL GOVERNANCE

The discussion in this chapter so far has focused on the commission of transnational profit-making crimes and on the organization of offenders involved in these crimes. This leaves one issue to be examined that ranks prominently in the public debate on organized crime in Europe: the transnational expansion of the spheres of influence of "mafia" organizations. In this context, mafias are not addressed as fraternal associations of criminals but as illegal governance structures that exercise some level of control over illegal and possibly also legal activities in a certain territory. The controversial question is to what extent these structures, which historically are local in nature, can replicate their position of power in another country.

Concerns that Italian mafia-type organizations such as the Sicilian Mafia, the Neapolitan Camorra, and the Calabrian 'Ndrangheta or Russian criminal groups such as the Moscow-based Solntsevskaya might colonize Europe have been a recurring theme for decades. These concerns typically surface in the wake of spectacular acts of violence such as the killing of six men outside an Italian restaurant in Duisburg, Germany, in August 2007. However, these events tend to be misleading. The victims in Duisburg, it turned out, were members of a 'Ndrangheta clan; however, they were murdered not in a quest for power in Germany, but in the course of a long-standing blood feud that pitted two families from the Calabrian town of San Luca against each other. The Duisburg murder was reportedly committed in revenge for the killing of a woman in San Luca a few months earlier (Fisher & Kiefer, 2007).

According to one view, mafias are unlikely to expand their territorial control across borders because of the specific sociopolitical context within which they have emerged (Gambetta, 1993, p. 251). According to another view, mafias are able to establish themselves in new territories provided a demand for criminal protection exists that is not met by domestic criminal organizations (Varese, 2011, p. 23).

Research on this issue is scarce and only two studies exist on the question of mafia transplantation within Europe that suggest that mafia organizations indeed tend to be unable to establish territorial control abroad.

The first study is Campana's (2011) previously mentioned investigation of members of a Camorra clan residing in the Netherlands and the United Kingdom. He found that while the clan provides illegal protection services at its home base in Italy in the form of, for example, protection against competitors and thieves, dispute settlement and debt collection, no evidence exists of any such activities being carried out abroad (2011, p. 219).

The second study, by Varese (2011), investigates the presence of members and associates of the Moscow-based Solntsevskaya in Italy and Hungary.

In the case of Italy, Varese (2011) found a picture similar to that described by Campana. Russian "mafiosi" residing in Italy aided members of Solntsevskaya in the laundering of money, but they made no attempt to establish any form of territorial control or to engage in any form of criminal protection in Italy (p. 81). In contrast, Varese argues that a successful "transplantation" of Solntsevskaya has taken place in Hungary in the 1990s citing evidence that a group led by a Ukrainian-born businessman with "solid connections with the Solntsevskaya's leaders" extracted protection payments from criminals and owners of legitimate businesses (2011, p. 92).

From the evidence presented by Varese (2011), however, it is not clear whether this can be attributed to Solntsevskaya as an organizational entity or is better interpreted as the work of individuals and groups operating within the context of Hungary's transition economy.

In the latter case, the example of criminals from the former Soviet Union operating in Hungary would better fit a more general pattern of multiethnic underworlds that appear to be characteristic of most if not all European countries. Criminals of particular ethnic and national backgrounds may achieve prominence in certain localities and certain illegal markets that would be more reflective of general migration patterns than of the migration of criminal organizations.

A separate issue is the expansion of outlaw motorcycle gangs in Europe. Organizations with origins in the United States—namely, the Hells Angels and Bandidos—have established chapters in Northwest Europe since the 1970s and 1980s. More recently, recruitment efforts have extended to Southern and Southeastern Europe, including Turkey and Albania (Ziercke, 2010, p. 701). Outlaw motorcycle gangs are fiercely territorial. However, it seems that territorial control is primarily sought within the context of the biker subculture in terms of the hegemony or exclusivity of one biker club in a given geographical area (Bader, 2011; Barker, 2007). Violent conflicts between outlaw motorcycle gangs have broken out as a result of territorial conflicts, for example, in Scandinavia in the 1990s (the "Nordic Biker War") and in Central Europe in the 2000s (Wright, 2006).

⁂ CONCLUSION

This chapter has examined transnational organized crime in Europe with regard to criminal activities, offender structures, and illegal governance. Transnational crimes connect Europe with other parts of the world and different countries on the European continent. The picture that emerges is that of a patchwork of trafficking routes and crime hotspots, involving criminals of different ethnic and national backgrounds. Offender structures take on a variety of forms, from purely market-based interaction to networks of criminally exploitable ties and, in some cases, more integrated criminal organizations. Mafia-like organizations such as the notorious Sicilian Mafia have a presence in various European countries as a result of the migration of individual members. However, in their role as illegal governance structures these mafia organizations tend to be confined to their territories of origin.

※ REFERENCEſ

Ampratwum, E. F. (2009). Advance fee fraud "419" and investor confidence in the economies of sub-Saharan African (SSA). *Journal of Financial Crime*, *16*(1), 67–79.

Antonopoulos, G. A. (2008). The Greek connection(s): The social organization of the cigarette-smuggling business in Greece. *European Journal of Criminology*, *5*(3), 263–288.

Antonopoulos, G. A., & Papanicolaou, G. (2009). "Gone in 50 seconds": The social organisation and political economy of the stolen cars market in Greece. In P. C. van Duyne, S. Donati, J. Harvey, A. Maljevic, & K. von Lampe (Eds.), *Crime, money and criminal mobility in Europe* (pp. 141–174). Nijmegen, the Netherlands: Wolf Legal.

Antonopoulos, G. A., & Winterdyk, J. (2006). The smuggling of migrants in Greece: An examination of its social organization. *European Journal of Criminology*, *3*(4), 439–461.

Bader, J. (2011). Outlaw motorcycle clubs. *Kriminalistik*, *65*(4), 227–234.

Barker, T. (2007). *Biker gangs and organized crime*. Newark, NJ: Matthew Bender.

Bruinsma, G., & Bernasco, W. (2004). Criminal groups and transnational illegal markets: A more detailed examination on the basis of social network theory. *Crime, Law and Social Change*, *41*(1), 79–94.

Campana, P. (2011). Eavesdropping on the mob: The functional diversification of Mafia activities across territories. *European Journal of Criminology*, *8*(3), 213–228.

Caulkins, J. P., Burnett, H., & Leslie, E. (2009). How illegal drugs enter an island country: Insights from interviews with incarcerated smuggler. *Global Crime*, *10*(1&2), 66–93.

Chu, B., Holt, T. J., & Ahn, G. J. (2010). *Examining the creation, distribution, and function of malware on-line* (Research report No. 23011). Washington, DC: U.S. Department of Justice. Retrieved from https://www.ncjrs.gov/pdffiles1/nij/grants/230111 .pdf

Coluccello, S., & Massey, S. (2007). Out of Africa: The human trade between Libya and Lampedusa. *Trends in Organized Crime, 10*(4), 77–90.

Decker, S. H., & Chapman, M. Townsend. (2008). *Drug smugglers on drug smuggling: Lessons from the inside.* Philadelphia, PA: Temple University Press.

Dowling, S., Moreton, K., & Wright, L. (2007). *Trafficking for the purposes of labour exploitation: A literature overview.* London, England: Home Office.

Düvell, F. (2008). Clandestine migration in Europe. *Social Science Information, 47*(4), 479–497.

Englund, C. (2008). *The organisation of human trafficking: A study of criminal involvement in sexual exploitation in Sweden, Finland and Estonia.* Stockholm: Swedish National Council for Crime Prevention.

European Monitoring Centre for Drugs and Drug Addiction. (2011). *Annual report 2011: The state of the drugs problem in Europe.* Lisbon, Portugal: Author.

European Monitoring Centre for Drugs and Drug Addiction & Europol. (2011). *Amphetamine: A European Union perspective in the global context.* Luxembourg: Publications Office of the European Union.

Europol. (2004, January). *An overview on motor vehicle crime from a European perspective.* The Hague, the Netherlands: Author.

Europol. (2007, February 21). *Major action against armed robberies: Europol support for Italian led operation "Baltico"* [Press release]. The Hague, Netherlands: Europol. Retrieved from http://www.europol.europa.eu/index.asp?page=news& news=pr070221.htm

Europol. (2011a). *EU organised crime threat assessment: OCTA 2011.* The Hague, the Netherlands: Author.

Europol. (2011b). *Europol warns of increase in illegal waste dumping, press release.* The Hague, the Netherlands: Author. Retrieved from https://www.europol .europa.eu/content/press/europol-warns-increase-illegal-waste-dumping-1053

Fisher, I., & Kiefer, P. (2007, August 31). Italian police raid gangs after pizzeria slayings. *International Herald Tribune,* p. 3.

Gambetta, D. (1993). *The Sicilian mafia: The business of private protection.* Cambridge, MA: Harvard University Press.

Gounev, P., & Bezlov, T. (2008). From the economy of deficit to the black-market: Car theft and trafficking in Bulgaria. *Trends in Organized Crime, 11*(4), 410–429.

Hornsby, R., & Hobbs, D. (2007). A zone of ambiguity: The political economy of cigarette bootlegging. *British Journal of Criminology, 47*(4), 551–571.

Hozic, A. A. (2004). Between the cracks: Balkan cigarette smuggling. *Problems of Post-Communism, 51*(3), 35–44.

Huisman, W., Huikeshoven, M., & van de Bunt, H. (2003). *Marktplaats Amsterdam.* The Hague, Netherlands: Boom Juridische Uitgevers.

Interpol. (2009). *Electronic waste and organised crime: Assessing the links.* Lyon, France: Author.

Joossens, L., & Raw, M. (2008). Progress in combating cigarette smuggling: Controlling the supply chain. *Tobacco Control, 17*(6), 399–404.

Junninen, M. (2006). *Adventurers and risk-takers: Finnish professional criminals and their organisations in the 1990s cross-border criminality*. Helsinki, Finland: European Institute for Crime Prevention and Control, affiliated with the United Nations (HEUNI).

Kaizen, J., & Nonneman, W. (2007). Irregular migration in Belgium and organized crime: An overview. *International Migration, 45*(2), 121–146.

Kelly, E. (2002). *Journeys of jeopardy: A review of research on trafficking in women and children in Europe*. Geneva, Switzerland: International Organization for Migration.

Kleemans, E. R., & de Poot, C. J. (2008). Criminal careers in organized crime and social opportunity structure. *European Journal of Criminology, 5*(1), 69–98.

Kleemans, E. R., & van de Bunt, H. G. (2002). The social embeddedness of organized crime. *Transnational Organized Crime, 5*(1), 19–36.

Kleemans, E. R., & van de Bunt, H. G. (2008). Organised crime, occupations and opportunity, *Global Crime, 9*(3), 185–197.

Kostakos, P. A., & Antonopoulos, G. A. (2010). The "good," the "bad" and the "Charlie": The business of cocaine smuggling in Greece. *Global Crime, 11*(1), 34–57.

Kukhianidze, A. (2009). Corruption and organized crime in Georgia before and after the "Rose Revolution." *Central Asian Survey, 28*(2), 215–234.

Lane, D. C., Bromley, D. G., Hicks, R. D., & Mahoney, J. S. (2008). Time crime: The transnational organization of art and antiquities theft. *Journal of Contemporary Criminal Justice, 24*(3), 243–262.

Larsson, P. (2009). Up in smoke! Hash smuggling the Norwegian way. In K. Ingvaldsen & V. Lundgren Sørli (Eds.), *Organised crime: Norms, markets, regulation and research* (pp. 63–82). Oslo, Norway: Unipub.

Lebov, K. (2010). Human trafficking in Scotland. *European Journal of Criminology, 7*(1), 77–93.

Leman, J., & Janssens, S. (2008). The Albanian and post-Soviet business of trafficking women for prostitution: Structural developments and financial modus operandi. *European Journal of Criminology, 5*(4), 433–451.

Liddick, D. R. (2011). *Crimes against nature: Illegal industries and the global environment*. Santa Barbara, CA: Praeger.

Lundin, S. (2012). Organ economy: Organ trafficking in Moldova and Israel. *Public Understanding of Science, 21*(2), 226–241.

Matrix Knowledge Group. (2007). *The illicit drug trade in the United Kingdom*. London, England: Home Office.

Miehling, R., & Timmerberg, H. (2004). *Schneekönig: Mein leben als drogenboss* [Snow King: My life as drug boss]. Reinbek bei Hamburg, Germany: Rowohlt Taschenbuch Verlag.

Nill, A., & Shultz, C. J. II. (2009). Global software piracy: Trends and strategic considerations. *Business Horizons, 52*(3), 289–298.

Nozina, M. (2010). Crime networks in Vietnamese diasporas: The Czech Republic case. *Crime, Law and Social Change, 53*(3), 229–258.

Paoli, L. (2003). *Mafia brotherhoods: Organized crime, Italian style*. New York, NY: Oxford University Press.

Paoli, L., & Reuter, P. (2008). Drug trafficking and ethnic minorities in Western Europe. *European Journal of Criminology, 5*(1), 13–37.

Powell, W. W. (1990). Neither market nor hierarchy: Network forms of organization. *Research in Organizational Behavior, 12*, 295–336.

Pullat, R. (2009). *Organized crime related drug trafficking in the Baltic Sea Region*. Tallinn, Estonia: Estonian Police Board.

Rieger, S. (2006, July). *Der Rolex-banden fall* [The Rolex gang case]. Seminar paper, presented at Berühmte Kriminalfälle Deutschlands—in strafrechtlicher und kriminalistisch-kriminologischer Analyse [Famous crime cases in Germany—under criminal law, forensic and criminological analysis], Fachhochschule, Villingen-Schwenningen, Germany.

Roth, J. (2009). *Mafialand Deutschland* [Mafia country Germany]. Frankfurt am Main, Germany: Eichborn.

Ruggiero, V., & Khan, K. (2006). British South Asian communities and drug supply networks in the UK: A qualitative study. *International Journal of Drug Policy, 17*(6), 473–483.

Ruggiero, V., & Khan, K. (2007). The organisation of drug supply: South Asian criminal enterprise in the UK. *Asian Journal of Criminology, 2*(2), 163–177.

Sagramoso, D. (2001). *The proliferation of illegal small arms and light weapons in and around the European Union: Instability, organised crime and terrorist groups*. London, England: Centre for Defence Studies.

Scheper-Hughes, N. (2004). Parts unknown: Undercover ethnography of the organs-trafficking underworld, *Ethnography, 5*(1), 29–73.

Schwirtz, M. (2008, July 31). Russian crime group fades, but retains a certain allure. *International Herald Tribune*, p. 4.

Silverstone, D. (2011). From triads to snakeheads: Organised crime and illegal migration within Britain's Chinese community. *Global Crime, 12*(2), 93–111.

Silverstone, D., & Savage, S. (2010). Farmers, factories and funds: Organised crime and illicit drugs cultivation within the British Vietnamese community. *Global Crime, 11*(1), 16–33.

Smit, M. (2011). Trafficking in human beings for labour exploitation: The case of the Netherlands. *Trends in Organized Crime, 14*(2–3), 184–197.

Soudijn, M., & Huisman, S. (2011). Criminal expatriates: British criminals in the Netherlands and Dutch criminals in Spain. In G. Antonopoulos, M. Groenhuijsen, J. Harvey, T. Kooijmans, A. Maljevic, & K. von Lampe (Eds.), *Usual and unusual organising criminals in Europe and beyond: Profitable crimes, from underworld to upper world—Liber Amicorum Petrus van Duyne* (pp. 233–246). Apeldoorn, the Netherlands: Maklu.

Soudijn, M. R. J., & Kleemans, E. R. (2009). Chinese organized crime and situational context: Comparing human smuggling and synthetic drugs trafficking. *Crime, Law and Social Change, 52*(5), 457–474.

Spapens, T. (2007). Trafficking in illicit firearms for criminal purposes within the European Union. *European Journal of Crime, Criminal Law and Criminal Justice, 15*(3), 359–381.

Surtees, R. (2008). Traffickers and trafficking in Southern and Eastern Europe: Considering the other side of human trafficking. *European Journal of Criminology, 5*(1), 39–68.

U.N. Office on Drugs and Crime. (2009). *Trafficking in persons: Analysis on Europe.* Vienna, Austria: Author.

U.N. Office on Drugs and Crime. (2010). *The globalization of organized crime: A transnational organized crime threat assessment.* Vienna, Austria: Author.

U.N. Office on Drugs and Crime. (2011). *World drug report 2011.* New York, NY: United Nations.

U.S. President. (2008). *National drug control strategy: 2008 annual report.* Washington DC: Author.

Van Duyne, P. C., & Nelemans, M. D. H. (2012). Transnational organized crime: Thinking in and out of Plato's cave. In F. Allum & S. Gilmour (Eds.), *Routledge handbook of transnational organized crime* (pp. 36–51). London, England: Routledge.

Vander Beken, T., Janssens, J., Verpoest, K., Balcaen, A., & Vander Laenen, F. (2008). Crossing geographical, legal and moral boundaries: The Belgian cigarette black market. *Tobacco Control, 17*(1), 60–65.

Vander Beken, T., & van Daele, S. (2009). Out of step? Mobility of "itinerant crime groups." In P. C. van Duyne, S. Donati, J. Harvey, A. Maljevic, & K. von Lampe (Eds.), *Crime, money and criminal mobility in Europe* (pp. 43–70). Nijmegen, the Netherlands: Wolf Legal.

Varese, F. (2011). *Mafias on the move: How organized crime conquers new territories,* Princeton, NJ: Princeton University Press.

Viuhko, M., & Jokinen, A. (2009). *Human trafficking and organised crime: Trafficking for sexual exploitation and organised procuring in Finland.* Helsinki, Finland: European Institute for Crime Prevention and Control, affiliated with the United Nations (HEUNI).

von der Lage, R. (2003). Litauische kfz-banden in der bundesrepublik Deutschland [Lithuanian motor vehicle gangs in the Federal Republic of Germany]. *Kriminalistik, 57*(6), 357–363.

von Lampe, K. (2006). The cigarette black market in Germany and in the United Kingdom. *Journal of Financial Crime, 13*(2), 235–254.

von Lampe, K. (2008). Organized crime in Europe: Conceptions and realities. *Policing, 2*(1), 2–17.

von Lampe, K. (2009). Transnational crime connecting Eastern and Western Europe: Three case studies. In P. C. van Duyne, S. Donati, J. Harvey, A. Maljevic, & K. von Lampe (Eds.). *Crime, money and criminal mobility in Europe* (pp. 19–42). Nijmegen, the Netherlands: Wolf Legal.

von Lampe, K. (2011). Re-conceptualizing transnational organized crime: Offenders as problem solvers. *International Journal of Security and Terrorism*, 2(1), 1–23.

von Lampe, K., & Johansen, P. O. (2004). Organized crime and trust: On the conceptualization and empirical relevance of trust in the context of criminal networks. *Global Crime*, 6(2), 159–184.

von Lampe, K., Kurti, M., Shen, A., & Antonopoulos, G. (2012). The changing role of China in the global illegal cigarette trade. *International Criminal Justice Review*, 22(1), 43–67.

von Lampe, K., van Dijck, M., Hornsby, R., Markina, A., & Verpoest, K. (2006). Organised Crime is . . . : Findings from a cross-national review of literature. In P. C. Duyne, A. Maljevic, M. van Dijck, K. von Lampe, & J. L. Newell (Eds.), *The organisation of crime for profit: Conduct, law and measurement* (pp. 17–42). Nijmegen, the Netherlands: Wolf Legal.

Weenink, A. W., Huisman, S., & van der Laan, F. J. (2004). *Crime without frontiers: Crime pattern analysis Eastern Europe 2002–2003*. Driebergen, the Netherlands: Korps Landelijke Politiediensten.

Williams, P., & Godson, R. (2002). Anticipating organized and transnational crime. *Crime, Law & Social Change*, 37(4), 311–355.

World Health Organization. (2010, January). Medicines: Counterfeit medicines (Fact sheet No. 275). Geneva, Switzerland: Author.

Wright J. (2006). Law agencies target criminality in European motorcycle gangs. *Jane's Intelligence Review*, 18(3), 32–35.

Zaitch, D. (2002). *Trafficking cocaine: Colombian drug entrepreneurs in the Netherlands*. The Hague, the Netherlands: Kluwer Law International.

Ziercke, J. (2010). Aktuelles Lagebild und Entwicklung der Gewaltkriminalität [Current situation and development of violent crime]. *Kriminalistik*, 64(12), 697–703.

5

Transnational Organized Crime in Africa

Mark Shaw

Playing its part in the age of globalization, Africa is more than ever a place of passage.

—Severino and Ray (2011, p. 52)

n the last decade, organized crime has emerged as one of the most compelling threats to stability, security, and development on the African continent. The evolution of organized crime into the multifaceted phenomena that it has become today was unimaginable a decade ago. Globalization and organized crime have flourished hand in hand—innovations in the former quickly being exploited for illicit gain by the latter.

Africa was long a source for criminal groups, most notably resilient and tenacious West African criminal networks now present in most of the globe's major cities. In the past decade, however, the continent itself has become a key transit point for drug shipments as well as a source for illegally procured natural resources and a point of origin for trafficking in human beings and the smuggling of migrants. In line with this trend, Africa's failed and weak states served as a breeding ground for an emerging set of criminal activities; the dramatic growth of cocaine trafficking through West Africa, for example, centered not on the regions big states, but on their smaller, impoverished and war-torn neighbors of Sierra

Leone, Guinea, Liberia, and Guinea-Bissau. More recently, control of illicit trafficking routes have emerged as an important dimension of the crises of the state in Mali and, more broadly in, respect of governing the Sahel as a whole.

But a broader and more important development is underway with profound implications for all areas of social policy, including confronting organized crime. Africa is now one of the fastest growing regional economies in the world. That growth has largely been driven by a resource boom, reshaping Africa's relations with the world but also bringing important changes to the nature of African state formation and the concentration of power in the hands of an increasingly wealthy economic and political elite (see Carmody, 2011). These trends in political economy are being paralleled by an unprecedented population growth rate. The population of Africa south of the Sahara will have multiplied by a factor of 10, from 180 million in 1950 to 1.8 billion in 2050. In the same period, China will see a growth of only 2.5 times, and India 4 times. This is, as a recent groundbreaking study notes, "a phenomenon with no equivalent in human history" (Severino & Ray, 2011, p. 13).

Globalization has drawn Africa deeper into the global economy, thereby making it both more susceptible to crime, but also increasing Africa's capacity to impact global stability and the global economy, as Somali piracy has dramatically exemplified. Furthermore, the fragile states paradigm is less obvious than it may have first appeared, with state capture and the compromising of key institutions becoming a more pressing concern than outright state failure. And emerging forms of crime on the continent may rely less on trafficking of physical goods and more on the trade in intangibles: Cybercrime and money laundering are flourishing in Africa in a context in which the continent is skipping over or "leapfrogging" older communication technologies and moving directly to new ones. Leapfrogging ahead in this way will have important benefits, but it will also have costs if it provides new avenues for criminal activity.

Africans have lived for too long in poverty. Rapid economic growth and technological advancement is something that must be welcomed. But the form that it takes in combination with (and as a contributor to) the rapid erosion of African states against a backdrop of huge social and demographic changes, suggests that organized crime in Africa may yet serve a defining role in shaping the future of life for ordinary people on the continent. Yet it is a surprisingly under analyzed phenomenon.

Although the pace of globalization makes it hard to project credibly into the next decade, this chapter briefly explores some of the nascent organized crime trends that should be of concern, because they make Africa particularly susceptible to organized crime:

- **Compromised states:** The combination of failed states and fragile states in Africa present an ideal breeding ground for organized crime to seed and take root.
- **Urban hubs:** The interplay between the major cities in the continent's emerging middle-income democracies—Lagos, Nairobi, and Johannesburg—and the zones of fragility across the continent facilitate subregional criminal activity.
- **Innovation and replication:** Loose borders, freedom of movement, and leapfrogging technology, coupled with organized crime's natural propensity for innovation, are creating potent criminal forces that have the potential to replicate themselves across the continent.

By way of conclusion, an argument is made that a new approach to tackling organized crime in Africa is required—one that recognizes the insidious nature of criminal groups and their ability to penetrate all aspects of state and civil institutions and that also acknowledges that a transnational crime cannot be tackled from a national perspective, but requires coordinated regional action. Although the threat is increasingly recognized, there is still considerable work to do to bolster weak state, subregional, and regional capacities.

ASSESSING THE SCALE OF ORGANIZED CRIME IN AFRICA

The growth of globalization and transnational organized crime are intertwined like the double helix of DNA—the latter lies like a cancer firmly in the genetics of the former. In the past decade, spurred by globalization trends and innovations, the global economy has doubled in size. But this growth has been matched, if not surpassed, by the growth of illicit activities and global criminal markets. In 2009, the World Development Report estimated the value of revenue accruing to organized crime to be $1.3 trillion. Using data for the same year, U.N. Office of Drugs and Crime (UNODC) conservatively estimated that transnational organized crime was generating an annual return in the region of $870 billion, an amount equivalent to 1.5% of global gross domestic product (GDP) at the time (UNODC, 2010). But all analysts agree that these figures can only be rising. Whatever the accuracy of these estimates, the increasing interconnectedness of the global economy and financial systems runs far ahead of the legitimate economy's ability to govern or regulate it (see the introduction to Spence, 2011), ensuring a fertile ground in which organized crime can flourish.

If the global economy has doubled since 2001, Africa has benefited disproportionately from this growth (see O'Neill, 2011, p. 4). Global GDP data have shown that countries in sub-Saharan Africa have enjoyed comparatively high levels of growth in contrast to overall global GDP levels, and in particular, the economies of low-income countries in Africa have barely felt the effects of the economic crises that have crippled more mature regions (International Monetary Fund, 2012). Although these positive trends should be celebrated and sustained, it must be recognized that economic growth in Africa has produced a series of new challenges as the continent, and its different subregional economies, becomes ever more integrated into the global economy. It is fundamental to understand the implications of Africa's connection to the global economy, both licit and illicit, if the vulnerabilities and threats in the next decade are to be well understood, because the disproportionate share of legitimate economic growth has been matched by the growth in illicit activities and organized crime.

Although it is complex to determine accurately the growth of the illicit economy, current estimates of illicit flows due to organized crime suggest a global figure in the region of an annual value of some $128 billion (UNODC, 2010). A conservative estimate of the proportion of these markets that have links to Africa (either as a transit zone, source, or destination) suggests that by 2010 Africa was linked in some way to between 7% and 10% of all global illicit flows.[1] Compared to Africa's share of the legitimate economy—where African trade accounts for only 3% of global trade in both goods and services and only 2.4% of global GDP[2]—it is clearly demonstrated that although Africa has benefited disproportionately from legitimate growth, *it has also a disproportionately high level of illicit flows linked to organized crime.*

Despite the growth of illicit activity on the continent, the past decade has seen surprisingly little literature on organized or serious crime and illicit trafficking in the African context. This could be partially attributed to the generally held view that organized crime was not a phenomenon that affected the continent, with the exception of two countries—Nigeria and South Africa. In these cases, in particular in South Africa, a growing literature and debate has focused on the causes of the problem and possible solutions (see, e.g., Altbeker, 2007; Gordon, 2006; Shaw, 2002). However, these studies, while beginning to document the nature and extent of organized crime, have considered the issue almost exclusively from a national perspective. This fails entirely to account for the fact that this is a transnational phenomenon, for which the borders of the nation state have no relevance. There remains to be written a single study of the nature, impact, and evolution of transnational organized crime across the African continent.

◈ NEW VULNERABILITIEſ

There are a number of reasons to be concerned with the growth of transnational organized crime—and accordingly the criminal groups that perpetuate them—the most pressing of which is the impact that these nonstate actors have had on stability, governance, and state building. A number of authors have considered the impact of organized crime and its implications for African state formation—the seminal work of Jean-François Bayart, Stephen Ellis, and others is relevant here—drawing the connection between corruption and the criminalization of Africa elites (Bayart, 2010; Bayart, Ellis, & Hibou, 1999).

Conventional wisdom has typically argued that failed states were pivotal to the growth of transnational organized crime groups. Certainly Somalia, described by British foreign secretary William Hague as "the world's most failed state,"[3] would reinforce that analysis. Somalia suffers under the triple threat of state failure, organized crime, and terrorism. The resurgence of piracy off the coast of Somalia is largely, if not entirely, attributed to the state's failure to provide viable livelihood options for its burgeoning youth population; 75% of the population in Somalia is under the age of 35. Somali pirates quickly found like-minded allies in organized criminal groups and networks based overseas, and piracy operations have become more sophisticated, organized, and effective. With the benefit of international funding, piracy has quickly transformed from an outmoded, home-grown criminal activity into a serious threat to global human and economic security. The international community's efforts to control the problem though military intervention have only now begun to bear fruit. Although the decline in incidents of piracy are directly related to security measures taken at sea, the longer term solution to the effective governance of Somalia must be on rebuilding Somali state institutions (and not just those in the criminal justice sector), seeking viable alternative livelihoods to piracy, and empowering local leaders to advocate within the community to reject pirates and piracy. In some respects, piracy has been an outlier in the development of organized criminal activity in Africa: It emerged quickly and visibly and attracted an international and (given other responses in the past) comparatively highly organized international response. The majority of forms of organized crime on the continent today can be classified more as "slow burners" but with important long-term impacts on economic, political, and social processes.

However, to point only to piracy as evidence of the connection between conflict and organized crime is to take an overly simplistic—and, frankly, optimistic—viewpoint. In the collapsed state of Somalia, the continuation of a protracted conflict has strong ties to the control of unregulated economic flows—and a network of economic beneficiaries. Prior to the recent bout of conflict, charcoal export volumes from southern Somalia were estimated at 3.5 to 4.5 million sacks per year, with 90% of the charcoal trade passing through the until recently Al-Shabaab-controlled port of Kismayo. The proceeds from the charcoal trade in Somalia dwarf anything made from piracy, but at the same time the trade's profitability has helped sustain the conflict in the context of a failed state.[4] Without a regulatory framework, legitimate state institutions, and security, viable economic activity becomes impossible unless violent protection is provided in parallel. And the protection of economic activity with violence has long been a defining feature of organized crime.

Although Somalia may appear to present strong evidence for the connection between conflict, failed states, and organized crime, in a broader survey, analysts have found that the relationship between organized crime and state failure is less than perfectly correlated. In fact, rather than thriving in a truly failed state, organized criminal groups find weak states more conducive to their operations. It appears that a modicum of security, stability, and infrastructure and the presence of formal but rudimentary state structures that are fragile and susceptible to corruption, present a better safe haven for illicit activities (see Patrick, 2011, chap. 4). Thus, although the last decade may have seen a marked decline in active conflict in the region, with major long-standing intrastate conflicts being successfully resolved, it is exactly as these countries move toward a more sustainable state building path that they are most vulnerable to the infiltration of organized criminal groups. The result is a plethora of states on the continent compromised by criminal money and influence.

The international community has been insufficiently aware and vigilant to this threat, and the impact on Africa's small, postconflict and fragile states has been severe. Illicit flows and their control by organizations resembling criminal groups or networks have become crucial not only in determining patterns of violence but also have acted as a disincentive for resolving conflicts and prevented the long-term consolidation of institutions. Resource flows to weak and fragile states during the Cold War perpetuated and sustained conflicts. In many cases, these flows have now been criminalized, but their impact has not changed. The considerable income generated from illicit activities and control over natural resources presents a powerful incentive to vested interests and armed groups to perpetuate conflict. Although the nature of this phenomenon has been explored in the literature on "greed and grievance," this analysis has not examined the broader criminal connections that make it possible. Without confronting this effectively, the international community has inadvertently empowered criminal actors at the expense of ordinary citizens and has allowed organized crime to become inextricably intertwined with legitimate state institutions (see Pugh & Cooper, 2004, p. 5).

The trappings of statehood of what has famously been called "quasi-states"—political entities granted international or juridical legitimacy despite lacking local legitimacy or control—have been used effectively as facilitators of organized crime (Jackson,1990). In a recent case, the president of Somalia's transitional federal government, which has only a fragile footprint in the country it seeks to represent, is accused in a July 2012 U.N. report of protecting a prominent pirate leader by issuing him a diplomatic passport. The report has criticized the "climate of impunity" that pirate kingpins enjoy both within Somalia and in their travels abroad.[5]

The phenomena that have thus emerged in the last decade, and that are evidenced not only in Africa, are the unprecedented levels of integration of organized criminal groups into all facets of society and the creation of what a recent analysis has termed "mafia states," described as cases where "government officials enrich themselves and their families and friends while exploiting the money, muscle, political influence, and global connections of criminal syndicates to cement and expand their own power" (Naím, 2012, pp. 100–101). In many African states, political, business, and criminal interests have become indistinguishable. In such cases, state institutions (or critical parts of them) have become compromised, a vehicle for profit involving criminal activities.

≋ COMPROMIƧED ƧTATEƧ

Nowhere is the phenomenon of compromised states better demonstrated than in West Africa, where an unhappy intersection of geographic location and a series of postconflict, weak, and fragile states (including Sierra Leone, Liberia, Guinea, and Guinea-Bissau) has turned the region into a major transit point for flows of illicit drugs. In a relatively short time, international drug cartels have used drug money to distort to various degrees the political and economic frameworks of the countries in the region. In each case, elements of the state are fighting back, perhaps most successfully in Sierra Leone, where the West has invested much in the postwar period in a stable democratic polity, but the challenge is enormous, with key institutions having become compromised. In the most extreme case, in Guinea-Bissau since the late 1990s, drug money has subverted governance altogether by ensuring that political competition for the control of the state is driven by a desire to control the drug trade. The result has been coup and countercoup and violent competition between elite groups over the resources that providing protection for cocaine trafficking generates. Guinea-Bissau is also a "window" to the wider region: Drugs entering the continent here have caused wider instability, for example, in surrounding states, including along the onward trafficking routes through the Sahel, Mali being the most visible case.

Thus, the threat has spread much more widely. Benin, for example, a recent report to the U.N. Security Council noted, has become a major port of embarkation for drug couriers. The country's "1989 km of land borders with Togo, Burkina Faso, Niger and Nigeria and 121 km of coastline on the Gulf of Guinea are very difficult to secure. Lagoons and rivers, which are sometimes used by criminals in speedboats, have also proved to be difficult to police and control."[6]

In 2009, an estimated 21 tons of cocaine, with a street value of $900 million, were thought to have been smuggled via West Africa to Europe. Unsurprisingly, given the volumes involved, which in this case are the approximate equivalent to the GDP of Sierra Leone and Guinea combined (Kemp, 2012), this has bought considerable access, influence, and, ultimately, state protection. Over time, it has become clear that elements within the formal institutional structure of the state have orientated themselves to protect the trade and by so doing ensuring their continued financial benefit. Senior police, military, and aviation officials, border controls, passport-issuing agencies, and customs offices, not to mention the wife and family of a president, prominent businesspeople, and politicians have all been implicated. In Guinea-Bissau designated trafficking kingpin, Jose Americo Bubo Na Tchuto, was reappointed Naval Chief of Staff, with considerable power to use military resources to protect trafficking routes; in Guinea, Ousmane Conté, son of the late president Lansana Conté, was officially labeled a drug kingpin by the U.S. government in 2010.

Criminal groups are disrupting democratic governance processes, by undermining already weak state authority and the rule of law by fueling corruption. Profits from the drug trade are funding electoral campaigns and political parties and generally affecting political and broader state-society relations. The increasing interwoven nature of politics, organized crime, and corruption poses a significant threat to the long-term development of democracy on the continent. (With some exceptions, the seeming impunity of African elites from prosecution and their ongoing connections to organized crime have undermined citizens' trust in democratic institutions, and both licit and illicit economic development may have bolstered some authoritarian regimes. Furthermore, the hijacking of legitimate political processes by criminal actors has a fundamental impact on the capacity of the country to achieve a sustainable rule-of-law framework and affects the sense of inclusion and enfranchisement of the population, which in turn makes citizens less likely to engage in institution-building activities, less likely to have trust in their state institutions, and thus more likely to engage in illicit activities themselves. Such trends, and their ability to perpetuate themselves, have long-term implications for future political and economic progress in Africa.

In compromised states, the policies and resource allocations of governments (or parts of them) are determined more by the influence of criminals than by the forces that would typically shape state behavior, and as such they blur the conceptual line between states and nonstate actors, as they move with the legitimacy, influence, and the power of a nation-state but make decisions that are not in the interest of the broader population or of national or regional stability. As a result, their behavior is difficult to predict, making them particularly dangerous actors in the international environment (Naím, 2012).

Organized crime will consistently seek new territory, new markets, and new spheres of influence in which to market its goods and exert control, and as noted, it is fragile states, not failed states, that will be the preferred target. Regrettably, the continent presents no shortage of choices: In the State Fragility Index, developed by the Center for Systemic

Peace, sub-Saharan Africa has the highest regional ranking for state fragility and has the largest number of states whose fragility is increasing in the postglobalization period (measured as being since 1995).

What does this mean in the longer term? Most immediately, it suggests that organized crime has penetrated and exploited the weakness of multiple fragile states, injecting resources and linking them to wider global criminal networks. Ironically, these resources and the local influence that they buy have strengthened some actors but weakened the overall ability of government institutions to act as states in the conventional sense. The ability to regulate trade, tax external companies, and control territories has all been compromised. Bigger regional states do retain this capacity to some extent, as well as some ability to project influence and stability, but subregional criminal economies have developed in which the "hinterland" of criminal accumulation in the smaller, weaker states is linked to major urban metropolises in the country's middle-income powers. These cities are themselves major hubs of criminal organization.

☒ URBAN HUBS

As noted in the relationship between Somalia and Kenya, where the criminal activities in one trigger a spillover into neighboring Kenya, there is also growing evidence that an overemphasis on the weak and failing states may underestimate the pivotal role that the middle-income countries are playing at regional level. Some of Africa's mega cities—Nairobi, Lagos, and Johannesburg—have become hubs for organized crime activity, and in fact, it is the combination of fragile states and powerful urban hubs that provides interconnections to the global economy that makes Africa a breeding ground for organized crime. The interaction between these regional hubs and regional criminal economies, and the role within these of weak and fragile states, requires much more attention.

Illicit transactions (like their counterparts in the licit economy) require a degree of infrastructure. Those who control and profit from criminal networks and illicit resource flows will not be found in fragile states, but living in the major cities. These in turn each exist in one of the continent's middle-income powers and the relationship between the economic dominance of each of these countries, the role of key cities, and the political economy of illicit activity in Africa are closely connected.

A feature of globalization is mobility and migration, and Africa is a continent that is characterized by very high migration, both transnational and internal. Urban growth rates are among the highest in the world averaging about 7% annually, with several of the major African cities having growth rates in excess of 10%; freedom of movement within certain regions and economic zones have made these cities true subregional melting pots. What this has meant is that traditional ways of life—particularly those of rural communities—are breaking down, and social identities and relations are changing in a variety of ways. The strength of social capital and trust in the community are two indicators that have long been proved to be negatively correlated to violent crime. Social capital is broadly defined as the set of rules, norms, obligations, reciprocity, and trust embedded in social relations, social structures, and society's institutional arrangements that enable its members to achieve their individual and community objectives. In the absence of social capital, and with insufficient economic opportunity, massive income inequality, and limited state-supported service delivery for social services, these urban hubs have become the malignant epicenters for the spread of organized crime across a subregion.

Although each region has its own dynamics, criminal networks, and resource flows at play, there are startling similarities in regard to the way that the inflow of criminal profits and other resources from fragile areas is channeled along trafficking routes into the urban hubs whose infrastructure allows them to be integrated into the formal system or moved beyond Africa's borders.

In West Africa, Nigerian criminal networks play an increasingly active role in the trafficking of cocaine and other commodities through the region, with the visible presence of Latin Americans now only a feature of the past. Profits from these activities along the fragile coastline are channeled back through the major urban center of Lagos and, to some extent, Accra and Dakar. The projection of trafficking through the increasingly unstable Sahel band and the weakening of state control over the northern rim in several states—most notably, Mali, Mauritania, and Niger, but also Nigeria itself—is providing a broader zone for illicit activities. The interaction with terrorism and insurgency provides further incentives and potency to the criminal activities and the perpetuation of instability through violent criminal acts.

In East Africa and the Horn of Africa, as has already been noted, Nairobi has become a center for the reception of illicit funds, both from illicit trafficking in the region but also from piracy. The city serves as a node for engagement with the outside world for four broad zones of state fragility: South Sudan, northern Democratic Republic of Congo (DRC) and Northern Uganda, eastern Congo, and Somalia. The Mombasa port is an important trafficking and smuggling center for drugs entering from South Asia. To demonstrate the extent of the relationship, in 2010 an impressive $2.1 billion found its way into the Kenyan economy without the government's being able to explain the source. A recent U.S State Department report concluded that the Kenyan financial system may be laundering more than $100 million a year, including proceeds of drug trafficking and piracy ransom money (Gastrow, 2011, p. 7). These are significant sums, and they have corrupted the foundations of the political system in Kenya, promoting corruption and violence. As a recent groundbreaking assessment notes, "Criminal networks have penetrated the political class and there are growing concerns about their ability to fund elections and to exercise influence in Parliament and in the procurement processes" (Gastrow, 2011, p. 8).

The criminal economy of Southern Africa is more complex. South African criminal networks, including a prominent set of Nigerian and other foreign groups, play an important role in trafficking drugs and other contraband to and through the country. The huge foreign diaspora in Johannesburg provides a network of connections across the region. The profits of illicit trafficking and criminal accumulation in the Democratic Republic of Congo and the broader region, including from Zimbabwe, filter through Johannesburg, with the city serving as a hub for communications and banking across the region. Organized crime in the region is characterized by the exploitation of natural resources and trafficking of other products, including weapons, cannabis, minerals, timber, and wildlife. It is estimated that some USD 200 million in gross revenues is generated annually from these activities.

South Africa provides an excellent case study demonstration for how a state can have comparatively strong institutions, economic performance, and social indicators, yet still present critical weaknesses that are easily exploited by criminal groups. It is a country where "the first and the developing world exist side by side," notes Misha Glenny (2009).

> The first world provides good roads, 728 airports . . ., the largest cargo port in Africa, and an efficient banking system. . . . The developing world accounts for the low tax revenue, over-stretched social services, high levels of corruption throughout the administration and 7,600 kilometres of land and sea borders that have more holes than a second hand dartboard. (pp. 238–239)

A recently released investigation into the activities of former associates of Viktor Bout, the notorious arms smuggler sentenced to 25 years in a U.S. prison in April 2012, showed how a "spider web of companies" has been established to facilitate illegal smuggling operations across southern Africa and beyond. Facing difficulties in South Africa itself, Bout's former associates targeted the conveniently located island hub of Mauritius to base their operations (Conflict Awareness Project, 2012). Following the release of the report, the Mauritian authorities have denied permission for the establishment of the aviation company that would have acted as a front for illegal activities (Roth, 2012).

The case of Bout's associates attempting to set up business in Mauritius is instructive. What is required for criminal activities in Africa is a solid base, a place to center operations and live comfortably, while directing activities. In this context, a series of burgeoning cities form the new hubs for criminal activity on the continent. Unlike Mauritius, however, it may be easier to escape attention where hard-pressed police have other priorities and where political protectors are paid to keep their mouths shut and the authorities from knocking at the wrong doors.

There is some historical basis in understanding this phenomenon. The formation of cities in Africa was not the basis for state creation, as may have been the case elsewhere in the world, with strong linkages between the cities and their hinterlands. Rather, the formation of urban areas in Africa was to service the needs of the colonizer, to provide ease of transit to the home state, and to command and control the resource base (see Herbst, 2000, pp. 13–14). These patterns have largely defined the future of the African city and are in part responsible for this pattern of urban hubs as a gateway to the trafficking of resources from the hinterlands where there is limited administrative reach or political control. This, coupled with the failure to create strong state institutions has created an opportunity for the control of illicit activities by nonstate groups.

In a negative spiral, the control and manipulation of these illicit resource flows will increasingly have a direct impact on patterns of violence within urban centers and will undermine the political strength within the state. Political violence in the slums of Nairobi cannot be disconnected from broader external illicit resource flows and their infiltration of the political process. With 70% of Africans below the age of 25 and a strong trend toward urbanization, the resulting concentration of unemployed young men comingled with organized criminal groups is a volatile mix, which in turn has opened the door to civil unrest, insurgency, and, in some cases, a greater propensity to extremism.

Unprecedented levels of urbanization and population growth are not the only trends marking the transformation of the continent. Mobile telephones and the Internet are dramatically changing the way in which Africans connect with each other and the world. That is creating new opportunities for organized crime.

〃 INNOVATE AND REPLICATE

In the introduction, organized crime was compared to a cancer that was intertwined within the genetics of globalization, and it is a distinct feature of organized criminal behavior that, like cancer, it infects those around it. Although the individual human costs may be more obvious in one region, countries rarely appreciate the spillover effects in others, whether an origin, transit, or destination country. As a recent UNODC (2010) report highlights, "Only when viewed globally are the net costs of trafficking apparent, and only national governments, not their organized crime substitutes, have any incentive to look global." (p. 35). For example, although Somalia may have been the locus for the rebirth of piracy, the seeming impunity of Somali pirates has paved the way for copycat crimes off the West African coast and deep into the Gulf of Guinea. Furthermore, many of the resultant effects of Somali piracy are playing out in neighboring Kenya. The building boom in Nairobi is said to be driven largely by the illicit proceeds of piracy, which is having a detrimental effect on legitimate economic activity in Kenya. Criminally inflated property booms price legitimate actors out of real estate markets, causing severe dislocations and economic distortions.[7]

As a consequence of being one of the fastest growing and developing continents on the globe, the susceptibility of sub-Saharan Africa to organized crime is high. Africa is well documented as having the potential to apply modern technological and communication innovations to leapfrog in terms of economic and social development; it is investing more in Internet and communication technology than is any other continent. In 2012, Angola achieved 4G broadband technology before most of Europe and North Africa. Somalia, the last country in Africa to access the Internet in August 2000, now has four Internet service providers (one each in Puntland and Somaliland and two in South Central) offering Internet access to more than 2 million users as of 2010.[8] Somalia also boasts one of the best and cheapest telecommunication industries in

Africa, which is no small feat in a continent hooked on the mobile phone. The most striking advances in information communication technology (ICT) in Africa have been in the use of mobile phone technology. Africa is now heralded as the world's fastest growing mobile phone market, as the number of mobile phone subscriptions increased from 16 million in 2000, to half a billion by 2010.

A potent example of the way in which innovations in technology are providing opportunity for the growth of criminal activities in Africa—both perpetuated by transnational networks and by homegrown criminal groups—comes in the area of cybercrime. As early as 2008, this was already a threat: A report on cybersecurity in Cote d'Ivoire noted that cybercrime in Africa is growing faster than on any other continent. Cybersecurity experts now estimate that 80% of PCs on the African continent are already infected with viruses and other malicious software ("Africa's Cyber WMD," 2010). And although that may not have been of great concern for the international economy a few years ago, the arrival of broadband service makes Africa a close neighbor in the virtual world. Three West African countries have become notorious for the perpetuation for crimes of identity theft, phishing, and Internet fraud. Nigeria, Ghana, and Cameroon are ranked among the top countries in the world where cybercrime activity is most prevalent. A recent survey of businesses operating online found that one quarter had stopped accepting certain countries due to repeated incidences of fraud—of these, 62% indicated Nigeria, followed by Ghana at 27% (UNODC, 2010).

The growth of communications access has provided benefit across a wide range of social and financial sectors, including the growth of phone banking through systems such as M-Pesa and *dahabshiil*; in the health sector (m-health), where phones are used for diagnosis and prescription for common ailments in rural communities; and even in the agricultural sector, where phones are used to establish fair market prices for commodities (Organisation for Economic Co-operation and Development, African Development Bank, & United Nations Economic Commission on Africa, 2009). The uptake of such technologies has been remarkable—in Kenya, 15 million consumers are subscribed to Safaricom's M-Pesa system, with the system registering 305 million transactions in 2010 with a total value in excess of $8.7 billion.

But although these technologies have improved the potential for development on the continent, they have also had a significant impact on criminality. Mobile finance systems are attractive to the consumer in part due to the security that they offer—informal businesspeople in Kenya are choosing to accept payments via M-Pesa rather than transact in cash, because it allows them to avoid carrying large amounts of cash, which makes them targets for robbery. However, criminals have quickly identified ways to exploit the technology for criminal activities, in particular enjoying the freedom of not needing to provide identification or to be required to conduct transactions in person. In Kenya, kidnappers have begun to demand ransoms via M-Pesa, subverting the traceability of the systems by registering their accounts with fraudulent identification. Similarly, there is an increasing prevalence of phone banking being used for extortion—known local businesspeople are sent a picture of their home or family members and a request for payment to an M-Pesa account. Corrupt traffic policemen in Nairobi have also exploited mobile finance, demanding that bribes be sent to intermediaries via M-Pesa.[9]

The freedom of movement between economic zones—such as in the Economic Community of West African States (ECOWAS) and South African Development Community (SADC) regions—allow for easy and swift dispersion of criminal activities and influence beyond national borders into those of neighbors. As innovations in the use of technology for criminal purposes are proven to be viable and successful in one country, evidence has shown that they are quickly replicated in others. Mobile phone crimes perpetuated in Kenya are seen in neighboring Uganda and Tanzania within months.

⫸ A NEW AGENDA

Structural deficiencies have made sub-Saharan Africa particularly susceptible to threats from transnational organized crime and trafficking. Many of these weaknesses can be attributed to years of economic mismanagement and lack of social investment, exacerbated by civil wars, which in some contexts have significantly diminished human capital, social infrastructure, and productive national development assets. Historical factors, such as corrosive nationalism and diverse colonial inheritance, coupled with national territories not correlated with traditional ethnic groups, have contributed significantly to the vulnerability. Together, these factors combined have exposed the subregion to the emergence of relatively new threats to peace, security, and sustainable human development, which at the same time undermine its capacity to respond effectively. Without being overly dramatic, organized crime could presently be argued to be the most significant threat to Africa's long-term development.

The traditional avenues for responding to organized crime have been to view it as a criminal justice or security issue, requiring strengthened cross-border and domestic law enforcement, borders, and intelligence capacity. However, clearly, in the face of the increasing entrenchment and interweaving of crime with political power and community identity, taking a narrow security-focused view has already been proved to be ineffective. The influence of organized crime on state structures is often compared with cancer, with the treatment being the same: to identify, isolate, and remove its growth before it kills the body (Shaw & Kemp, 2012). To achieve this will require new and innovative responses that go far beyond the crime-fighting lens and that activate regional, continental, and subregional strategies across a broad range of sectors, including a diverse group of stakeholders.

Too many plans, programs, and strategies to counter transnational organized crime target only one or a limited number of countries in a subregion, and the focus is usually on the weak and fragile states. Although it is crucial to focus on those most affected, this alone will not solve the problem nor prevent its spread. Traffickers, with their infinite resources, technology, and drive to exploit new opportunities, have shown themselves capable of constantly adapting to and developing new routes and new markets. For example, as capacity is strengthened in the central West African states of Guinea, Guinea-Bissau, Liberia, and Sierra Leone, the problem is displaced elsewhere, thus increasing pressure on other, more vulnerable states, such as Benin. Of growing concern now is the Sahel band—the stretch of northwestern, semiarid states with typically weak state authority, resulting in significant human insecurity, which includes Mauritania, Mali, and Niger. One reason for this is that efforts remain largely country focused. There are few initiatives that allow for the countries of the region to share the burden among themselves, an approach that is more likely to be effective, given that these approaches are more likely to be perceived as the shared responsibility of developed and developing countries rather than externally imposed responses that carry little national ownership.

The response to piracy, although not fully successful in serving to address the roots of the problem, has demonstrated the capacity of a region to respond in a coordinated manner to an emerging organized crime threat. Kenya, Mauritius, and the Seychelles came together to provide a criminal justice framework under which pirates could be held, tried, and incarcerated and from which they could ultimately be transferred back into Somalia once the capacity had been sufficiently built.

This model would help to mitigate the interplay between fragile states and their neighbors, and the international community has a key role to play in supporting capacity building in the stronger states to investigate, try, and convict offenders from weaker or fragile ones, thereby creating a bulwark around the weaker state and preventing a system of impunity for organized crime being established.

A system like this, however, must be understood as a two-step strategy that will publically target illicit forces on the first track, while national capacity and regional coordination can be developed along the second. Considerable and sustained investment of resources will be required for both tracks if lasting results are to be achieved. The first track can offer some immediate and symbolic success stories—such as the prosecution of prominent suspects—which can serve as a marker of progress while the longer term processes of strengthening and stabilizing relevant national and regional institutions takes place. In this, the piracy response has served as a good practice, when Somaliland was able to accept its first prisoners transferred from the Seychelles into a model prison in Hargeisa in February 2012.

Establishing systems for regional prosecutions could also be effective in West Africa, where the weakened or overtly corrupted state institutions in certain countries are unable to provide effective justice. A brief review of some of the processes that have emerged around several of the high-profile drug-trafficking cases in West Africa, including judicial processes or commissions of inquiry with prosecutorial powers, have clearly demonstrated that the national criminal justice systems are unable to try or sentence any senior political figures or mafia bosses in the drug-trafficking chain, even when there seems to be more than sufficient evidence of their involvement. Prosecutions stick only at the mid- to low level of criminal activity. Failures to achieve successful prosecutions serve as a clear message to traffickers and those who collude with them that they have the impunity to act. The importance of symbolic initiatives has been mentioned above; at the top of this list is the effective prosecution, within the framework of the rule of law, of high-level suspects.

To develop effective continental and subregional responses will require a concerted effort to put crime and citizen security more firmly on the agenda of the African Union and the Regional Economic Commissions as a development issue. ECOWAS's response in the case of cocaine trafficking has been prominent, but West Africa still suffers from multiple initiatives that are often uncoordinated and with almost no capacity to ensure the effective collection of data on emerging trends, as well as the impact of current initiatives to strengthen institutions. In short, there is much greater scope for seeking regional solutions to a challenge that is transnational. Development actors whose focus is often only on national response must build in cross-border dimensions in their responses. The private sector and civil society groups also have a role to play. For example, in response to the increasing threat of exploitation of mobile phone and banking technology for crime, the ICT regulators and operators lobbied for the establishment of the East Africa Communications Organisation. This intergovernmental group has proved effective in leading a coordinated movement to register all SIM cards in Kenya, Uganda, and Tanzania—a move targeted specifically at reducing crime.

As noted, although it is clearly crucial to solving the problem of organized crime and trafficking, a focus exclusively or predominantly on law enforcement assistance is too narrow. Moreover, such a response, when viewed in light of the high levels of corruption that reduce the political will to fight the problem, may in the end prove to be a waste of scarce resources. Millions of dollars have already been spent on law enforcement training in the West Africa region, for example, but such support often takes place in a broader vacuum and in a fragmented bilateral context that may have little impact in the end. Pure law enforcement responses are also too narrowly conceived given the scope of the challenge sketched out. Whatever the differences in approaches to policing, there is a single defining feature: Police institutions are confined to particular jurisdictions and are designed to focus on the needs of a specific community. Globalization and technological change mean that the boundaries of the community are no longer the same—they are transnational—which means that law enforcement, already weak in the national context, is greatly challenged to respond to the problem. Even in the most highly developed relationships, for a variety of reasons, but most notably due to issues of national sovereignty, cooperation across national borders is a challenge. Therefore, to rely solely on law enforcement responses is to apply an ill suited tool to face the challenge.

⁂ STRENGTHENING COMMUNITY RESPONSES

In the absence of effective state institutions, targeting community-level initiatives to create an environment that is inhospitable to organized crime and corruption may be a better, more effective entry point.

Culturally driven, traditional approaches to governance and justice rein-force frameworks of community resilience and traditional social safety nets. Community advocacy, norms, and values have shown to be a remarkably potent tool in reducing criminal behavior; for example, communities in Puntland have proved successful in expelling pirates from the community through the use of social pressures from community leaders and elders. Therefore, reinforcing support to traditional community structures can provide momentum against organized crime influences where state institutions or political will might be lacking. Furthermore, identifying and rebuilding the trust disconnect between state institutions and communities is an important strategy for longer term sustainable, crime-free development.

Almost all the responses to the growth of organized crime and illicit trafficking in Africa have been reactive. Warnings from the UNODC that cocaine trafficking was increasingly a major threat in West Africa were not taken seriously for some time, largely because of the multiple other development priorities on the table. The speed of globalization and related developments has kept the international community on the back foot: Organized criminal networks are dynamic, flexible, and opportunis-tic, and current approaches—particularly in the degree to which criminals are making use of cyberspace—will not be sufficient on their own to address the problem. Technological changes mean that we are dealing with an unprecedented set of new challenges, and more proactive and innovative approaches will be needed to tackle the emerging crimes such as piracy, toxic waste dumping, and cybercrime.

To achieve more proactive and effective responses to organized crime, dedicated capacity for analysis of transnational organized crime flows, trends, drivers, and impact in the region is crucial. This is an area of policy that is often driven by guesswork. But as the scale of the problem grows, there is an urgent requirement to increase information collection and analysis and translate these into effective policy responses. Most studies have a tendency to approach the very multidimensional problem of transnational organized crime through one narrow lens—one domi-nated by a discourse of transnational terrorism. This may, in part, have contributed to policy and operational responses that are grounded in a narrow interpretation of security, leaving only peripheral considerations for the political, social, and economic impacts of organized crime and drug trafficking. A dedicated capacity for data collection and analysis across the continent would allow for an effective assessment of organized crime drivers, vulnerability, and the basis for a comprehensive needs assessment as a framework on which strategic planning can be built. In an age of greater Internet connectivity on the continent, civil society can play a key role here. Supporting regional observatories to monitor illicit trafficking is one way of promoting the role of civil society groups, particularly given the role the media needs to play in drawing attention to crime and corruption. Furthermore, the establishment of a focal point for sharing information, producing agreed-on assessments and monitoring progress will provide both information and incentives for promoting cooperation/nonduplication in capacity-building efforts on the ground.

In conclusion, Africa is a continent threatened by multiple crime types, crime that has interwoven itself deeply into the fabric of political, economic, and social frameworks. It is no longer relevant or even possible to provide a short-term response to illicit trafficking and organized crime. Nor is it appropriate to argue that these activities are somehow not criminal, but instead as something intrinsic to "doing business in Africa," a product of complex social, economic, and political developments. That is the same for organized crime everywhere. Now sustained economic growth holds the prospects of raising much of the continent from poverty; if organized crime imbeds itself permanently in this growth phase, it will distort African development for years to come, further encouraging inequality, the alienation of citizens, the promotion of violence, and the endangerment of legitimate trade. Africa deserves better. But this is a long-term struggle, which must rely on the better collection and analysis of information to proactively target emerging challenges and build agreed-on responses based on a shared understanding of the problem. It must engage with all sectors of society, the state, and the community, and most important, it must be addressed at a continental level if a sustainable solution is to be found. It will not be an easy challenge; it is one that will only get more difficult over time. The time to begin the intensive course of treatment to eradicate this cancer must begin today.

〰 NOTE∫

---

1. This is an admittedly rough calculation across all the criminal markets analyzed in the UNODC report by determining the proportion of each market's linkage to Africa. The resulting figure is nothing more than a guide, given that it excludes prominent criminal markets (marijuana) as well as a host of internal African illicit markets (stolen cars, firearms, or cattle rustling, for example). Nevertheless, as a

broad rule of thumb, it provides some indication of the continent's immersion in the emerging global criminal economy.

2. Economic Commission for Africa and the African Union, *Economic Report on Africa 2011*, Addis Ababa, 2011. U.N. Office of the Special Advisor to Africa and NEPAD-OECD Africa Investment Initiative, *Africa Fact Sheet: Main Economic Indicators*, 2011.

3. In an official visit to Mogadishu in February 2012.

4. Based on interviews conducted by the author in Somalia in November 2011.

5. Report of the Monitoring Group on Somalia and Eritrea pursuant to Security Council Resolution 2002 (2011), Advanced Copy, United Nations, June 27, 2012.

6. Security Council, S/2012/45, Report of the United Nations assessment mission on piracy in the Gulf of Guinea (7 to 24 November 2011), January 19, 2012, p. 10.

7. Global Agenda Council on Organized Crime: 2010-11 Term Report, World Economic Forum, Geneva, 2011.

8. See http://www.eitictlabs.eu/.

9. I am indebted to Matthew Herbet of STATT, who conducted research on the telecommunication sector and opportunities for criminal exploitation in East Africa in April 2012. This research is published at http://www.statt.net/2012/07/mobile-finance-and-citizen-security/.

\\\\ REFERENCES

Africa's Cyber WMD. (2010, March). Foreign policy. Retrieved from http://www.foreignpolicy.com/articles/2010/03/24/africas_cyber_wmd

Altbeker, A. (2007). *A country at war with itself: South Africa's crisis of crime.* Johannesburg, South Africa: Jonathan Ball.

Bayart, J-F. (2010). *The state in Africa: The politics of the belly* (2nd ed.). Cambridge, England: Polity Press.

Bayart, J-F. Ellis, S., & Hibou, B. (1999). *The criminalisation of the state in Africa* (S. Ellis, Trans.). Oxford, England: J. Currey.

Carmody, P. (2011). *The new scramble for Africa.* Cambridge, England: Polity Press.

Conflict Awareness Project. (2012, July). *Viktor Bout's gunrunning successors: A lethal game of catch me if you can.* Retrieved from http://conflictawareness.org/wp-content/uploads/2012/08/ConflictAwarenessProjectReport-13August2012.pdf

Gastrow, P. (2011). *Termites at work: Transnational organised crime and state erosion in Kenya.* New York, NY: International Peace Institute.

Glenny, M. (2009). *McMafia: Seriously organised crime.* London, England: Vintage.

Gordon, D. (2006). *Transformation and trouble: Crime, justice and participation in democratic South Africa.* Ann Arbor: University of Michigan Press.

Herbst, J. (2000). *States and power in Africa: Comparative lessons in authority and control.* Princeton, NJ: Princeton University Press.

International Monetary Fund. (2012, January 24). *World economic outlook update.* Retrieved from http://www.imf.org/external/pubs/ft/weo/2012/update/01/index.htm

Jackson, R. (1990). *Quasi-states: Sovereignty, international relations and the third world.* Cambridge, England: Cambridge University Press.

Kemp, W. (2012, March 5). As crime in West Africa spreads, response requires regional cooperation. *International Peace Institute Global Observatory.* Retrieved from http://www.theglobalobservatory.org/analysis/231-as-crime-in-west-africa-spreads-response-requires-regional-cooperation.html

Naím, M. (2012, May/June). Mafia states: Organised crime takes office. *Foreign Affairs,* pp. 100–101.

Organisation for Economic Co-operation and Development, African Development Bank, & United Nations Economic Commission on Africa (2009). *The African economic outlook (AEO) 2009 on innovation and new technologies in Africa.* Paris, France: OECD Printing Press.

O'Neill, J.-J. (2011). *The growth map: Economic opportunity in the BRICs and beyond.* London, England: Penguin.

Patrick, S. (2011). *Weak links: Fragile states, global threats and international security.* New York, NY: Oxford University Press.

Pugh, M., & Cooper, N. (2004). *War economies in a regional context: Challenges of transformation.* London, England: Reiner.

Roth, A. (2012, July 17). Mauritius bars ex-associates of arms dealer. *New York Times.* Retrieved from http://www.nytimes.com/2012/07/18/world/africa/mauritius-rejects-application-from-arms-dealers-associates.html

Severino, J. M., & Ray, O. (2011). *Africa's moment.* Cambridge, England: Polity Press.

Shaw, M. (2002). *Crime and policing in post-apartheid South Africa: Transforming under fire.* Bloomington: Indiana University Press.

Shaw, M., & Kemp, W. (2012). *Spotting the spoilers: A guide to analyzing organized crime in fragile states.* New York, NY: International Peace Institute.

Spence, M. (2011). *The next convergence: The future of economic growth in a multispeed world.* New York, NY: Farrar, Straus & Giroux.

U.N. Office of Drugs and Crime. (2010). *The globalization of crime: A transnational organized crime threat assessment.* Vienna, Austria: Author.

World Bank. (2011). *World development report 2011: Conflict, security and development.* Washington, DC: Author.

6

Transnational Organized Crime in Asia and the Middle East

*Richard H. Ward and Daniel J. Mabrey**

Although transnational organized crime has a relatively long history in Asia and the Middle East, the turn of the century has marked not only growth in organized criminality but also a greater emphasis on new forms and new adaptations of technology to foster cross-border and international crime. The emergence of China as a global economic power has also had consequences on a government coping with major changes in crime and corruption. For many of the developing economies of Asia, organized crime continues to be a troubling issue, characterized by corruption, unstable or weak governments, and corruption in the boardrooms and offices of international corporations. In many cases, criminal justice systems have neither the funding nor the technology necessary to cope with increasingly sophisticated criminal activity.

*AUTHORS' NOTE: The authors would like to express their appreciation to Dr. Cindy Moors for her assistance in the preparation of an earlier version of this chapter and to John Hitzeman and research assistants Angelica Zdonek, Rachel Putorti, and Michael Figorito.

In the Middle East, where the so-called Arab Spring has brought down governments in Egypt and Libya[1] and threatened many other countries, organized criminality has flourished as justice systems and law enforcement organizations have been overthrown or handicapped by coping with public disorder. The result has been the formation of new organized crime enterprises that operate on a global scale.

Nevertheless, in many countries throughout Asia and the Middle East, organized criminal groups have long histories, in some cases dating back hundreds of years. In virtually all cases, these groups have been evolutionary, adapting to changing political conditions, warfare (both domestic and international), and perhaps most important, to the development of technology, communication, travel, and the emergence of a global economy. Criminal activities have been fueled by major advances in social media, new forms of sophisticated technology, and the inability of international organizations, such as Interpol (International Criminal Police Organization), the United Nations Office on Drugs and Crime (UNODC), the World Bank, and regional organizations to combat sophisticated criminal activities.

A number of countries have been the focus of transnational criminal activity, particularly in the areas of drug trafficking, illegal immigration, arms trafficking, the exploitation of women and children, internet schemes, fraud, kidnapping, child pornography on the Internet, and widespread public and private corruption. Behind most of these activities are organized and enterprise criminal groups. In Asia, some examples include the triads and tongs in Hong Kong and China, the Yakuza in Japan, the United Bamboo Gang in Taiwan, warlords in Myanmar, the Nam Cam Gang in Vietnam, and other ethnic entrepreneurs throughout Asia. In the Middle East, where terrorism has also contributed to the destabilization of governments, there have been links established between organized crime and violent groups.[2]

In many cases, symbiotic relationships between groups have resulted in a global network of organized criminal activity. Cooperation in various forms of criminal trafficking, money laundering, and illegal enterprises involving technology (e.g., cybercrime) are the most common forms of these relationships. In adapting to a new world order, many criminal groups in Southeast Asia and the Middle East have reinvented themselves, both to evade international law enforcement efforts and to take advantage of new "markets" throughout the world.

At the heart of these criminal activities is the world market in illegal drugs, ranging from poppy production for heroin to new demands for psychotropic substances, such as methamphetamines and other forms of "designer" drugs—for example, methylamphetamine (commonly known as Ecstasy), gamma hydroxybutyrate (GHB), Rohypnol, ketamine (Special K), Methcathanone (Cat), and mescaline.

With the opening of China to the West in the 1980s and the fall of the Soviet Union in December 1991, a growing market in illegal immigration and the exploitation of women and children have also become lucrative sources of income for organized crime. The technological advances of the past decade have fostered child pornography, money laundering, and Internet scams. Organized crime groups have become an integral part of this burgeoning international phenomenon.

It is widely assumed that organized crime cannot exist to any substantial degree in the absence of corruption, and many countries find themselves facing growing levels of government, judicial, and police involvement in corrupt activities that support criminal enterprises.

This chapter examines Asian and Middle Eastern organized criminal activities and their impact on the global economy and international criminal justice systems, largely from the perspective of developing nations, industrialized countries, and democratization. Although these three variables are not mutually exclusive, they do reflect in large measure a typology that relates to criminal activity. Of particular interest is the increasing involvement of terrorist groups in organized crime to help fund their operations. Crime in developing countries, although less likely to be transnational in nature—with the exception of illegal migration, exploitation of women and children, and to some degree, drug trafficking—is expanding. Crime in industrial countries, whether democratic or autocratic, is characterized by more sophisticated criminality and organized crime. There is also likely to be more cross-border or transnational crime. Countries that have placed a greater emphasis on the rule of law and democratic freedoms have seen increases in street-level crime, such as robbery and burglary, and are more likely to be plagued by sophisticated international organized crime groups. The impact of Arab Spring has also contributed to disorder and opportunities for organized crime. To understand some of these relationships, it is important to be familiar with the cultural, political, and economic environments of different countries and how they contribute to organized criminal activity. Because a number of countries in the Middle East are still in transition, coverage has focused largely on those countries where organized crime is well established or adjusting to change. The first section focuses on Asia, and the second focuses on the Middle East.[3]

※ AJIAN ORGANIZED CRIME

To understand organized crime in Asia, one must recognize that different legal structures and the justice systems of different countries, particularly police, courts, and corrections, have an impact on public order and crime control. Methods of training, education, and selection of personnel in each of these areas frequently differ among countries. The following analysis is illustrative rather than exhaustive and provides a brief overview of the justice systems and transnational crime in select Asian countries[4]:

- China (The People's Republic of China)
- Hong Kong (The People's Republic of China)
- Japan
- Cambodia
- Republic of Korea
- Myanmar (formerly Burma)
- Taiwan (Republic of China)
- North Korea
- Singapore
- Philippines
- Thailand
- Vietnam

China

The People's Republic of China (PRC), with a population of more than 1.5 billion, is the most populous country in the world and has evolved since its inception in 1949 from a relatively isolated country to a burgeoning superpower. The criminal justice system has undergone numerous changes from the time when the country opened up to the West in the late 1970s and early 1980s. Although crime in China is relatively low by Western standards, the country has experienced an increasing crime problem due in no small measure to a growing economy and the ability of organized crime to move more freely throughout the country and globally. China's centralized police service, under the Ministry of Public Security, numbers more than 1.5 million personnel. Judicial and correctional services come under the Ministry of Justice. Over the past 30 years, these two ministries have undergone sweeping changes, modeled in many ways on European and American concepts of criminal justice. The criminal laws and judicial process have also undergone key revisions, although, in practice, there is a major difference between the written legal system and the actual practices of the system.

Organized crime in China is now well entrenched but generally takes two similar forms. The first involves criminal activity by well-organized gangs such as the triads, frequently in cooperative ventures involving black-market activities, drug trafficking, cybercrime, and smuggling. These gangs are also involved in extortion of small businesses. Criminal syndicates and street gangs make up the second form of Chinese organized crime and are involved in more localized or cross-border crimes such as prostitution, illegal emigration, slavery, and other organized forms of vice. Many of China's crime groups are family oriented, of limited size, and more likely to work in cooperation with established crime groups.

Historically, Chinese law enforcement officials maintained that organized crime was virtually eliminated under the leadership of Mao Zedong, but it is doubtful that organized crime ever left the country; rather, the triad societies,[5] which moved to Hong Kong following the fall of the Kuomintang government,[6] maintained a clandestine presence on the mainland.

Data relative to the increase of triad activity in China are becoming more available, and newspapers are more likely to report major cases. Chinese street gangs are more prone to violence, and Misha Glenny (2008a), an investigative reporter, notes that "increasingly, the [Japanese] *yakuza* outsource the punitive deployment of violence to Chinese gangs" (p. 312). Chinese gang members are imported to carry out attacks in Tokyo, Yokohama, and Osaka.

Triads have established drug-trafficking networks with the Bamboo Union gangs in Taiwan, the Yakuza in Japan, and drug cartels from Mexico and South America. The U.S. Bureau for International Narcotics and Law Enforcement Affairs reported that China is a major transit point for illegal narcotics produced in the Golden Triangle, and in 2011, the largest number of seizures of Southeast Asian heroin continue to occur within the country (Bureau of International Narcotics and Law Enforcement Affairs, 2012). The southern areas of China will also continue to be major transit routes for Southeast Asian heroin as well as for domestic drug use. Heroin is trafficked into and through China from Thailand, Myanmar, and Laos. Despite death sentences for traffickers and a widespread war on drugs, police and government corruption has increased dramatically over the past decade. China is also a major source country for precursor chemicals such as ephedrine, pseudo-ephedrine, and acetic anhydride and is a major producer of crystal methamphetamine.

The number of registered drug addicts in China is about 1.5 million, with heroin being the primary drug of choice (U.N. Office on Drugs and Crime, 2012b). Drug trafficking is one of a number of crimes punishable by death in China. Unemployment, and what is commonly referred to as the "floating population," has created migration to the cities and contributes to the crime problem.

The exploitation of women and children for sex and human trafficking by organized criminal groups represents another major problem for China. Yunnan, Sichuan, and Guizhou provinces are the principal areas from which many women are kidnapped and sold into slavery. Within the country, prostitution has become a major source of revenue for the poor, and as drug addiction has increased, the problem has become more widespread. In the larger cities, organized crime has taken over much of the trade, and corruption of police and others, such as hotel employees and cab drivers, has contributed to the problem.

Illegal emigration has also become a lucrative business for organized crime, and the smuggling of individuals to all parts of the world has become commonplace. Chinese organized crime groups, especially the triads, are deeply involved in the human trade business. Traffickers, known as "snakeheads," are part of a global network, wherein an individual may pay as much as $30,000 or more to enter the United States. Within the United States, a well-organized criminal network has been developed to foster illegal immigration.

Chinese triads have taken over the smuggling of illegal immigrants from smaller "mom and pop" organizations as an increasingly attractive alternative to drug trafficking because it promises multibillion dollar profits without the same severe penalties if caught. Earnings from illegal immigrant trade are estimated to total USD 3.2 billion per year, yet it is punishable in the United States by a maximum sentence of only 5 years in jail. Most who are convicted under current laws serve very short sentences (Bolz, 1995, p. 147).

Thousands of minor gangs throughout the country are also involved in a wide range of illegal thefts and commerce violations. For example, in Hunan Province, a 20-member gang monopolized the seafood market beginning in 2007, making almost a million dollars (6.4 million yuan) until they were arrested in 2010 and the 30-year-old leader was sentenced to 19 years in prison (Zhang & Cao, 2011).

As gangs have become more sophisticated, and travel easier, gangs have broadened their activities and cooperate with other criminal groups. Shanxi Province in Northern China, Guangdong Province, and the autonomous region of Guangxi Zhuang in the South of China are high-crime areas in the country.

The increase in drug trafficking and other organized criminal activities in China has contributed largely to government and police corruption. Despite severe penalties and a number of ongoing crackdowns, the problem has become increasingly severe. Corruption in China has become a mainstream issue with the 2011–2012 crackdown on corruption of government officials and within the Ministry of Public Security.

Hong Kong

In 1997, Hong Kong was returned to the People's Republic of China, ending a 100-year lease to the United Kingdom. Under the transition agreement, the Chinese government established a policy of "one country, two systems," agreeing that the former colony would continue to follow a legal system based on British common law for a period of 50 years. As one of the most successful communities in Asia, Hong Kong has one of the most advanced criminal justice systems in the world. Nevertheless, it continues to be the center of triad activity in that part of the world.[7]

With a police force of more than 33,000 personnel, this relatively small geographic city has a population of more than 7 million (2011 estimate). The judicial system, based on British common law, allowed a relatively independent judiciary to be adopted under Chinese control, which is exercised through an administrator appointed by the government.

Compared to crime in Mainland China, Hong Kong's generally has a higher juvenile crime rate but a lower overall crime rate (Xu, 2011). Theft is the most significant criminal activity. However, Hong Kong is a densely populated city, and when compared with other large cities, the crime rate is comparable.

One of the more interesting criminal justice units in Hong Kong is the Independent Commission Against Corruption (ICAC), an independent body established when Hong Kong was under British control. ICAC's reputation for fighting corruption is unparalleled, and the organization has some extraordinary powers to conduct investigations. Over the years,

Hong Kong has been rated as one of the least corrupt places in the world. The Chinese government has continued to support ICAC and its activities. ICAC holds an international conference every 4 years to bring together experts from a wide range of countries to observe the anticorruption activities in this unique city.

Japan

Japan is one of the most advanced governments in Asia, with a well-trained and well-organized criminal justice system that is adversarial with a presumption of innocence until proven guilty. The political system has been influenced by 19th-century German and British parliamentary models, and the country's constitution was rewritten by U.S. advisers following World War II. The legal system incorporates aspects of the legal systems of Germany and France as well as the United States model.

A sluggish economy over the past decade and revelations about the influence of organized crime, the Yakuza or *Boryokudan*, in government and business have cast a cloud over crime control efforts. The Yakuza influence has infiltrated banks, real estate agencies, corporations, and government, prompting major scandals. In 2008, the Japanese National Police Agency estimated that there were more than 80,000 active members. In 2012, the U.S. Treasury Department implemented a plan to freeze the assets of Japan's Yamaguchi-gumi, the largest of the Yakuza crime families, noting that the group earns "billions of dollars from prostitution and weapons, drugs and human trafficking" (Younglai, 2012).

The Yakuza have a strong presence in Japan's private sector. In 2008, the National Police Agency identified more than 800 Yakuza front companies in Tokyo alone. These included investment and auditing firms, construction companies, banks, and even pastry shops. The Japanese Securities and Exchange Surveillance Commission has an index with more than 50 listed companies that have ties to the Yakuza.

Cambodia

Turmoil, civil war, and repressive governments have dominated Cambodia for more than 40 years, and many of those in the educated and legal community fled the country during the 1970s. Rival political parties dominate the justice system, and the lack of clear legal systems and procedures contributes largely to corruption, political influence, and arbitrary criminal justice policies.

The major transnational criminal activities in Cambodia are controlled primarily by Chinese and Myanmarese organized crime groups and are closely tied to drug and human trafficking. Cambodia has been repeatedly cited by the U.S. Drug Enforcement Administration (DEA) as a source country for the growth of marijuana, which is trafficked mainly in Europe, and as a transit country on the international drug market for the distribution of Southeast Asian heroin. Heroin is moved from Laos and Thailand through Phnom Penh as part of the global drug trade.

Law enforcement efforts against organized crime in Cambodia are largely ineffectual. Statistical information about organized crime in Cambodia is questionable at best. Law enforcement agencies are underfunded and lack even basic training in criminal investigation and drug control efforts, a problem further compounded by endemic corruption.

Within the country there has been a significant increase in the use of methamphetamines by young people, prompting the government to take an active role in working with international agencies in antidrug activities. Nevertheless, the existence of widespread corruption hampers enforcement efforts. Gambling, prostitution, and money laundering have also fostered the existence of global organized crime networks in the country.

Organized crime groups control prostitution, and the exploitation of women is a major problem within Cambodia. Children are often victims of forced prostitution and are sold or "rented" to customers as sex slaves.

Republic of Korea

South Korea, with a population of 49.7 million (2011 estimate), employs a civil law system wherein written laws are the primary source of reference, as opposed to statutes or ordinances. The criminal law classifies crimes into five broad categories: crimes that breach the national interest, crimes that breach the social interest, crimes of a personal nature, tax-related crimes, and drug crimes. Children between the ages of 14 and 20 are handled under the juvenile legal system.

Organized crime in Korea has a unique history when compared to that of other Asian nations. As Korea began to modernize in the 1800s, the population swelled and began to concentrate in urban centers where unemployed young men banded together and idled about city streets.

These groups of young men were called *Keondal,* meaning scamps, and they worked in places like bars, gambling houses, and construction sites. The *Keondal* were not considered criminal groups, even though they engaged in criminal activities and violence among each other. Because they honored loyalty and faithfulness, they would sometimes help the weak and the poor. Much like the Japanese Yakuza, the lives of *Keondal* are an attractive source of material for movies and are admired by some Korean youth.

In the 1960s, organized crime groups emerged as an influential power in entertainment districts and quickly became associated with politicians, who used them as their personal henchmen to attack political rivals. The military government in Korea at the time arrested over 13,000 members of these political gangs and temporarily stamped out organized crime in Korea.

Throughout the 1970s and 1980s, Korean organized crime groups developed into nationwide organizations, with some groups even extending their activities to foreign countries through associations with the Yakuza and other organized crime groups in the United States. This led the Korean government to declare a "war" against organized crime. Members could be arrested and punished for forming, joining, or even affiliating with criminal organizations.

Drug trafficking is the main criminal enterprise for Korean organized crime, with most shipments originating in drug factories in China and Japan before being smuggled into countries throughout Asia and into the United States. According to the U.S. Department of State (2012), Korea is neither a major user nor a producer of dangerous drugs. Drug use among Korean youths has steadily increased in recent years.

Myanmar

Myanmar is a major opium-producing country, and under the leadership of a military junta, is one of the most lawless countries in Asia. The military-controlled criminal justice system is rife with corruption. In 2011, the U.S. government eased restrictions on the government in an attempt to foster change and establish closer ties to combating drug trafficking and human rights abuses.

Drug production and trafficking is controlled by several "armies," which in effect are perhaps the largest organized crime groups in the world. Armed ethnic groups such as the United Wa State Army (UWSA), the Kokang Chinese, and the Myanmar National Democratic Alliance Army (MNDAA) control the cultivation areas, refine opium into heroin, and also produce methamphetamine. These heavily armed ethnic groups generally promise to eliminate opium production in the course of their negotiations with the government. Drug production in those areas continues nonetheless.

Myanmar is also a major source of women and children (many of whom are under the age of 18), who are trafficked to Pakistan and Thailand by organized crime groups. Many victims are lured by job placement agencies, frequently controlled by organized crime groups, and other young girls are simply abducted from hill tribes and exported into the sex trade (Hughes, Sporcic, Mendelsohn, & Chirgwin, 1999).

⟡ OTHER AJIAN COUNTRIEJ

Although this chapter focuses on the countries previously named, organized criminal groups have expanded into most countries in Asia in one form or another. Globalization has opened new markets and a variety of new forms of organized criminal activity that ranges from the production of counterfeit goods to Internet crime. In Taiwan, organized crime is controlled largely by Bamboo Union Gangs. These gangs have close relationships with triad groups in China and Hong Kong and are primarily involved in drug trafficking (methamphetamine and heroin) from mainland China.

North Korea, despite its relative isolation, has been identified as a haven for state-sponsored organized crime involving counterfeit currency, cigarettes, and drugs as well as drug and human trafficking. Reportedly, the government works in cooperation with Russian, Japanese, and Chinese organized crime groups.

In contrast to most countries in Asia, the tiny country of Singapore stands as one of the few places where strict law enforcement and a strong central government impose stringent fines, extended prison sentences, and capital punishment to maintain public security. In 1973, the Misuse of Drugs Act established severe penalties for drug violations, including long prison sentences and capital punishment for trafficking and production of drugs. The Philippines and Thailand have long been havens for the sex industry, both domestically and internationally. Organized crime groups control virtually every aspect of commerce in women and children. Thousands of women are sent to other countries.

Thailand's sex industry is one of the most notorious in the world and is a multibillion-dollar industry. Organized crime groups have imported an estimated 1 million women from China, Laos, and Vietnam to Thailand. An estimated 400,000 children under the age of 16 work in brothels, bars, and nightclubs. Global criminal networks involved in Thailand's drug trafficking, money laundering, and prostitution operate from China, Hong Kong, Japan, and Singapore.

Most of the transnational organized crime groups operating in Vietnam are from bases in other Asian countries, but there are a growing number of Vietnamese organized gangs (namely, affiliates of the Nam Cam Gang), many of which display characteristics of the more sophisticated groups in Hong Kong and China. Accordingly, corruption of public officials and the police is increasing. Vietnam is ranked by the United States among the top 26 drug-producing and drug-trafficking countries in the world ("Seven Vietnamese Police Officers," 2000). The U.S. Department of State identified Vietnam repeatedly over the last decade as a transit point and production entity for heroin. Heroin from Laos, Myanmar, China, and Thailand and marijuana from Cambodia are frequently moved through Vietnam by organized crime groups.

⧠ TRANSNATIONAL CRIME IN THE MIDDLE EAST[8]

Turmoil in the Middle East has severely impacted the ability of many criminal justice organizations to cope with more traditional criminality, and in many ways organized criminal groups have been immune to investigation and prosecution. The economies of countries in the region range from very poor in Yemen, Syria, and Afghanistan (which is also considered to be in Central Asia) to wealthier nations, including Saudi Arabia, Turkey, and Iran. Russia has been included in this compendium because parts of the country, including Chechnya, are more closely aligned with Middle Eastern countries and are influenced by Russian organized crime groups (but see also the coverage of Russia in Chapters 2 and 4). Although Islam is the predominant religion in most of the countries, Christianity and Judaism originated in this part of the world.

The following list of countries is selective, providing an overview of nations in various stages of governance and economic development, a number of which have been torn asunder by public protests and the formation of new governments or changes in the political and legal structures:

- Egypt
- Israel
- Republic of Lebanon
- Libya
- Saudi Arabia
- Republic of Turkey

Egypt

The fall of the Hosni Mubarak government in 2011 and the aftereffects of a major change in the government's structure were characterized by military control and efforts to establish a democratic model that has been difficult to achieve. Senior government and police officials, including Mubarak (who served as president from 1981–2011), were put on trial and in 2012 Mubarak was sentenced to life imprisonment. The country continues to be mired in conflict with the Supreme Council of the Armed Forces holding almost complete control.

The Egyptian police structure and legal system was primarily secular, drawn initially from a British model of law enforcement. However, a growing acceptance of Muslim law has become popular within the country as evidenced by the influence of the Muslim Brotherhood in political activities. Widespread charges of police brutality and assassinations during the 2011 revolution brought to light many abuses and corruption of government officials, the police, and the state security operation. When the government fell in 2011, the military took control to restore order pending a scheduled election in June 2012 and a return to civilian control. Elections for a new parliament in 2011 resulted in Islamist parties gaining close to 70% of the seats, but their power was limited by the military. Historically, the Supreme Council for the Armed Forces (SCAP) has played a key role in the politics and security of Egypt. "Underneath its autocratic surface, modern Egypt was effectively a military state" (Wright, 2012, para. 7). All of its presidents since the monarchy was overthrown in 1952 have been from the military. The officer class controls as much as a third of the economy and seeks to maintain control under a new civilian government.

Organized criminal activity in Egypt has historically been local or regional, influenced in no small measure by the military, which controls or plays a role in many of the large businesses. Black-market activities and corruption of and by government officials (kickbacks, bribery, and white-collar crime) have been common, Activities by organized gangs involve illegal immigration of women from Africa or Eastern Europe for use as domestic servants or who are transited through the country to Israel as laborers or servants. In recent years, Egyptian organized crime has expanded drug-trafficking operations in cooperation with other international groups, as both a transit point and for internal distribution.

Israel

The criminal justice system in Israel draws on English common law, civil law, and Jewish law; criminal cases are adversarial in nature, handled by professional judges. A modern police service of about 35,000 (and about 70,000 volunteers) is responsible for traditional law enforcement operations, working against organized crime, and counterterrorism. The police are under the administrative control of the Ministry of Internal Services and the Ministry of Public Security. A number of senior government officials have been convicted of corruption over time, and police corruption has generally been limited to relatively minor charges.

For its size, with a population smaller than most states in America, Israel's organized crime connections are global. A number of groups, or syndicates, are active within the country and carry on illegal activities throughout the world, including the United States. Among their activities are the following:

- Prostitution and trafficking in women
- Money laundering
- Protection and extortion rackets
- Loan sharking
- Drugs and arms dealing
- Fencing stolen goods
- Operating casinos and other forms of gambling inside and outside Israel (Israeli Mafia, 2012)

A major factor in the development of transnational organized crime was an influx of Russian Jews with connections to the Russian Mafiya, who introduced new and more sophisticated forms of money laundering, a drug transit point, and human trafficking (Glenny, 2008b). Israeli ties to the United States also afforded an opportunity to develop contacts within financial markets and legitimate businesses as a means of money laundering. Computer sophistication has enabled organized gangs to hack into Israeli credit card companies, government facilities, and personal accounts of officials. In addition to carrying out financial scams to support terrorist groups, cyber attacks on the country's banks and critical infrastructure have been more frequent in recent years.

The Republic of Lebanon

Lebanon is a country torn by war and periods of conflict between the 18 religious groups recognized by the government. With fewer than 5 million people, the government structure includes leadership positions occupied by members of specific religious groups and a 128-seat legislature, half of which is Muslim and the other half, Christian.[9] The citizens of Lebanon enjoy a relatively high standard of living, and the country's financial system is one of the strongest in the region.

Organized crime in Lebanon is often overshadowed by the criminal activities of the largest terrorist group in the country, Hezbollah. Hezbollah, or Party of God, is a Shiite Muslim organization based in Lebanon as a political party and classified as a terrorist group by the United States and other, mostly Western, countries.[10] As funding from Iran and Syria has dwindled because of internal strife and sanctions by numerous governments, Hezbollah has turned to organized crime as a means of financial and weapons support:

On June 13, 2011, in Kuala Lumpur, Malaysia, [Cetin] Aksu and [Bachar] Wehbe signed a written contract for the purchase of 48 American-made Stinger SAMs, 100 Igla SAMs, 5,000 AK-47 assault rifles, 1,000 M4 rifles, and 1,000 Glock handguns, for a total price of approximately $9.5 million. During the course of the weapons negotiation, Wehbe stated that he was purchasing the weapons on instructions from Hizballah. Shortly thereafter, Wehbe and others caused approximately $100,000 to be transferred to the CSs as a down payment for the weapons purchase, including a $50,000 wire transfer to an undercover bank account. (U.S. Drug Enforcement Administration, 2011)

One of the more sophisticated money-laundering cases in recent years involved a scheme by Hezbollah to fund their organization through drug trafficking and "laundering" money through an elaborate scheme involving the purchase of used cars in the United States that were sold in Africa. Investigative auditors discovered about 200 accounts described as suspicious because of their links to Hezbollah. Funds were moved through a Lebanese Canadian bank and involved a large number of Lebanese immigrants living in the United States and other countries. A suspect arrested by the FBI was accused of laundering money for Hezbollah, as well as for Colombian cartels and Mexico's Los Zeta gang. The global demand for illegal drugs furthered the global monetary networks established in South American countries and West Africa, eventually moving through Portugal, Spain, or Syria and Lebanon. The scheme, according to officials, centered on the Lebanese Canadian bank and was discovered when the bank's assets were sold and auditors discovered "nearly 200 accounts that appeared to add up to a giant money-laundering operation, with Hezbollah smack in the middle, according to American officials" (Becker, 2011).

Saudi Arabia

One of the richest countries in the world, Saudi Arabia is a monarchy managed by the king and royal family, who hold positions as ministers within the government. The country has a low crime rate, due in large part to strong Islamic religious ties among the populace, the majority of whom are Sunni, and a modern law enforcement system backed by a strong criminal intelligence capability. The justice system is based on Sharia law. The Ministry of Interior is responsible for the police and criminal investigation and presents cases before the Sharia courts. Nevertheless, the country has not been immune to terrorism in the past and continues to maintain a strict security system. Most of the local crime is committed by foreign workers who are admitted to work in relatively low-level jobs, and organized criminal activity within the country is minimal. Capital punishment by beheading is viewed as a strong deterrent to crime.

Organized criminal activity involves gambling, human trafficking, hostage taking, selling black-market goods, such as liquor (which is illegal in the country), and to a limited degree, drug trafficking, all of which are capital offenses in the country. In September 2011, police arrested a group of drug smugglers using a glider to smuggle Captagon pills (an amphetamine type stimulant) into the country (Al-Sulami, 2011). Seven Pakistani and Indian suspects were arrested in October 2011 in connection with an illegal gambling and lottery racket (Al-Tamimi, 2011).

Human trafficking in Saudi Arabia has been a source of concern by the U.S. State Department, resulting in a number of changes in recent years to come into compliance with the Victims of Trafficking and Violence Protection Act of 2000. The use of skilled and unskilled labor in the kingdom is common, and commercial sex exploitation involves organized criminal gangs working in cooperation with local recruitment agencies. According to reports, the judicial system, which operates under Sharia Law, does not adequately protect immigrants from abusive treatment and sexual advances. Police officers do receive training in cases involving exploitation and abuse of children, women, and workers.

In 2011, the Naif Arab University established a chair "to study and combat the menace of drug abuse in Saudi Arabia." Although drug abuse in the kingdom is considered relatively low, Saudi hospitals have treated 72,000 addicts, and there are indications that a small number of students are drug abusers (Ali Kahn, 2012).

Republic of Turkey

With a population of almost 80 million people, Turkey falls into the Middle East or East Asia and claims close ties to countries in both the Middle East and Asia. The criminal justice structure has usually followed a Western orientation, and the national police organization, under the Ministry of Interior, is progressive in terms of training and technology. Human rights issues, charges of police abuse of authority, the use of excessive force, and torture have been subjects of concern by a number of international groups, including Human Rights Watch and Amnesty International. The country has applied for membership in the European Union and has one of the most stable economic structures in the region.

The police structure operates under the General Directorate of Security with responsibility for traditional law enforcement functions, including organized crime and aspects of counterterrorism. The Gendarmerie, a "third force" that is quasi-military and under jurisdiction of the Ministry of Interior, performs similar to the French Gendarmerie and the Carabinieri in Italy and carries out law enforcement and counterterrorism operations in smaller towns and the Anatolia region, where terrorism is prevalent. Both organizations, as well as military commands, maintain intelligence operations coordinated by the Turkish National Intelligence Organization.

Turkish organized crime activity is legendary (Cengiz, 2010; Demiroz & Kapucu, 2012; Galeotti, 2012). International gangs are involved in drug trafficking and illegal immigration, and smuggling of goods is prevalent, much of which is carried out by street gangs. A crackdown on gangs, a major priority of the police and Gendarmerie over the past decade, has resulted in as many as 20,000 arrests since 2000.

⩔ SUMMARY: ORGANIZED CRIME IN ASIA AND THE MIDDLE EAST

The most significant trend in criminal activity over the past decade has been the growing influence of international and transnational organized crime groups. China's rapid economic gains have also fostered a broad range of criminal activities in virtually every aspect of illegal transactions that involve smuggling, Internet crime, emigration, forgery, and drug trafficking.

The UNODC, in a 2010 press release, noted that

> factors including the region's geographical location, income inequality, rapid urbanization and instability have increased the vulnerability of the Middle East and North Africa to organized crime and drug abuse. Criminal justice systems are under-resourced and prison conditions need to be improved. There is also a lack of data on drugs and crime. (U.N. Office on Drugs and Crime, 2010, para. 3)

Within the individual countries that have spawned organized criminal activity, many groups have expanded their operations because of inadequate criminal justice systems and high levels of police corruption. Many of these groups have histories over several hundred years, involving growing networks that span the globe and work cooperatively to foster their criminal enterprises and money-laundering efforts. The problem is further compounded by the implications of the Arab Spring movements and a growing trend in which terrorist groups work with organized crime groups or have established their own crime groups to fund their activities.

Al-Queda in the Maghreb (AQIM), for example, has turned to "abductions, hostage-taking operations, drug smuggling and bank robberies" as a means funding terrorist operations:

> Experts and officials from various countries have expressed fear that Al Qaeda's operations have become a vital source of income to fund its attacks around the world. Moreover, experts in Algeria have raised the issue of the current overlap between AQIM and drug smugglers as a result of terrorists offering protection to drug smuggling gangs across the desert. (Al Shafey, 2011)

More sophisticated forms of enterprise crime are evident, particularly as result of the increasing role that the Internet plays in cybercrime, money laundering, and identity theft. Human smuggling, corruption, and the changing nature of the drug trade also find extensive involvement by criminal groups. There is no effective mechanism in many of these developing countries to conduct sophisticated criminal investigations into organized crime. Many of the police and security forces lack both the training and technology necessary to carry out such investigations.

Corruption of police and government officials has become endemic. Corruption takes many forms and may involve different levels of government as well as the private sector. In some countries, such as Japan, government corruption is tied largely to the private sector, which in turn is influenced in large measure by the Yakuza. Low pay and status contributes to widespread police and government corruption; the exploitation of women and children, the illegal sex trade, and child pornography represent ongoing threats that have expanded across the globe.

Improved international law enforcement networks have been strengthened through the efforts of the United Nations, Interpol, UNODC, and other global organizations. In the private sector, groups such as the American Society of Industrial Security (ASIS), which includes many members from multinational and global corporations, have also become more active in fostering cooperation and intelligence sharing. A number of countries have expanded the practice of assigning law enforcement officials to other countries to work closely with their counterparts in the host country, focusing on the investigation of transnational organized criminal groups. The United States is the largest participant in assigning federal agents to other countries. The DEA, the U.S. Customs Service, the Federal Bureau of Investigation (FBI), the Immigration and Naturalization Service (INS), the Secret Service (responsible for counterfeiting), and the U.S. Postal Inspection Service are but some of the American agencies with representatives abroad.

The U.S.-initiated International Law Enforcement Academies (ILEA) in Budapest, Bangkok, and Gabarone have cooperative relationships with host countries to provide training to police. The ILEA in Roswell, New Mexico, has trained police officials from more than 40 countries in management and focuses on strategic approaches to controlling international crime. Likewise, exchange programs such as those offered by the Office of International Criminal Justice (OICJ) at the University of New Haven and other colleges and universities present criminal justice practitioners and academics the opportunity to study the successes and failures of other countries.

Despite these efforts, Asian criminal organizations have continued to expand their activities, in many cases teaming up with criminal enterprise organizations from countries throughout the world, including Asian groups, such as the Yakuza and Chinese tongs, the American and Italian mafia, Colombian and Mexican cartels, the Russian Mafiya, and emerging groups in the Middle East and Eastern Europe. Organized crime is now firmly entrenched in the global community.

⁂ NOTES

1. At the time of this writing Syria has been engaged in a major civil insurrection resulting in the loss of thousands of lives in attempts to overthrow the government.

2. For example, Al-Queda in the Islamic Maghreb (AQIM) has been linked to drug trafficking, money laundering, kidnapping for ransoms, and arms trafficking (Al Shafey, 2011).

3. The countries selected reflect different political and economic systems.

4. For a more comprehensive description of justice systems throughout the world see *The World Factbook of Criminal Justice Systems* at http://bjs.ojp.usdoj.gov/content/pub/html/wfcj.cfm, and Das and Palmetto (2006) *World Police Encyclopedia*.

5. Triad societies have their roots in 17th-century China.

6. The Kuomintang government, under the leadership of Chiang Kai-Shek, moved to the island of Taiwan and formed a new country, which is in dispute today, as the Chinese government maintains that Taiwan is still a province of China.

7. With the transition to Communist rule many of the triad groups relocated to other parts of the world, although there continues to be a triad presence in the former British colony.

8. The Middle East encompasses between 18 and 40 countries depending upon various definitions. The largest countries in the region, with approximate populations, include Egypt (77 million), Turkey (78 million), Iran (71 million), Iraq (31 million), Saudi Arabia (23 million), Syria (22 million), Yemen (24 million), Afghanistan (32 million), Algeria (33 million), Kazakhstan (15 million), Pakistan (170 million), Sudan (31 million), and Uzbekistan (27 million).

9. By law, the president must be a Maronite Christian; the prime minister, a Sunni Muslim; the Speaker of Parliament, a Shia Muslim; and the Deputy Speaker, Greek Orthodox.

10. Hezbollah's primary goal is the destruction of Israel, and over the years the group has established a strong political presence and a formidable paramilitary organization. In addition to using suicide bombers, the group has fired rockets and missiles into Israel.

※ REFERENCES AND FURTHER READING

Al Shafey, M. (2011, January 17). Al-Qaeda and organized crime: Two sides of the same coin. *Alawsat, Asharq.* Retrieved from http://www.asharq-e.com/news.asp?id=23813

Al-Sulami, Md. (2011, September 28). Ban on gliders after drug bust. *Arab News.* http://www.arabnews .com/node/392756

Al-Tamimi, S. (2011, October 16). Seven nabbed in gambling racket raid. *Arab News* http://www .arabnews.com/node/394999

Ali Khan, S. (2011, October 18). Naif Arab university chair to study and combat drug menace. *Saudi Gazette,* p. 1.

August, O. (2001, February 12). China locking addicts in mental hospitals. *London Times,* p. D13.

Becker, J. (2011, December 13). Beirut bank seen as a hub of Hezbollah's funding. *New York Times.* Retrieved from http://www.nytimes.com/2011/12/ 14/world/middleeast/beirut-bank-seen-as-a-hub-of-hezbollahs-financing.html?page wanted=all&_r=0

Bolz, J. (1995). Chinese organized crime and illegal alien trafficking: Humans as a commodity. *Asian Affairs: An American Review, 22*(3), 147–158.

Bremner, B. (1996, January 1). How the mob burned the banks. *Business Week,* p. 42.

Bruno, A. (2003). Unique gang organizations: The Yakuza. *Court TV—Crime Library.* Retrieved from http://www.trutv.com/library/crime/gangsters_outlaws/gang/yakuza/1.html

Bureau of International Narcotics and Law Enforcement Affairs. (2012, March 7). 2012 INCSR: Country reports: Afghanistan through Costa Rica, Retrieved from http://www.state .gov/j/inl/rls/nrcrpt/2012/vol1/184098.htm

Cengiz, M. (2010). *The globalization of Turkish organized crime and the policy response* (Doctoral dissertation). Available from ProQuest Dissertations and Theses database. (UMI No. 3435745)

China: Beijing authorities recover millions of dollars in anti-graft crackdown. (2003, January 15). *BBC Monitoring Asia Pacific*. Retrieved from Lexis Nexis Database. http://www.accessmylibrary.com/ coms2/summary_0286-22434606_ ITM

China reports new HIV/AIDS statistics. (2001, August 24). *Xinhua News Agency*. Retrieved from Lexis Nexis Database. Retrieved from://www.china .org.cn/english/18028.htm

Ching-Ching, N. (2003, January 24). China struggles to combat drug use: Heroin becomes a scourge in poor regions of the country where its use is soaring among her young. *Los Angeles Times*, p. E6.

Coalition against trafficking in women. (1998). *CATW-Asia Pacific Newsletter*, *1*(2).

Das, D. K., & Palmetto, M. (Eds.). (2006). *World police encyclopedia*. New York, NY: Routledge.

Demiroz, F., & Kapucu, N. (2012). Anatomy of a dark network: The case of the Turkish Ergenekon terrorist organization. *Trends in Organized Crime, 15*, 271–295.

Drug Enforcement Administration. (2002a, March). *Drug intelligence brief: Cambodia country brief*. Washington, DC: Author.

Drug Enforcement Administration. (2002b, March). *Drug intelligence brief: China country brief*. Washington, DC: Author.

Drug Enforcement Administration. (2002c, March). *Drug intelligence brief: Myanmar country brief*. Washington, DC: Author.

Federal Bureau of Investigation. (2003, April). Organized crime: The FBI perspective. *Crime and Justice International, 19*(72), 13–16.

Floating brothels popular in Taiwan. (1998, July 22). *Associated Press*. Retrieved from Lexis Nexis database.

Forced labor in Burma. (2002, March 19). *Boston Globe*, A18. Retrieved from Lexis Nexis database.

Galeotti, M. (2012). Turkish organized crime: From tradition to business. In D. Siegel & H. van de Bunt (Eds.), *Traditional organized crime in the modern world: Responses to socioeconomic change* (Vol. 11, pp. 49–64). New York, NY: Springer.

Glenny, M. (2008a). *McMafia: A journey through the global criminal underworld*. New York, NY: Knopf.

Glenny, M. (2008b). *McMafia: Seriously organised crime*. London, England: Vintage Books.

Greitens, S. C. (2012, March 4). A North Korean Corleone. *New York Times*, p. A4.

Hsieh, D. (2001, November 22). Corruption in China's police force intolerable, says minister. *The Straits Times* (Singapore), p. A2.

Hughes, D. M., Sporcic, L. J., Mendelsohn, N. Z., & Chirgwin, V. (1999). Burma/ Myanmar. *World factbook on global sexual exploitation*. Coalition against Trafficking in Women. Retrieved from www.catwinternational.org/fb/Burma-Myanmar.html

Human Trafficking in Saudi Arabia. Retrieved from http://en.wikipedia.org/w/ index.php?title= Human_trafficking_in_Saudi_Arabia&oldid= 460233429

Israeli mafia. (2012). Retrieved from http://en.wikipedia.org/wiki/Israeli_mafia

Juvida, S. F. (1997, October 12). Philippines—children: Scourge of child prostitution. *IPS-Third World News*. Retrieved from Lexis Nexis Database: http://www .ipsnews.net/1997/10/philippines-children-scourge-of-child-prostitution

Lacey, R. (2009). *Inside the kingdom: Kings, clerics, modernists, terrorists, and the struggle for Saudi Arabia*. New York, NY: Penguin Books.

Liu B., & Elliott, D. (1998, June 29). Trying to stand on two feet. Special report, Women. *Newsweek*, p. 48.

Mabrey, D. J. (2003, March). Human smuggling from China. *Crime and Justice International, 19*(71), 5–11.

Minister vows to further curb police misconduct. (1999, November 4). *China Business Information Network*. Retrieved from Lexis Nexis Database.

Moriyama, D. (1999). Criminal justice system in Japan: Present situation and issues. *News and Views from Japan. Japanese Mission to the EU*. Retrieved from http://www.eu.emp-japan.go.jp/interest/crimju.htm

Morrison, S. (2003, April). Approaching organized crime: Where are we now and where are we going? *Crime and Justice International, 19* (72), 4–10.

National Police Agency. Criminal Investigation Bureau. (2002, October 10). Criminal trends. *Japan Information Network*. Retrieved from http://www .jinjapan.org/stat/category_14.html

Park, Y. K. (2001). *Transnational organized crime and the countermeasures in Korea*. Resource Material Series No. 58 of the 116th International Training Course. UNAFEI. Harumi-cho, Fuchu, Tokyo, Japan.

Peters, G. (2009). *Seeds of terror: How heroin is bankrolling the Taliban and Al Queda*. New York, NY: St. Martin's Press.

Police corruption cases in Japan doubled in 2000. (2001, February 9). *Global Financial Times*. Retrieved from Lexis Nexis Database.

Schauble, J. (2001, August 28). China facing increase in drug use. *The Age* (Melbourne), p. 13.

Serio, J. D. (2008). *Investigating the Russian mafia*. Durham, NC: Carolina Academic Press.

Seven Vietnamese police officers sacked for drug use. (2000, March 4). *Bernama: The Malaysian News Service*. Retrieved from Lexis Nexis Database http:// www.accessmylibrary.com/article-1G1-59962601/7-vietnamese-police-officers .html

Tat-wing, P. Y. (2001). *Triads*. Resource Material Series No. 58 of the 116th International Training Course. UNAFEI. Harumi-cho, Fuchu, Tokyo, Japan.

U.N. Office on Drugs and Crime. (2010, May 3). UNODC strengthens partnership in the Middle East and North Africa, Retrieved from http://www.unodc .org/southerncone/en/frontpage/ 2010/05/03-unodc-reforca-a-parceria-no-oriente-medio-e-no-norte-da-africa.html

U.N. Office on Drugs and Crime. (2012a). *UNODC strengthens partnership in the Middle East and North Africa.* Retrieved from http://www.unodc .org/unodc/ en/frontpage/2010/May/unodc-strengthens-partnership-in-the-middle-east-and-north-africa.html

U.N. Office on Drugs and Crime. (2012b). *World drug report 2012.* Retrieved from http://www.unodc .org/unodc/en/data-and-analysis/WDR-2012.html

U.S. Department of State, Bureau for International Narcotics and Law Enforcement Affairs. (2012, March 1). *International narcotics control strategy report.* Washington, DC: Author. Retrieved from http://www.state.gov/j/inl/rls/ nrcrpt/2012/

U.S. Department of Justice, Bureau of Justice Statistics. (1997). South Korea. In *World factbook of criminal justice systems.* Retrieved from http://www.ojp.usdoj .gov/bjs/pub/ascii/wfbcjsko.txt

U.S. Drug Enforcement Administration. (2011, July 26). Manhattan U.S. Attorney announces arrests in DEA narco-terrorism undercover operations. Retrieved from http://www.justice.gov/dea/divisions/nyc/2011/nyc072611.shtml

Wright, R. (2012, January 21). After Tahrir: Finishing the revolution. *Wall Street Journal.* Retrieved from http://online.wsj.com/article/SB100014240529702045 5590457716881177803592 8.html

Xu, J. (2011). Hong Kong: The state of criminology. In C. J. Smith, S. Zhang, & R. Barberet (Eds.), *Routledge handbook of international criminology* (pp. 411–418). New York, NY: Routledge.

Younglai, R. (2012, February 23). UPDATE 1-U.S. blocks yakuza godfather from its markets. Reuters. Retrieved from http://www.reuters.com/article/2012/ 02/23/usa-treasury-crime-idUSL2E8 DN8BI20120223

Zhang, Y., & Cao, Y. (2011, May 20). Criminals target resources, logistics, and manipulate village elections. *China Daily.* http://www.chinadailyapac.com/ article/gangs-muscling-key-activities

7

Transnational Organized Crime in Oceania

Roderic Broadhurst,
Mark Lauchs, and Sally Lohrisch

This chapter briefly outlines the context and nature of transnational crime within the large and diverse region of Oceania. The region encompasses more than 8.5 million square kilometers (or 3.3 million square miles) and is composed of 25 island nations with varied histories, cultures, economies, and political and legal systems. Oceania can be broadly divided into four geographical regions: (a) Australia (including Norfolk Island) and New Zealand, Melanesia (Fiji, New Caledonia, Papua New Guinea, Solomon Islands, Vanuatu), (b) Micronesia (Guam, Kiribati, Marshall Islands, Federated States of Micronesia, Nauru, Northern Mariana Islands, Palau), and (c) Polynesia (American Samoa, Cook Islands, French Polynesia, Niue, Pitcairn, Samoa, Tokelau, Tonga, Tuvalu, Wallis and Futuna Islands).[1] Australia is the largest nation in the region, both in terms of population and geographical size, followed by Papua New Guinea and New Zealand. The umbrella term *Pacific Island countries* (PICs) is used to describe the numerous nations of the Pacific Ocean; here we use PIC to refer to the island nations composing Micronesia, Melanesia, and Polynesia (except New Zealand and Hawaii).[2]

Australia and New Zealand are the most economically significant nations in the region. They share many legal, economic, and political similarities as former British colonies and dominions, having inherited the common law and Westminster systems. Australia is the largest economy in Oceania, with a population of over 22 million and an annual gross domestic product (GDP) of USD 1.6 trillion. It is a nation of mature and stable political, legal, and economic systems. New Zealand has 4.3 million residents and a GDP of $127 billion. Papua New Guinea, the only other large nation in Oceania, has 6.6 million people, but its GDP is only USD 9.5 billion. Australia's GDP per capita in 2011 was over $40,000, New Zealand's $27,000, but the next highest is Fiji with $4,600. Thus, most of the PICs have both small populations and developing economies. The quality of governance also varies greatly across the region. Transparency International's (2011) Corruption Perceptions Index 2011, which ranks countries by their perceived levels of corruption, shows Oceania's diversity of governance with Australia and New Zealand ranked as having low risks of corruption, whereas the Solomon Islands and Papua New Guinea ranked among the highest risk. New Zealand was ranked at Number 1 (indicating the lowest risk) in the index out of 159 countries. After Australia (which was ranked at Number 8), the next Oceanic country Samoa was ranked at 69. The remaining nations rate among countries with the highest perceived risk of corruption, with Tonga at 95, Solomon Islands 120, and Papua New Guinea at 154.

Australia maintains a relatively large immigrant intake, including from its neighbor New Zealand and to a lesser extent, the other nations of Oceania. Consequently, it has a diverse ethnic population with the migrant community constituting a fifth of its total population, the highest proportion of any country with a population of 20 million or greater (United Nations, n.d.). In both Australia and New Zealand, the migrant population exceeds the indigenous Aboriginal and Maori population. This is not the case among the PICs, where indigenous populations predominate. An exception is Fiji, however, where about 38% of the population is of Indian origin.

The PICs are made up of 20,000 to 30,000 islands, some as small as coral atolls, scattered throughout the Pacific Ocean. Large parts of the Pacific Islands are geographically isolated, sparsely populated, and vulnerable to natural disasters (McCusker, 2006, p. 1).

These nations have varied histories and distinct cultures and societies. Language is diverse throughout the region and within states. For example, 841 languages are found in Papua New Guinea (PNG), 63 languages are found in the Solomon Islands, and in Vanuatu there are over 100 tribal languages. Political and legal systems also differ in the region from monarchies, to military juntas, and democracies. In addition, many of the PICs are viewed as "emerging states"; that is, they are experiencing ongoing economic, political, and legal instability resulting from recent independence from European colonial powers, which is exacerbated by the ongoing effects of globalization (Australian Federal Police [AFP], 2006; Browne, 2006).

Given these factors, the region has been described as the "arc of instability" (AFP, 2006). Examples of political instability in the region include Fiji, which has experienced four coups in the last quarter century, a number of constitutional crises, and continued instability.[3] The Solomon Islands have also been destabilized by a coup and civil war, and an Australian- and New Zealand–led peacekeeping and stabilization mission has been in place since 2003 (see Regional Assistance Mission to Solomon Islands). A constitutional crisis has also unfolded in PNG in 2011–2012 with a failed mutiny of elements of the PNG Defence Force and the arrest of the chief justice arising from conflict between groups in support of rival premiers (Fox, 2012). Generally, political instability has manifested itself in poor governance and corruption in several jurisdictions in the region. There is also significant economic underdevelopment, with high rates of unemployment and concerns regarding appropriate fiscal management (including suitable public sector controls, development of private sector industries and opportunities, appropriate aid management, and regional integration) (Browne, 2006). These underlying political and socioeconomic weaknesses are vulnerabilities that have also been exploited by criminal entrepreneurs.

Unemployment rates are very high in the PICs, running at 70% of youth and 80% of males across the islands (Senate Foreign Affairs Defence and Trade References Committee [SFADTRC], 2010, pp. 7–8). While there is disagreement by observers as to whether unemployment will lead to increases in crime rates (SFADTRC, 2010, p. 10), increased urbanization and inequality are known drivers of crime (Newman, 1999). Ethnic tensions are also high across the region. PNG experiences frequent intertribal conflicts, especially in the volatile highlands, and other PICs, such as Fiji, see clashes between indigenous and migrant Chinese and Indian communities (SFADTRC, 2010, p. 12).

Oceania is not a major global economic or trade hub. However, its importance is growing with the economic shift toward the Asia Pacific region and the contemporary emergence of a multipolar model of global political and economic power (U.N. Office on Drugs and Crime [UNODC], 2011b, p. 43). Indeed, Oceania is potentially an important region, strategically situated near the global powerhouse economies of China and India, while also having strong ties to traditional powers such as the United States and the United Kingdom. Australia, the regional middle power, in particular retains strong economic links with both traditional and emerging economies and is one of China's leading trading partners while retaining strong alliance with the United States.

Australia and New Zealand's high GDPs makes them attractive markets for drug, vice, money laundering, and other contraband associated with criminal activity. The PICs lack both the money and population to become significant criminal markets. Nonetheless, they play a special role in the criminal environment as transit points and safe operational bases for transnational criminal activity—offering the "comparative advantage in illegality" (Windybank, 2008, p. 32).

⟍ ORGANIZED CRIME GROUPS

The reporting of organized crime in Oceania varies according to the levels of development in the different nations; thus there is more information about Australia than the rest of the region. In 2004, the Australian Crime Commission identified 97 organized crime groups in Australia, most of which operate in Sydney and Melbourne (Broadhurst, Gordon, & McFarlane, 2012). Traditionally, the PICs see little serious organized crime; however, "evidence is often anecdotal, contradictory, or fragmented. Drug seizures, for instance, provide some information on how drug traffickers operate, but the real extent of the problem remains unknown." (Windybank, 2008, p. 33) Transnational crime networks are more likely to operate in the PICs because of these nations' poverty, instability, and low levels of development. However, cultural and ethnic differences across the region preclude any consistency in how criminal groups operate (McCusker, 2006, p. 2). The forms of transnational crime that have been identified in the PICs appear to be facilitated by the increasing role of foreign investment and influence in PNG and other resource rich countries of the region rather than indigenous crime groups transcending cultural, linguistic, and ethnic differences in the PICs. Investors mainly from East Asia (primarily the People's Republic of China [PRC] and Taiwan) and India (AFP, 2005) may also bring in their wake Triad-like groups. Despite the lack of reliable information, it is possible to identify some key players in Oceania transnational crime.

Outlaw Motorcycle Gangs

Outlaw motorcycle gangs (OMCGs) operate throughout Australia and New Zealand. OMCGs such as the Rebels, Finks, and Hells Angels are recognized as an organized crime threat (Australian Crime Commission [ACC], 2012) and have attracted increased attention from law enforcement. Since their establishment in Australia and New Zealand in the 1960s (Parliamentary Joint Committee on the Australian Crime Commission [PJCACC], 2007, p. 8; Veno & Gannon, 2010, p. 24), OMCGs have evolved from motorcycle enthusiast clubs into significant participants in illicit/criminal markets (ACC, 2011). The extent of the organized crime threat that OMCGs pose is unclear (PJCACC, 2007, pp. 22–27; Veno & van den Eynde, 2008), but some Australian OMCGs have links with OMCGs in the United States, Canada, and Scandinavia who are involved in significant criminal enterprises. Whether OMCGs are primarily established for criminal purposes or whether the structures and interpersonal associations of the OMCGs simply facilitate criminal activity (Barker, 2011) has created challenges for effective countermeasures. Nevertheless, the visibility and profile of the OMCGs show they play a major role among the criminal macro networks (Spapens, 2010) that facilitate serious crime in Australia and New Zealand. Recent high-profile homicides involving competing OMCGs prompted South Australia and New South Wales, for example, to introduce association or consorting laws to help suppress these groups. Generally a range of law reforms focusing on serious and organized crime has been enacted in Australia to address witness protection, tainted wealth, and the interception of communication (see Ayling & Broadhurst, 2012, for details).

Some OMCGs spread to Australia and New Zealand as part of the franchising of the gangs by American organizers and through the absorption of local homegrown gangs. In fact, New Zealand was the first international location outside the United States where the Hells Angels established a chapter (Veno & Gannon, 2010). However, despite this international connection, the operations of OMCGs at the local chapter level are largely autonomous, with strategic direction from the national leadership (ACC, 2011; Crime and Misconduct Commission [CMC], n.d.). Australia has chapters of the "Big Four" OMCGs: the Hell's Angels, Bandidos, Outlaws, and Pagans (Quinn & Forsyth, 2011). Australia also has homegrown OMCGs, such as the Rebels, Finks, and Coffin Cheaters, who are not aligned with an international brand but have been established and operate within Australia (Veno & Gannon, 2010, p. 70).

Recent reports indicate that the Rebels, Australia's largest OMCG, is establishing chapters in New Zealand (Oakes, 2012; Organised & Financial Crime Agency New Zealand [OFCANZ], 2011; Robertson, 2011). There are also reports showing that some OMCGs have been establishing chapters and more permanent connections throughout Southeast Asia, notably in Thailand (Oakes, 2012; Robertson 2011).

It is estimated that there are about 40 active OMCGs in Australia (Veno & Gannon, 2010, p. 56); however, there is uncertainty about the precise numbers of chapters and "patched" members. There are between 100 and 200 chapters of the large clubs (ACC, 2012; Veno & Gannon, 2010, p. 56). Estimates of total OMCG membership range from between 2,500 (Veno & Gannon, 2010, p. 57) and 4,000 (ACC, 2011). These diverging numbers reflect the difficulty in ascertaining membership numbers and/or actual shifts in membership (through attrition or recruitment variations, etc.). Once exclusively Caucasian, the OMCGs have diversified to include Middle Eastern ethnic groups and Pacific Islanders and do business with Chinese organized crime groups (Ayling & Broadhurst, 2012).

Members of these OMCGs are thought to engage in a broad spectrum of criminal activities from drug trafficking (especially the domestic production of amphetamines and cannabis) to money laundering, fraud and identity crime, firearms offenses (including firearms trafficking), extortion, vehicle-related crime (primarily vehicle "rebirthing"), and prostitution. Membership of these OMCGs is often used as leverage to further these activities through enhanced criminal associations and networks. These groups also engage in the legitimate economy and have infiltrated the maritime, private security, entertainment, natural resources, and construction industries (ACC, 2011).

Other Groups

Traditional mafia groups are rare in Oceania. There is evidence of 'Ndrangheta and other Italian mafia-like groups in Australia and some indication that Taiwan- or PRC-based Triad-like groups such as the Four Seas operate in Fiji and PNG. These groups seek to exploit the relative vulnerability of PICs. A few reports refer to these groups as triads or mafia (Bashir, 2010; Callick, 2010), while others note them to simply be groups of "Chinese nationals." Whatever their origin and structure, these groups corrupt officials to obtain work permits, visas, investment approvals, and passports to facilitate their movement (AFP, 2006, p. 6). The three main criminal industries in the region are narco-trafficking, people trafficking, and firearms trafficking, with reports of other significant activities, including environmental crime, money laundering, and vice-related activities such as gambling and prostitution (Schloenhardt, 2006). There are reports of Chinese nationals participating in all such criminal endeavors (AFP, 2006; Lindley & Beacroft, 2011; McCusker, 2006; Squires, 2005).

Although it is difficult to ascertain the morphology of these Chinese nationals engaged in criminal activity in the Pacific Islands, many have international links that are exploited in the furtherance of their activities. For example, a large methamphetamine laboratory discovered near Suva, Fiji, in 2004 was being run by local Fijians (including Fijian Chinese) and a Hong Kong Chinese, with the operation apparently financed through Hong Kong. No specific Triad group has been identified. There are also examples of Chinese nationals in the region facilitating human trafficking from their native provinces in China (Lindley & Beacroft, 2011, p. 3).

There is also evidence of other criminal groups operating within the Pacific region. In December 2011, it was reported that the Speaker of the Tongan Parliament had been implicated in assisting a Colombian national relocate to Tonga; this Colombian national was alleged to be a member of a transnational drug syndicate, and his purpose for being in Tonga was to coordinate the transit of cocaine from South America, using Tonga as a transit destination for markets in Australia and China (McKenzie & Baker, 2011).

PICs also have homegrown criminal gangs such as the Rascals in PNG. Although the level of organization of these gangs is unclear, they are recognized as a crime threat (Fickling, 2004). This is particularly true in PNG and the Solomon Islands where these gangs have conducted bank robberies, arms trafficking, drug cultivation and trafficking, and card skimming (Schloenhardt, 2006). Goddard (2005) notes the traditional view that such activities are reflections of underdeveloped economies and/or perceived social inequalities. However, he suggests such crimes in PNG may be motivated by local gift culture (Goddard, 2005, p. 110) and notes that the proceeds of social activities (including crime) are shared "to enhance prestige, repay gift-giving and engender future obligation."

Gang activity is also prominent in New Zealand, although the number of members in these gangs is not clear (Refugee Review Tribunal, 2009). An estimated 30 adult gangs currently operate throughout New Zealand

and are involved in diverse and far-reaching criminal activity, including illicit drug trafficking, burglary and theft, extortion, and environmental crime and are characterized by their use of significant violence. This violence is generally directed at other gang members and is used to facilitate criminal activities or related to territorial disputes (New Zealand Government, 2010; Refugee Review Tribunal, 2009). Youth gangs also engage in illicit drug distribution, burglary, and vehicle-related crime in New Zealand and may act as "feeders" into adult gangs (Gower, 2008).

Two significant adult gangs in New Zealand are the Mongrel Mob (established in the mid-1960s in Hastings) and Black Power (established around 1970 in Wellington), which are both dominated by Pacific Islanders and Maoris (Bellamy, 2009, p. 2). These groups share similarities with OMCGs in their organization and structure (specifically, their use of chapter, or local-level, divisions or operations), use of colors/patches to delineate membership, and specific areas of territorial operation (Refugee Review Tribunal, 2009).

The exact number of members of these groups is also unknown, but a combined figure (for Mongrel Mob and Black Power) of 2,600 was estimated in 2007. It was also estimated that this membership was spread across 145 chapters throughout New Zealand (Callinan, 2007). Interestingly, there is some evidence of aspirations for international expansion by the Mongrel Mob. In the 1980s, they tried to establish a chapter in Perth, Western Australia, but were unsuccessful after being targeted for violence and intimidation by local OMCGs such as the Coffin Cheaters (Refugee Review Tribunal, 2009).

Other migrant ethnic-based organized crime groups operate in the region, including a number of prominent groups in Australia that tend to be active in specific areas of criminality. The Romanians have a lengthy involvement in drug trafficking in Australia (ACC, 2011; CMC, n.d.). Lebanese groups have been active in illicit drug trafficking (especially hashish) and extortion in Australia since the 1960s (Morton & Lobez, 2007). Similarly, Vietnamese groups have had long-standing involvement in drug trafficking, including heroin and cannabis. Infamous groups such as the 5T dominated criminal activity (including drug trafficking, extortion, illegal gaming) in parts of Sydney (Australian Broadcasting Corporation, 1997). Generally, organized crime groups in Australia "continue to evolve from being communally based, strongly hierarchical and easily defined by ethnicity or ethos, towards more flexible, loosely associated and entrepreneurial networks" (ACC, 2007, p. 10).

☆ TRANJNATIONAL OFFENJEJ

Illicit Drugs

The most significant organized crime threat in the Oceanic region is the illicit drug industry. Although the scale of this issue is relatively small compared to other global regions, the illicit market remains locally significant. Also, Oceania ranks significantly globally in terms of prevalence rates, with one of the highest prevalence rates of the use of amphetamine-type stimulants (ATS) and cannabis in the world. Australia and New Zealand are the target markets for drug importation in the region. Most importation is for ATS and precursor chemicals such as (pseudo) ephedrine from Europe, India, and China; heroin from West and Southeast Asia; and cocaine from South America. Cannabis is grown and transported within the region (UNODC, 2011b).

Cannabis is easily available in Australia, and the market is supplied predominantly by local crops (McLaren & Mattick, 2007, p. 26). It is the most common illegal drug in Australia, with about one third of the community estimated to have admitted to use of cannabis (Tresidder & Shaddock, 2008). Similarly, cannabis is grown extensively in New Zealand in sufficient supply to meet the entire home demand for the drug (Wilkins & Casswell, 2003). The second most common drug in Australia is MDMA (3,4-methylenedioxy-N-methylamphetamine), also known as "ecstasy," with 22% of 20- to 29-year-olds claiming to have used it—one of the highest rates in the world (Asia & Pacific Amphetamine-Type Stimulants Information Centre [APAIC], 2009a). Australians pay a much higher price for the drug than customers in other Western Countries. This premium attracts suppliers to the market (AFP, n.d.-c). New Zealand also has one of the highest rates of use of ATS in the world (APAIC, 2009b). Precursor chemical demand has even been met by the importation of ContacNT, a Chinese drug with concentrated levels of pseudoephedrine. New Zealand Customs Service estimates that 10 million tablets were imported in 2008. However, "pill shopping" (where cheaper drugs are sought in the illicit marketplace) is still prevalent among younger age groups (Stringer, 2009).

Since the turn of the century, ATS have taken over the market from opiates in Australia, with speed, the powder form of the drug, being the most common variant. However, usage rates are comparatively low at 2% to 4% of the population (APAIC, 2009a). Interestingly, only 3% of police detainees use MDMA ecstasy compared with 21% using other forms of ATS—a reversal of the trend in the general population (APAIC, 2009a). Once again, most of the market is supplied from producers within the country, whereas crystal methamphetamines are imported from Canada and Southeast Asia (AFP, n.d.-a). Only 2% of New Zealanders use ATS and are supplied mostly by local producers (APAIC, 2009b).

Heroin is still used in both countries even though its market share has fallen following a fall in availability. It is now used by only an estimated 0.2% of Australians (APAIC, 2009a). Unlike Europe and North America, Australia and New Zealand are supplied from the Golden Triangle in Southeast Asia (AFP, n.d.-b). Cocaine also has a very small market in Australia with only 1% of the population using the drug (APAIC, 2009a), but there are signs of an increase in use of cocaine along with availability (Australian Associated Press [AAP], 2009; Ross, 2007).

The PICs suffer from underresourced police services, and high levels of corruption among politicians and public officials may occur (Rolfe, 2004, p. 7). This makes them attractive locations to operate drug redistribution and grow and/or manufacture such drugs as well as provide money-laundering facilities (Reid, Devaney, & Baldwin, 2006).

Transshipment of drugs assists drug syndicates by allowing them to disguise the point of origin of their cargo. This can take place on land or at sea. "Some five thousand vessels cross the region on any given day. Large shipments can be transferred from a mother ship into smaller boats that speed to isolated atolls to await transit to the next destination" (Windybank, 2008, p. 33). Because of the geographic proximity to the PIC's, Asian organized crime gangs are involved in drug operations in the region (Rolfe, 2004, p. 7). Similarly, South American gangs are involved in transshipment of cocaine via the Pacific (Ranmuthugala, 2002, p. 17). Drugs seized in Fiji are usually destined for Australia and New Zealand. In 2000, 357 kg of heroin was seized in Suva. The shipment was associated with Chinese nationals. The large methamphetamine seizure in 2004 was made possible and organized by ethnic-Chinese Fijian citizens, and it potentially involved corrupt immigration and customs officials (The Age, 2004). As noted, there are no reliable figures on how much transshipment is occurring (SFADTRC, 2010, pp. 59–60). The prime target markets for drugs in Pacific are the large Western economies such as the United States, Canada, Australia, and New Zealand (AFP, 2005, p. 7; Windybank, 2008, p. 33). The PIC's currently have very low levels of drug use among the population, although there are signs that ATS, notably "ice" is becoming popular throughout the region, particularly with Rascal gangs in PNG (Windybank, 2008, p. 34).

An indication of the scale of drug manufacture can be found in the discovery of a large methamphetamine factory in Suva, Fiji, in 2004. At the time, this was the largest methamphetamine lab found in the Southern Hemisphere. This factory's ATS production was distributed to Europe, the United States, Australia, and New Zealand. It was capable of producing approximately 500 kg of methamphetamine each week (Associated Press, 2004). Yet, the most common illicit drug activity in the Pacific remains the cultivation of cannabis, which can be grown all year round in the equatorial Pacific climate (Ranmuthugala, 2002; Reid et al., 2006). Most cannabis cultivation is for domestic consumption; however, there is an increasing involvement of organized crime. Most extensive cultivation of cannabis occurs in the PNG and Fiji. Most of the trade in cannabis is from PICs to the large Western markets, and there have been documented cases of trades of guns from Indonesia, Southeast Asia, and Australia for cannabis from the PNG (Reid et al., 2006, p. 649).

People Smuggling

The PICs also play a role in people smuggling to the southwest Pacific (Australia and New Zealand) and northeastern Pacific (Canada and the United States of America). Australia is the primary target for people smugglers in Oceania. It has a reputation for taking refugees and a very high percentage of those who arrive and claim refugee status are resettled, with the majority staying in Australia. It is one of the top three refugee resettlement countries in the world and allocates places to refugees who are able to reach Australian territory (by boat or plane) under a Special Humanitarian Program (Parliamentary Library, 2011).

In the last decade most smuggled persons arriving in Australia were from the Middle East, who traveled overland or by plane and transited through Indonesia. They usually had a visa to visit Indonesia and some had their entire trip organized by the smugglers (UNODC, 2011a, pp. 18–19).

People smuggling is facilitated through the PICs. It is relatively easy to enter a PIC and obtain a passport. In some countries, such as PNG, there have been cases of public officials selling passports illegally. "In 2002 the database and passport-making machine were stolen from

Papua New Guinea's immigration department. It was an inside job. Of twelve officials implicated in the scam, only one was charged. Not long after, streams of Chinese migrants began arriving" (Windybank, 2008, p. 35). However, other PICs openly sell passports as a means of obtaining foreign currency. Tonga raised $20 million from such a program (Rolfe, 2004, p. 8). Travelers, once in a nation such as Fiji, have in the past found it is easier to obtain a visa to Australia than from their home country (Fiji Broadcasting Corporation, 2010). In addition, passport and identity fraud are used to support people-smuggling activities (AFP, 2005, p. 7)

China is often cited as a source country of illegal migrants into the PIC, and organized crime groups allegedly facilitate the passage of Chinese illegal migrants. The routes include going via Micronesia to get into the United States, PNG to get into Australia, and Polynesia to get into New Zealand (Rolfe, 2004, p. 7). Chinese crime groups were thought to have prepared for such activities by sending associates to PICs in the late 1990s to facilitate people smuggling. Smugglees enter by overstays or false passports, although some use bribery to buy citizenship. Many intend to go on to Australia, although most Pacific islands are transit points to the United States and Canada (Windybank, 2008, pp. 34–35).

People Trafficking

People trafficking in Oceania provides for both the sex and construction business. Most people trafficking in Australia and New Zealand is associated with sex trafficking. In Australia, the majority of trafficked sex workers end up in Sydney. A 2004 estimate stated that between 300 and 1,000 women are trafficked into Australia each year (Phillips, 2008, p. 3). Arrests and convictions for trafficking offenses are, however, relatively infrequent, and over several years (2004–2008) as few as 34 prosecutions undertaken (David, 2008, 2010). Most of these women come from Southeast Asia and China, are typically brought to the country on legitimate student or holiday visas, and then employed in legal and illegal brothels around the country (David, 2008, 2010; Phillips, 2008, p. 3).

In recent years, Australian states and territories have legalized prostitution. One of the outcomes of this has been a reduction in organized crime involvement in prostitution. At present, there is little evidence of organized crime in the legal sex industry on the Australian Gold Coast, which is a major tourist location (CMC, 2011). There are growing numbers of Asian women in the illegal sex industry but no evidence that they are trafficked. Charges were laid in 2009 against Chinese, South Korean, and Thai nationals for organized illegal prostitution but not sex trafficking:

> Most of the organizers of Asian prostitution detected by PETF [Prostitution Enforcement Task Force] are from the same country as the sex workers, or at least speak the same language, but there have been some cases of Australian-born organizers operating a number of Asian sex workers. (CMC, 2011, p. 21)

There is no information as to the number or the scale of operations involving the forced labor of trafficked people in Australia. However, this does not include situations where foreign visitors on work visas are exploited once in the country—for example, being invited to stay to work under false claims of high wages and good working conditions (Lindley & Beacroft, 2011, p. 3; Phillips, 2008, pp. 11–12).

PICs are used as transit points for people trafficking to other target nations, but few people end up in Australia because of relatively effective border controls (Larson, 2010, p. 5; Lindley & Beacroft, 2011). There is evidence of people being brought into PICs by legal and illegal means, usually by facilitators (both organized crime and small-scale operators) outside the country. Most of the trafficking is either between islands or from Asia to the PICs, and often for sex work (Lindley & Beacroft, 2011, pp. 3–4; Sasako, 2007). There have also been reports of child sexual exploitation associated with the logging industry in the PICs, where children are sexually exploited as prostitutes in logging camps (Larson, 2011).

Illegal Weapons Smuggling

Australia and New Zealand have very strict firearm laws and relatively small markets for illegal firearms. However, there is weak law-and-order capacity in PNG, which facilitates illegal activity. In PNG, firearms, both modern high-powered models and homemade, are used in ethnic and tribal fighting, robberies, extortion, and intimidation, including during elections (Singirok, 2005). Most of the illegal weapons are concentrated in the Enga and the Southern and Western Highlands, and most armed crime occurs in the cities and Highlands (Singirok, 2005, p. 2). Parliamentarians also use guns to intimidate voters and other members of Parliament. The situation was so common that in 2004,

Parliament was suspended because of the concern that high-powered weapons were on parliamentary grounds. Illegal ownership and sale of guns and ammunition are encouraged by weak gun registration laws and practice and the high tariff on weapons and bullets, which in turn keeps selling guns and ammunition through legitimate retail outlets from being economical (Singirok, 2005, pp. 4–5). Guns are also available due to poor management of military and police arsenals. It is easy to bring guns into PNG from Australia through the Torres Strait and the "dogleg" region between PNG, Australia, and Indonesia. Demand is also driven by rebel groups in West Papua (Irian Jaya) and the Solomon Islands (Singirok, 2005). In the Solomon Islands militia groups obtained the police armories in Auki and Guadalcanal (SFADTRC, 2010, p. 15). The Solomon Islands are still heavily supplied by guns and grenades left over from the Second World War (Singirok, 2005).

Financial Crime

Financial crime takes two forms: (a) economic crime targeting the finances of victims and (b) use of the financial system to disguise profits from criminal activity. Financial crime is an increasingly sophisticated criminal activity, driven in part by the rapid expansion of e-commerce and, consequently, manifest in Oceania as well. The small size of the PIC populations and inexperience of governments has led to nations becoming victims of financial scams, including unprofitable mines and in one case, a musical (Ranmuthugala, 2002, p. 17).

The involvement of organized crime in these activities is unclear because the majority of known offenders were individuals not associated with organized crime. Detailed data are not available on the extent of financial crime; for example, there is very little information about money laundering on the public record because investigators do not release detailed information on cases (CMC, 2009, p. 11). A decade ago, there was extensive offshore banking in the PICs with some earning the dubious reputation as safe havens for tainted wealth. The underregulated financial services that once proliferated in PICs such as Vanuatu, Nauru, and Fiji have all been closed with international assistance following blacklisting by the Financial Action Task Force (FATF). PICs are still avenues for money laundering (SFADTRC, 2010, p. 61). A 2008 estimate put the value of money-laundering transactions in Australia at between $2 billion and $4.5 billion per year (Choo, 2008, p. 3).

Excise avoidance is common throughout the region. The most lucrative product is smuggled tobacco from Southeast Asia into the high tobacco tax nations of Australia and New Zealand. Raw tobacco, or "chop-chop," is available from nations such as the Philippines and can fetch a 10,000% profit when sold in Australia with minimal risk of apprehension or a prison term. Tobacco is also smuggled in its processed form as cigarettes, both legitimately branded and counterfeit. Most smugglers of tobacco are also involved in "drugs, money laundering, identity fraud, and car re-birthing" (Scollo & Winstanley, 2008).

Cybercrime

In Australia in 2010–2011, 6.2 million households had broadband access (Australian Bureau of Statistics, 2011). While this brings many social benefits, it also increases Australia's exposure to cybercrime. Australia is subject to the full gamut of cybercrime, including hacking, malware, Botnets, DDoS attacks, phishing, and spam (House of Representatives Standing Committee on Communications, 2010, p. 33). According to the Australian Institute of Criminology, 14% of Australian businesses were attacked at least once in 2006–2007. However, malware continues to be the predominant security threat to individuals and corporations in Australia (Choo, 2011, p. 2). There is also a continued presence of advance-fee frauds being perpetrated via the Internet (AFP, 2005). It is estimated that West African–based advance-fee fraudsters take $100 million from Australia every year (Queensland Police Service, 2010).

Illegal Fishing

Illegal fishing is a threat to the region (AFP, 2005) and ranges from a failure to comply with laws and regulations by commercial fishermen to illegal fishing by unregistered fishermen (Putt & Nelson, 2009). Organized crime tends to concentrate on the trade in high-value seafood (rock lobster, abalone, and shark fin in Australia) and the provision of seafood products that are not legally on the market (Putt & Nelson, 2009).

It is difficult for small PICs to prevent illegal fishing in their exclusive economic zones (EEZ), making illegal fishing a significant transnational crime in the region. It takes the form of authorized fishing vessels operating outside the terms of their license and unlicensed vessels fishing in the EEZs. PICs have small populations and vast areas of ocean in their EEZs. PNG has 19 square kilometers of sea for every one square kilometer of land; Tuvalu has almost 28,000 square kilometers of seas for every square kilometer of land (SFADTRC, 2010, pp. 55–57) both are underequipped to police these zones.

〰 CONCLUSION

Oceania has a relatively low level of crime prevalence, yet in the smaller and underdeveloped PICs, transnational crime has become increasingly common—risk contained but potentially dangerous if state failure or fragility undermines law enforcement capacities. We predict that as the pace of globalization quickens and the demand for raw materials and resources grows, some parts of the Pacific will be prone to criminal enterprises run by both indigenous and foreign crime groups. Australia and New Zealand will remain attractors of illicit goods, notably ATS, but will in turn be source countries for diminishing fish stock such as bêche-de-mere and abalone as well forest timber. Finally, the role of states such as Australia and New Zealand in helping to maintain law enforcement capacities throughout the region will be crucial if organized crime in Oceania is to be kept in check while demand for illicit resources grow.

〰 NOTES

1. The preceding geographical divisions are those used by the U.N. Statistical Division; they may not reflect all geographical understandings of the region.

2. New Zealand is discussed separately from the PICs due to its distinct historical background that has influenced its contemporary economic, political, and legal systems. Hawaii is not discussed in this chapter because of its political affiliation with United States.

3. Three coup d'états in Fiji occurred in May and September of 1987, 2000, and 2006. The most recent constitutional crises occurred in 2009 when an Indian-led political party won most seats in the legislature, precipitating the closure of Parliament by the mainly indigenous Fiji Armed Forces in 2006. Fiji remains under military rule, although elections are to be held in 2014.

⦚ REFERENCEƒ

The Age. (2004). Pacific an ideal launch pad for drugs. Retrieved from http://www
.theage.com.au/articles/ 2004/06/19/1087595786691.html?from=storylhs

Asia & Pacific Amphetamine-Type Stimulants Information Centre. (2009a).
Australia. Retrieved from http://www.apaic.org/index.php?option=com_content
&view=article&id=132&Itemid=140

Asia & Pacific Amphetamine-Type Stimulants Information Centre. (2009b).
New Zealand. Retrieved from http://www.apaic.org/index.php?option=com_con
tent&view=article&id=134&Itemid=142

Associated Press. (2004). Southern hemisphere's biggest meth lab smashed.
Taipei Times. Retrieved from http://www.taipeitimes.com/News/world/
archives/2004/06/10/2003174485

Australian Associated Press. (2009). Cocaine use rising in Australia: Report.
Retrieved from http://news.theage.com.au/breaking-news-national/cocaine-
use-rising-in-australia-report-20090612-c541.html

Australian Broadcasting Corporation (Writer) & Altschwager, I., & Le, D.
(Producers). (1997). Cabramatta [Television series episode]. In *Four corners.*
Sydney, New South Wales, Australia.

Australian Bureau of Statistics (ABS). (2011). Household use of information technology, Australia 2010–11. Retrieved from http://www.abs.gov.au/AUSSTATS/
abs@.nsf/Latestproducts/8146.0 Media%20Release12010-11?opendocument&tabn
ame=Summary&prodno=8146.0&issue=2010-11&num=&view=

Australian Crime Commission. (2007). *Inquiry into the future impact of serious
and organised crime on Australian Society.* Submission to the Parliamentary
Joint Committee on the Australian Crime Commission. Canberra, Australian
Capital Territory, Australia: Australian Crime Commission.

Australian Crime Commission. (2011). Outlaw motorcycle gangs. Retrieved
from Australian Crime Commission http://crimecommission.gov.au/sites/
default/files/files/omcgs.pdf

Australian Crime Commission. (2012). *How serious is the threat posed by
outlaw motorcycle groups?* Retrieved from www.crimecommission.gov.au/
node/71

Australian Federal Police. (2005). A new network in the Pacific. *Platypus, 89,*
5–7.

Australian Federal Police. (2006). *Submission 16: Inquiry into Australia's aid
program in the Pacific.* Submission to Parliamentary Inquiry. Retrieved from
http://www.aph.gov.au/Parliamentary_Business/Committees/House_of_
Representatives_ Committees?url=/jfadt/pacificaid/subs.htm

Australian Federal Police. (n.d.-a). Amphetamines. Retrieved from http://www
.afp.gov.au/policing/drug-crime/amphetamines.aspx

Australian Federal Police. (n.d.-b). Heroin. Retrieved from http://www.afp.gov.au/policing/drug-crime/heroin.aspx

Australian Federal Police. (n.d.-c). MDMA. Retrieved from http://www.afp.gov.au/policing/drug-crime/mdma.aspx

Ayling, J., & Broadhurst, R. (2012). Organized crime in Australia and New Zealand. In L. Paoli (Ed.), *Oxford handbook of organized crime* (pp. 151–170). Oxford, England: Oxford University Press.

Barker, T. (2011). American based biker gangs: International organized crime. *American Journal of Criminal Justice, 36*, 207–215.

Bashir, M. (2010, March 25). Chinese stunned, *Papua New Guinea Post Courier*. p. 3

Bellamy, P. (2009). *Young people and gangs in New Zealand*. Retrieved from http://www.parliament.nz/en-NZ/ParlSupport/ResearchPapers/b/c/7/00PLSocRP09021-Young-people-and-gangs-in-New-Zealand.htm

Broadhurst, R., Gordon, A., & McFarlane, J. (2012). Transnational and organised crime in the Indo-Asia Pacific. In F. Alum & S. Gilmour (Eds.), *Handbook of transnational organised crime* (pp. 143–156). London, England: Routledge.

Browne, C. (2006). *Pacific island economies*. Washington, DC: International Monetary Fund.

Callick, R. (2010, January 5). Triads arrested after PNG shooting, *The Australian*, p. 3.

Callinan, R. (2007, July 5). Tribal trouble, *Time*. Retrieved from http://www.time.com/time/magazine/article/0,9171,1640583,00.html

Choo, K.-K. (2008, September). Money laundering risks of prepaid stored value cards. *Trends & Issues in Crime and Criminal Justice*, No. 363. Available from http://www.aic.gov.au/documents/E/5/9/%7BE59FC149-DBEF-46DE-AFF4-5653992E88BE%7Dtandi363.pdf

Choo, K.-K. (2011, February). Cyber threat landscape faced by financial and insurance industry. *Trends & Issues in Crime and Criminal Justice, No. 408*. Available from http://www.aic.gov.au/publications/current%20series/tandi/401-420/tandi408.html

Crime and Misconduct Commission. (2009). *Money laundering and organised crime in Queensland Crime Bulletin Series*. Brisbane, Queensland, Australia: Crime and Misconduct Commission.

Crime and Misconduct Commission. (2011). *Regulating Prostitution: A follow-up review of the Prostitution Act 1999*. Brisbane, Queensland, Australia: Crime and Misconduct Commission.

Crime and Misconduct Commission. (n.d.). *Inquiry into the future impact of serious and organised crime on Australian society*. Submission to the Parliamentary Joint Committee on the Australian Crime Commission. Retrieved from www.aph.gov.au/Parliamentary_Business/Committees/Senate_Committees?url=acc_ctte/completed_inquiries/2004-07/organised_crime/submissions/ sublist.htm

David, F. (2008). *Trafficking of women for sexual purposes. Research and Public Policy Series.* Canberra, Australian Capital Territory: Australian Institute of Criminology.

David, F. (2010). *Labour trafficking. Research and public policy series.* Canberra, Australian Capital Territory, Australia: Australian Institute of Criminology.

Fiji Broadcasting Corporation. (2010, February 11). Fiji crackdown on illegal immigrants [Radio news item].

Fickling, D. (2004). High levels of rape, robbery and murder help keep Port Moresby, the Capital of New Guinea, at the wrong end of the hardship table. *The Guardian* (London), September 22, 16.

Fox, L. (2012, April 17). PNG's constitutional crisis set to continue [Radio news item]. Australian Broadcasting Corporation. Retrieved from http://www .radioaustralia.net.au/international/radio/program/pacific-beat/pngs-constitutional-crisis-set-to-continue/906008

Goddard, M. (2005). *Unseen city: Anthropological perspectives on Port Moresby, Papua New Guinea.* Canberra, Australian Capital Territory, Australia: Pansanus Books.

Gower, P. (2008, January 19). Gang presence growing since early days in Otara. *New Zealand Herald.* Retrieved from http://www.nzherald.co.nz/nz/news/article.cfm?c_id=1&objectid=10487652

House of Representatives Standing Committee on Communications. (2010). *Hackers, fraudsters and botnets: Tackling the problem of cyber crime.* Canberra, Australian Capital Territory: Parliament of the Commonwealth of Australia.

Larson, J. (2010, November). Migration and people trafficking in southeast Asia. *Trends & Issues in Crime and Criminal Justice,* No. 401. Available at http://www.aic.gov.au/documents/D/8/6/%7BD868274B-2F97-45DB-BA32-3DBB7290 A7C 4%7Dtandi401.pdf

Larson, J. (2011, April). The trafficking of children in the Asia-Pacific. *Trends & Issues in Crime and Criminal Justice,* No. 415. Available at http://www.aic .gov.au/publications/current%20series/tandi/ 401-420/tandi415.html

Lindley, J., & Beacroft, L. (2011, November). Vulnerabilities to trafficking in person in the Pacific Islands. *Trends & Issues in Crime and Criminal Justice,* No. 428. Available at http://www.aic.gov.au/publications/current%20series/tandi/421-440/tandi428.html

McCusker, R. (2006, March). Transnational crime in the Pacific Islands: Real or apparent danger? *Trends & Issues in Crime and Criminal Justice,* No. 308. Available at http://www.aic.gov.au/publications/current%20series/tandi/301-320/tandi308.html

McKenzie, N., & Baker, R. (2011, December 17). Tongan speaker helped drug team, say police. *Sydney Morning Herald.* Retrieved from http://www.smh.com .au/national/tongan-speaker-helped-drug-team-say-police-20111216-1oyrg .html

McLaren, J., & Mattick, R. (2007). Cannabis in Australia—Use, supply, harms and responses *Monograph series*. Sydney, New South Wales: Australian Government Department of Health and Ageing.

Morton, J., & Lobez, S. (2007). *Gangland Australia*. Melbourne, Victoria, Australia: Victory Books.

New Zealand Government. (2010). *Organised crime in New Zealand*. Retrieved from www.ofcanz.govt.nz/publications/organised-crime-new-zealand-2010

Newman, G. (Ed.). (1999). *Global report on crime and justice*. New York, NY: Oxford University Press.

Oakes, D. (2012, March 15). Bikie gangs expanding into south-east Asia. Retrieved from http://www.theage.com.au/national/bikie-gangs-expanding-into-southeast-asia-20120314-1v3lk.html#ixzz1x AtiN8iY

Organised & Financial Crime Agency New Zealand. (2011). Rebels not welcome here [Press release]. Retrieved from http://www.ofcanz.govt.nz/publications

Parliamentary Joint Committee on the Australian Crime Commission. (2007). *Inquiry into the future impact of serious and organised crime on Australian society*. Canberra, Australian Capital Territory, Australia: Senate Printing Unit.

Parliamentary Library. (2011). Refugee resettlement to Australia: What are the facts? *Background Note*. Canberra, Australian Capital Territory: Parliament of Australia.

Phillips, J. (2008). *People trafficking: An update on Australia's response. Research paper*. No. 5. Canberra, Australian Capital Territory, Australia: Parliamentary Library. Retrieved from http://parlinfo.aph.gov.au/parlInfo/search/display/display.w3p;adv=yes;orderBy=date-eFirst;page=0;query=%22People%20trafficking%22%202008%20SearchCategory_Phrase%3A%22publications%22;rec=6;resCount=Default

Putt, J., & Nelson, D. (2009, June). Crime in the Australian fishing industry. *Trends & Issues in Crime and Criminal Justice*, No. 366. Available from http://www.aic.gov.au/publications/current%20series/tandi/361-380/tandi366.html

Queensland Police Service. (2010). *Annual Report 2009-2010*. http://www.police.qld.gov.au/services/reportsPublications/annualReport/20092010/default.htm

Quinn, J. F., & Forsyth, C. (2011). The tools, tactics, and mentality of outlaw biker wars. *American Journal of Criminal Justice, 36*, 216–230.

Ranmuthugala, D. (2002). Security in the South Pacific: The law enforcement dimension. *Platypus*, No. 77, 10–17.

Refugee Review Tribunal. (2009). *Country advice—New Zealand*. Canberra, Australian Capital Territory: Australian Government.

Reid, G., Devaney, M., & Baldwin, S. (2006). Drug production, trafficking and trade in Asia and Pacific Island countries. *Drug and Alcohol Review, 25*, 647–650.

Robertson, J. (2011, October 14). Australian bikies Hells Angels and Bandidos club members own nightspots in Thailand tourist centres. Retrieved from http://www.news.com.au/australian-bikies-hells-angels-and-bandidos-club-mem bers-own-nightspots-in-thailand-tourist-centres/story-e6 freoof-1226166279473

Rolfe, J. (2004). *Oceania and terrorism: Some linkages with the wider region and the necessary responses* (Working paper No. 19). Wellington, New Zealand: Centre for Strategic Studies. Retrieved from http://www.victoria.ac.nz/css/docs/Working_Papers/WP19.pdf

Ross, J. (2007). *Illicit drug use in Australia: Epidemiology, use patterns and associated harm* (2nd ed.). Canberra, Australian Capital Territory, Australia: National Drug & Alcohol Research Centre.

Sasako, A. (2007). Are the Chinese Triads taking over Honiara? *Islands Business.* Retrieved http://www.islandsbusiness.com/islands_business/index_dynamic/containerNameToReplace=MiddleMiddle/focusModuleID=17965/overide SkinName= issueArticle-full.tpl

Schloenhardt, A. (2006). Drugs, sex and guns: Organised crime in the South Pacific. In N. Boister & A. Costi (Eds.), *Regionalising international criminal law in the Pacific* (pp. 159–184). Wellington: New Zealand Association for Comparative Law (NZACL) and Association of Comparative Legislation of the Countries of the Pacific (ALCPP).

Scollo, M. M., & Winstanley, M. H. (2008). *Tobacco in Australia: Facts and issues* (3rd ed.). Carlton, Victoria, Australia: Cancer Council Victoria.

Senate Foreign Affairs Defence and Trade References Committee. (2010). *Security challenges facing Papua New Guinea and the island states of the southwest Pacific.* Canberra, Australian Capital Territory, Australia: Senate.

Singirok, J. (2005). The use of illegal guns: Security implications for Papua New Guinea. *State Society and Governance in Melanesia.* Canberra, Australian Capital Territory, Australia: Research School of Pacific and Asian Studies, ANU.

Spapens, T. (2010). Macro networks, collectives, and business processes: An integrated approach to organized crime. *European Journal of Crime, Criminal Law and Criminal Justice, 18*, 185–215.

Squires, N. (2005, February 26). South Pacific islands seen as soft touch by Chinese gangsters, *South China Morning Post.* Retrieved from http://www.scmp.com/article/490451/south-pacific-islands-seen-soft-touch-chinese-gangsters

Stringer, D. (2009, May 1). The National Drug Intelligence Bureau battling against billion dollar "P" trade. Retrieved from http://www.policeassn.org.nz/newsroom/publications/featured-articles/-national-drug-intelligence-bureau-battling-against-billion-

Transparency International. (2011). *Corruption perception index 2011.* Retrieved from http://cpi.transparency.org/cpi2011/results/

Tresidder, J., & Shaddock, C. (2008). *Policing and cannabis use in Australia.* Retrieved from http://ncpic.org.au/ncpic/publications/aic-bulletins/article/policing-and-cannabis-use-in-australia

United Nations. (n.d.). Oceania. Retrieved from http://www.un.org/migration/presskit/factsheet_oceania.pdf

U.N. Office on Drugs and Crime. (2011a). *Smuggling of migrants by sea.* Vienna, Austria: Author.

U.N. Office on Drugs and Crime. (2011b). *World drug report 2011.* New York, NY: Author.

Veno, A., & Gannon, E. (2010). *The brotherhoods: Inside the outlaw motorcycle clubs (Full throttle edition).* Crows Nest, New South Wales, Australia: Allen & Unwin.

Veno, A., & van den Eynde, J. (2008). *Submission 10: Parliamentary Joint Committee on the Australian Crime Commission Inquiry into the legislative arrangements to outlaw serious and organised crime groups.* Canberra, Australian Capital Territory, Australia.

Wilkins, C., & Casswell, S. (2003). Organized crime in cannabis cultivation in New Zealand: An economic analysis. *Contemporary Drug Problems, 30,* 757–777.

Windybank, S. (2008). The illegal Pacific, Part 1: Organised crime. *Policy, 24*(2), 32–38.

8

Terrorism and Transnational Organized Crime

Gus Martin

Transnational organized crime in the modern era is an intricate system of billion-dollar enterprises providing diversified illicit services and products on the global market. Organizationally, some illegal enterprises are decentralized and cellular in their operations, whereas others are highly sophisticated and organized as illicit enterprises. The latter organizations have joined together from time to time to create criminal cartels and transnational associations that try to regulate "product lines" such as military-grade weapons, refined cocaine or heroin, and human cargo. Those specializing in illicit trafficking ply their trades in a global economy where classic laissez faire market forces allow them to thrive on supplying illegal commodities to satisfy the seemingly insatiable international demand for arms, drugs, and exploitable humans.

In the international security arena, insurgent movements and terrorists often obtain resources covertly from sources such as the security services of sympathetic governments. For example, the BBC reported in February 2012 that a classified NATO analysis concluded that Pakistan's Interservices Intelligence (ISI) was deeply involved in providing direct assistance to the Taliban in Afghanistan (Sommerville, 2012). However, security services are not always optimal as patrons because they use insurgent movements as international proxies, and as proxies the provision of resources is constrained by the politics of the state patron. Transnational criminal organizations offer a less constraining alternative.

Demand by insurgent movements and terrorists for military-grade weapons—universally necessary for self-preservation or promoting violent political agendas—motivates criminal organizations to court a fervent customer base. From the perspective of transnational criminals, insurgent movements and terrorists are wealthy customers in a potentially lucrative market. From the perspective of their infamous clientele, transnational organized crime provides a reliable pipeline for funneling the requisite tools of a violent trade. Hence, arms trafficking represents a natural nexus between international traffickers and political pariahs; it is simply a question of doing business. Such symbiosis is logical and unsurprising.

The global drug trade is a similar, yet much more anarchic, nexus between transnational organized crime and violent political insurgency. Three patterns of participation in the drug trade encourage this anarchic nexus: first, traditional patterns of drug production and trafficking in which criminal enterprises are motivated by enormous profit margins; second, the relatively recent trend of participation in the drug trade by committed political insurgents and terrorists as a modus to fund their revolutionary agendas; and, third, narco-insurgencies in which criminal enterprises directly threaten the internal security of drug-producing nations. The first and third patterns of participation in the drug trade are typically competitive rather than collaborative, and the motivations driving drug-related political violence are predominantly related to profits. Narco-insurgencies are characterized by internecine warfare among traffickers and extreme resistance against governments pursuing policies of drug suppression. Unlike cooperative associations among arms traffickers and insurgent customers in a relatively collaborative global arms market, participation in the drug trade can be quite volatile. The reason for this is logical: Illicit drugs are a tremendously profitable source of revenue for those who successfully etch market niches. In essence, "Terrorists may sometimes join others in the traffic in drugs; [and] drug-lords may sometimes commit acts of terrorism against one another in coalition with others, or use violence against governments" (Martin & Romano, 1992, p. 79).

Inciting this anarchic environment are political insurgents and terrorists who are keen to trade drug profits for weapons and other martial materiel.

This chapter explores the relationship between terrorism and transnational organized crime by considering three foci of inquiry. First, an examination is made of fundamental conceptual considerations, explicating convergence between illicit enterprise and asymmetrical insurgency in the age of globalization. Second, an examination is made of baseline incentives that link demand by revolutionary customers for requisite tools of the terrorist trade and supply from transnational organized crime. Third, an examination is made of criminal enterprise in modern terrorist environments, recounting the recent past as prologue to the modern environment, along with a regional analysis of the global scope of the problem.

TERRORISM AND TRANSNATIONAL ORGANIZED CRIME: CONCEPTUAL CONSIDERATIONS

Collaboration between terrorists and transnational criminals poses a genuine threat to national and international security. This is because such groups are innately covert, guarded, and antiestablishment in their behavior and organizational configuration. Criminal enterprises have created and operate within covert global networks and are expert at trafficking in drugs and weapons sold to well-heeled clients. From their perspective, the covert market consistently generates enormous profits from reliable customer bases. These attributes of the modern global environment cause security experts to concede that transnational organized crime is able and willing to provide weapons and other goods to insurgents or terrorists. Facts confirm this conclusion. For example,

> In March 2005, Ukrainian prosecutors reported that members of Ukrainian transnational organized crime smuggled 18 Soviet-era cruise missiles to China and Iran in 2000 and 2001, respectively. The officials further reported that at least 12 of the missiles are capable of carrying a 200-kiloton nuclear warhead. (Martin, 2013, p. 289)

Two considerations form a conceptual framework for understanding the symbiotic relationship between terrorists and transnational organized crime: (1) illicit enterprise and political convergence and (2) illicit enterprise and asymmetrical insurgency.

Illicit Enterprise and Political Convergence

Until recently, the demarcation between criminal enterprise, political insurgency, and illegal trafficking was observable and explicable; in the modern era, this demarcation has become blurred. Extremist politics and transnational criminal enterprise now intersect in the illicit global market, resulting in participation by some political extremists in arms and drug trafficking. Market-driven mutual interest has led to the creation of cooperative pacts between traditional criminal enterprises and politically motivated insurgent movements. These mutual interests and cooperative pacts have been termed *political convergence* by experts. Although evidence exists that political convergence occurs, there is debate about

> whether those terrorists who take on criminal traits for purposes of terrorism . . . actually *become* criminals—and vice versa. There are two schools of thought in this debate. One . . . argues that convergence does exist and can remain permanent. The other . . . argues that terrorism and crime are very different in their motivations and that therefore convergence is at best very infrequent. To the extent that interaction takes place, it is simply an alliance of convenience. (Grabosky & Stohl, 2010, pp. 7–8)

Both perspectives in the debate have merit. However, the operational hypothesis of this discussion is that political convergence between terrorists and transnational criminals occurs when purveyors of illicit commodities collaborate with insurgent customers to create cooperative balance between terrorist demand and criminal supply. This association forms a pattern of cooperation in which purveyors and customers aggressively seek to mutually benefit from their illicit compact.

When considering patterns of cooperation, it is important to recognize that the illicit compact is not necessarily the result of vertical organizational configurations in which directives are delivered from heads of criminal organizations to subordinates; the same is true for terrorist consumers. To the contrary, mid-level and low-level operatives often act as independent entrepreneurs, thus establishing "a *leaderless nexus* . . . between criminal and terrorists" (Dishman, 2006, p. 368) resembling a relatively flat and cellular organizational configuration. Such arrangements are quite flexible and adaptive to the shifting sands of terrorist and counterterrorist environments, especially in comparison to the political vagaries that may affect the reliability of support from state patrons.

Political convergence results in terrorist violence when political insurgents or criminal organizations are challenged by oppositional government policies or (in the case of narco-insurgencies) competitive enemy interests. Cases of terrorist violence perpetrated by participants in the illicit arms and drug trades are well documented, the characteristics of which may be subsumed under the following three descriptive models:

- Profit-motivated traditional criminal enterprises
- Politically motivated criminal-political enterprises
- Narco-insurgencies

The underlying attributes that distinguish the three models (aside from motive) are the following: First, traditional criminal enterprises are composed of illicit businesses whose participants normally desire a minimal amount of public attention for their activities. Second, criminal-political enterprises are composed of dissident movements that frequently desire a high public profile for their activities. Third, narco-insurgencies are anarchic environments exhibiting the seemingly contradictory desire to achieve minimal attention from state authority on drug transactions by warning them off with public (and violent) demonstrations of the narcos' prowess. As indicated in Table 8.1, when the decision is made to engage in extremist violence, the activity profiles of traditional criminal enterprises, criminal-political enterprises, and narco-insurgencies are distinguishable in their motives, goals, targets, personnel, and degrees of political agitation.

Profit-Motivated Traditional Criminal Enterprises

Traditional criminal enterprises include Italian organized crime groups, the Japanese Yakuza, Chinese triads, the American La Cosa Nostra, Southeast Asian drug lords, and the Russian mafia groups. Fortunately,

> most of these enterprises have been politically passive and have engaged in political violence reactively rather than actively. In essence, the likelihood of antistate violence by these organizations depends on the social and political environments of their national bases of operation. (Martin, 2007, p. 290)

The principal objectives for traditional criminal enterprises are to maximize proceeds from their criminal endeavors and defend the viability

Table 8.1   Illegal Enterprise and Political Convergence

Descriptive Models

The actions of the three descriptive models for illegal enterprise and political convergence can be contrasted in several ways. When the decision has been made to engage in terrorism, their activity profiles become distinguishable.

The following table illustrates differences between these environments in their motives, goals, targets, personnel, and degrees of political agitation.

	Activity Profile				
Environment	Motives	Goals	Targets	Personnel	Political Agitation
Traditional criminal enterprises	Financial	Passive government	Active governments	Criminals	Reactive and anonymous
Criminal-political enterprises	Political	Revolutionary victory	Agents and symbols of oppression	Dissident activists	Active and public
Narco-insurgencies	Financial political	Passive government; market domination	Active governments; market rivals	Criminals; trained mercenaries	Reactive and public

of their illicit commerce. Because they are driven by the prospect of lucrative financial returns, profit-motivated enterprises become involved in political conflict only within the context that they wish to establish secure markets and trafficking routes for their illicit trade.

Thus, traditional criminal enterprises usually do not seek to ruin political systems but rather to diminish the intensity of state-sponsored suppression campaigns or otherwise co-opt these systems for the benefit of the criminal enterprise. Traditional criminal enterprises are usually uninterested in active political involvement, other than to corrupt or pacify government officials and thereby palliate the perception of their activities. They desire a seamless market for their business, and regimes that are either too enervated to interfere with the illicit environment or lack the will to do so are unlikely to be targeted by traditional criminal enterprises. On the other hand, traditional criminal organizations have vigorously opposed suppression operations that significantly damage their illegal business environment. Such opposition is not a ubiquitous consequence, but many incidents have occurred. Comparative analyses indicate that these patterns of behavior are significantly influenced by the political and historical environments of specific nations (Siegel & van de Bunt, 2012).

Politically Motivated Criminal-Political Enterprises

During the Cold War, the Soviet Union and Eastern bloc provided covert support for aligned governments and revolutionary groups in their rivalry with the United States and West. Such "proxy war" was a common feature of the Cold War. Terrorist groups received financial and other support from the Soviet Union and its allies until the late 1980s, when the Soviet Bloc collapsed and Communist-supported insurgencies were left without state patronage. Absent such patronage, terrorist groups turned to alternative means for funding their causes.

With the end of the Cold War, antistate political insurgents and terrorists increasingly became direct participants in transnational organized crime. Insurgents and terrorists operating from Asia, Latin America, and elsewhere repeatedly occupied or controlled drug-producing territory, or engaged in other criminal activity such as seizing hostages for ransom, bank robbery, and kidnapping. From the perspective of political dissidents, such participation is a practical evolutionary progression. Simply explained, politically motivated extremists calculated that a considerable degree of independence and flexibility can be established via participation in drug trafficking or other transnational enterprises on the illicit market. In this way, their status as proxies for state patrons is greatly reduced or obviated.

Trading in drugs or arms is quite profitable, and dissidents have become capable of establishing economic autonomy from state patronage if a niche is found in an illicit market. Evidence of this phenomenon began in the immediate aftermath of the Soviet collapse. For example, in 1989 the U.S. Drug Enforcement Administration tracked

> Chinese-made AK-47 assault rifles from their points of legal importation to private gun dealers in California to their illegal smuggling to drug-traffickers in Mexico and Colombia. The report notes that drugs were sometimes used instead to pay the smugglers for the weapons. (Martin, & Romano 1992, p. 69)

This system of illicit bartering continues to be a regular pattern of interaction and is evident in many high-profile arrests and prosecutions of drug traffickers (Apodaca, 2012).

Narco-Insurgencies

The drug trade has produced environments wherein previously traditional criminal enterprises have evolved to resemble insurgents who use terrorist violence against state security forces, rival participants in the drug trade, and civilians. The terms *narco-insurgency, narco-guerrilla,* and *narco-terrorism* accurately mirror the scale of violence perpetrated by drug lords against government personnel and competitors. Narco-insurgencies characteristically exhibit the same paramilitary violence used in classic political insurgencies, including extreme brutality directed against perceived sympathizers of rival organizations. In narco-insurgent environments, criminal organizations boldly confront state security officers and agencies, regularly using advanced military hardware and tactics which rival government tactics and resources. The narco-insurgencies in Colombia during the 1980s and in Mexico during the 2000s are classic examples of such direct confrontation (Bowden, 2002; Grillo, 2011). Narco-insurgencies represent a particularly violent consequence of global demand for drugs on the behavior of criminal organizations vying for dominance in the illicit global market.

Illicit Enterprise and Asymmetrical Insurgency

Asymmetrical insurgency refers to irregular, unanticipated, and seemingly indiscriminate acts of terrorist violence. Threat scenarios plausibly forecast that terrorists seek to obtain and employ state-of-the-art weapons, attack unexpected targets, inflict substantial damage, and develop unpredictable and unconventional tactics. Furthermore,

> The dilemma for victims and for counterterrorism policy makers is that by using these tactics, the terrorists can win the initiative and redefine the international security environment. In this way, the traditional protections and deterrent policies used by societies and the global community can be surmounted by dedicated terrorists. (Martin, 2013, p. 245)

A central objective of asymmetrical insurgency is to intrude on normative patterns of interaction in the global community and within societies. In this regard, terrorists attempt to reframe the global security environment by launching destabilizing strikes against high-value symbolic targets. They have adapted their own structural and tactical profiles considerably to exploit international political and informational interconnectivity. For example, sophisticated networking via the Internet—and media exposure through cable news systems—present an exceptional opportunity for terrorists to threaten the global community immediately, easily, and with minimal vulnerability for the insurgent movement. In this regard,

> The modern era is one of immense potential for dedicated extremists who possess sophisticated technical, operational, and public relations skills. In addition, self-supported terrorist networks have emerged within the context of modern integrated economies and regional trade areas. These new attributes define *globalized terrorism*. (Martin, 2007, p. 645)

The impetus driving the expansion of asymmetrical insurgency is uncomplicated: Revolutionary insurgents cannot prevail using conventional tactics against state-level opponents. The calculus for success against such opponents is measured by social disruption and promulgation of the terrorists' message. Hence, the doctrine of asymmetrical insurgency permits the acquisition of weapons of mass destruction (WMD) and military-grade arms, the infliction of wholesale casualties, and undiscerning victimization. It is an attractive option because "the weaker forces are seeking total war, encompassing all segments of society" (Haselkorn, 2000). The expansion of asymmetrical insurgency is in fact occurring because violent extremists conclude that global interconnectivity greatly magnifies the effect of their acts of violence—all that is required is proper manipulation of, and violence against, informational and political nodes.

Clearly, as the terrorists' desired scale of destruction has increased using asymmetrical measures, so has their need for critical resources to carry out such high-intensity and high-profile attacks. This is especially true because of recurrent lack of consistency and trust in state sponsorship. Sustaining a movement's viability and access to requisite tools of the trade requires financial resources and reliable sources of supply. For this reason, some terrorist groups and movements such as the Liberation Tigers of Tamil Eelam (Sri Lanka), FARC (Colombia), The Abu Sayyaf Group (the Philippines), and Al Qaeda have engaged in criminal activity as a tactical decision to acquire needed cash to support themselves and purchase materiel on the illicit global market. Because of the globalized nature of the New Terrorism, collaboration with transnational criminal traffickers and other illicit endeavors helps sustain asymmetrical insurgencies. Modern globalized terrorism represents a transformation from recent history when criminal activity by dissidents was more isolated and less coordinated—in the post-9/11 world, the promise of self-sustaining criminal enterprise arguably provides an attractive motivation for participation in the illicit global market (Dishman, 2001).

In the modern era, neither terrorists nor transnational organized crime groups owe loyalty to sovereign states, and the demand on the illicit market for drugs and weapons creates natural affinities driving illicit enterprise and asymmetrical insurgency (Williams, 1995). These affinities are discussed in the following contexts:

- Demand: Requisite Tools of the Terrorist Trade
- Supply: Transnational Organized Crime and Revolutionary Customers

Demand: Requisite Tools of the Terrorist Trade

The motivation behind, and objectives of, asymmetrical insurgency encourage the acquisition and use of high-yield weapons and the selection of targets that may comprise sizable civilian populations. Enemy populations and symbolic interests can now be targeted with much greater effect than was possible in the recent past; terrorists simply require the resources and perseverance to do so. A foremost purpose behind many asymmetrical attacks is to create the greatest number of casualties as possible. Terrorists are no longer necessarily attempting to force the overthrow of governments or demanding new policies as ultimate goals. Rather, their immediate objective is often simply to maximize the number of injured and dead victims and thereby intimidate and unsettle substantial sectors of targeted interests.

The "gun and the bomb" typically have been employed by terrorists as primary weapons since the 19th century. However, in the modern era, the lethality of weapons available to terrorists is greatly superior, and the selection of targets is more indiscriminate and less surgical. Modern arms found in terrorist arsenals consistently include firearms, explosives, rocket-propelled grenades, vehicular bombs, and suicide bombs. Technologically advanced arms are sometimes used, such as antiaircraft rockets and sophisticated triggering instruments for explosives. Few WMDs have been used by terrorists, although threat scenarios consistently posit the use of chemical, biological, radiological, or nuclear devices.

Strong demand exists among violent extremists for firearms and common explosives. Types of firearms frequently sought by terrorists include the following:

- Submachine guns are common in the arsenals of domestic security services. Modern models such as the Israeli UZI and American Ingram are used by police and other services. However, models from the World War II–era models are smuggled by transnational criminals and used by terrorists.
- Assault rifles are designed for use by military services and are commonly found in terrorist and insurgent arsenals. The famous AK-47 became synonymous with revolutionary movements because of its widespread use by insurgents and terrorists. It was produced in large quantities and distributed globally.
- Rocket-propelled grenades (RPGs) are relatively cheap self-propelled munitions common to the arsenals of insurgents and terrorists. Like the AK-47, the RPG-7 is widely used by dissident movements. It was produced in large quantities by the Soviets, Chinese, and other communist nations.
- Precision-guided munitions (PGMs) are self-propelled munitions capable of being guided by infrared or other tracking systems. The American-made Stinger was delivered to Afghanistan during the Soviet invasion and was extremely effective against Soviet helicopters and other aircraft. The Soviet-designed SA-7 Grail is an effective surface-to-air missile, and along with the Stinger it poses a considerable threat to commercial airliners.

Types of explosives desired by terrorists include the following:

- Readily available commercial and industrial explosives such as dynamite and TNT are common.
- Plastic explosives such as Semtex and Composite-4 are puttylike compounds that can be easily shaped. Semtex is a very powerful plastic explosive originating from the former Czechoslovakia. It was trafficked on the international market during the Cold War, and a large quantity obtained by Libya was subsequently delivered to terrorists, including the Irish Republican Army. Composite-4 (C-4) originates from the United States. Although it is more difficult to obtain than Semtex, it has been used to great effect by terrorists. For example, C-4 was used by terrorists in the attack against the American destroyer USS *Cole*.

- Ammonium nitrate and fuel oil (ANFO) explosives are constructed by soaking ammonium nitrate fertilizer in fuel oil and adding other compounds and explosives to intensify the explosion. ANFO explosives consist of hundreds of pounds of ammonium nitrate and therefore are commonly used in car or truck bombs. Timothy McVeigh's device was a two-ton bomb.

A subject of continuing apprehension is the trafficking in radiological materials and other potential components for WMDs. Four types of WMDs are typically discussed as possible threats: biological, chemical, radiological agents, and nuclear weapons. They are described as follows:

- Biological agents are "living organisms . . . or infective material derived from them, which are intended to cause disease or death in man, animals, and plants, and which depend on their ability to multiply in the person, animal, or plant attacked (Stern, 2000, p. 6).
- Chemical agents are "chemical substances, whether gaseous, liquid, or solid, which are used for hostile purposes to cause disease or death in humans, animals, or plants, and which depend on direct toxicity for their primary effect" (Stern, 2000, pp. 21–22).
- Radiological agents are materials that emit radiation that can harm living organisms. To become threatening to life or health, these radioactive substances must be "ingested, inhaled, or absorbed through the skin" in sufficient quantities (Stern, 2000, p. 26).
- Nuclear weapons are high-explosive military weapons using weapons-grade plutonium and uranium. Explosions from nuclear bombs devastate the area within their blast zone, irradiate an area outside the blast zone, and are capable of sending dangerous radioactive debris into the atmosphere that descends to earth as toxic fallout.

Supply: Transnational Organized Crime and Revolutionary Customers

The trafficking of arms is a lucrative and attractive business for transnational organized crime. Transferring weapons to areas of conflict is an ancient vocation, and in the modern era, transnational organized crime is instrumental in aiding and abetting the delivery of arms and other materiel to terrorists and warring adversaries.

The collapse of the Soviet Union effectively opened the global market to trafficking in Eastern Bloc weapons, and literally tens of millions of small arms are believed to have been delivered to terrorists and insurgents around the globe. For example, illicit trafficking in Soviet-era arms in Africa was instrumental in increasing the scale of violence in Rwanda, Congo, Sudan, and other states. Elsewhere, Chinese-manufactured AK-47 assault rifles that were legally imported by private arms dealers in the United States have been smuggled to drug lords in Colombia and Mexico. In the recent past, sympathetic Americans and organized crime groups regularly smuggled weapons to the Irish Republican Army. Significantly, American-manufactured small arms are smuggled to Latin America and are widely used by Mexican narco-insurgents (Martin & Romano, 1992).

Trafficking in radioactive material is also an enterprise of transnational organized crime, and quantities have been seized by law enforcement officials. After the dissolution of the Soviet Union, and well into the 1990s, Soviet radioactive materials were seized on multiple occasions in various locations in Central and Eastern Europe. These materials included highly enriched uranium, beryllium, and lithium (Rounds, 2000).

CRIMINAL ENTERPRISE IN TERRORIST ENVIRONMENTS

Terrorists and other insurgents have historically resorted to criminal activity to sustain their campaigns. Bank robberies by political extremists are not uncommon, carried out in the recent past by notable movements such as the PLO's Force 17, West Germany's Red Army Faction, the Irish Republican Army, the Aryan Republican Army in the United States, and the Japanese Red Army. Although bank robberies can provide substantial sums of money, they do not provide a steady stream of financial support for the cause. In comparison, drug production and trafficking offer the possibility of structuring a system of self-sustaining autonomy for political extremists. The drug trade also supports a self-perception among revolutionaries that they are using their enemies' vices against them, thereby subverting them by enabling domestic drug consumption. The quality of violence emanating from participants in the lucrative drug trade has been characterized as *narco-terrorism*, signifying "forms of terrorism that are linked to the production of illegal drugs, either through the use of drug profits to fund political violence or the use of violence and terror to protect and preserve illegal drug production" (Sullivan, 2011, p. 413). Other crime-related methods of financing terrorist activities include "taxation" (i.e., extortion), kidnapping for ransom, laundering or redirecting money through charitable fund-raising, and producing "knock-off" counterfeit goods.

Such criminal activity reflects growing logical and tactical realities stemming from, and as a consequence of, declining state sponsorship of insurgencies and the proliferation of nonhierarchical networked terrorist environments. Table 8.2 summarizes examples of criminal enterprise in terrorist environments.

Regional Considerations: The Middle East

Islamist and nationalist organizations in the Middle East have used extortion, bank robbery, laundering, and drug trafficking to generate revenue for their movements. Hezbollah and other organizations consider these ventures to be justifiable appropriations used to hurt their adversaries—principally, the West and Israel. Collaborations with transnational organized crime facilitate these activities. Two cases underscore the extent to which Middle Eastern groups have allied themselves with transnational criminal networks. These are the Beka'a Valley in eastern Lebanon and, ironically, the Tri-Border Area in South America.

Lebanon's Beka'a Valley

Beginning in the 1970s, the Beka'a Valley in Lebanon became a crossroads of state terrorism, nationalist and Islamist extremism, drug trafficking, and currency counterfeiting. This is an important nexus because when the Syrian army occupied the valley in 1976, the Syrians created a protected haven for organizations, including Iran's Revolutionary Guards; Palestinian nationalists, such as the Popular Front for the Liberation of Palestine—General Command and the Abu Nidal Organization; Palestinian Islamist organizations, such as Hamas and Palestine Islamic Jihad; and other disparate movements, such as the Japanese Red Army and the Kurdistan Workers' Party.

The valley is a historic hub for producing hashish and opium. It is a relatively modest producer of these substances in comparison to much larger industries in Asia and elsewhere, but income has been instrumental

Table 8.2 Criminal Enterprise in Terrorist Environments

Criminal enterprise in terrorist environments is conducted by traditional criminal enterprises and criminal-political enterprises. They are differentiated primarily by motive, with traditional criminal enterprises motivated by profit and criminal-political enterprises motivated by a dissident cause.

The following table summarizes the activity profiles of several criminal enterprises.

| Group and Type | Activity Profile | | |
	Criminal Enterprise	Motive	Quality of Violence
Taliban (Afghanistan: criminal-political)	Opium and heroin production	Consolidate the movement; promote jihad	
Tamil Tigers (Sri Lanka: criminal-political)	Arms and drug trafficking	National independence	Terrorism, insurgency
Myanmar groups (traditional criminal)	Opium and heroin production	Profit; regional autonomy	Insurgency
The Abu Sayyaf Group (Philippines: criminal-political)	Kidnapping, extortion, drug trafficking	Jihad against the Filipino government	Terrorism, insurgency
Italian organized crime (traditional criminal)	Broad variety of activities	Profit	Terrorism, extortion, intimidation
Russian mafia (traditional criminal)	Broad variety of activities	Profit	Terrorism, extortion, intimidation
Irish dissidents (criminal-political)	Drug trade	Republicanism or loyalism	Terrorism
Kosovo Liberation Army/ National Liberation Army (criminal-political)	Arms and drug trafficking	Albanian nationalism	Terrorism, insurgency
Colombian cartels (traditional criminal)	Drug trade	Profit	Narco-terrorism
FARC (Colombia: criminal-political)	Drug trade	Revolution	Terrorism, insurgency
AUC (Colombia: criminal-political)	Drug trade	Counterinsurgency	Terrorism, counterinsurgency
Shining Path (Peru: criminal-political)	Drug trade	Revolution	Terrorism
Mexican narcotraficantes (traditional criminal)	Drug trade	Profit	Narco-terrorism

in sustaining extremist organizations in the valley. Hezbollah has been implicated in drug trafficking, which allowed them to generate income when support from patrons such as Iran became inconsistent. Beka'a Valley drugs have been transported to Israel, North Africa, Europe, and the United States. Lebanese drug production declined significantly beginning in the 1990s, but the traditional trade has continued.

The Beka'a Valley also became notorious for the quality of its currency counterfeiting industry, in particular the production and distribution of large quantities of high-quality dollars on the international market. The quality of the valley's counterfeiting industry greatly influenced the redesigning of U.S. paper currency in the 1990s.

The Tri-Border Area

Middle Eastern extremists such as Lebanon's Hezbollah have received millions of dollars from the proceeds of sympathizers living in Latin America, particularly from a region known as the Tri-Border Area. The Tri-Border Area is where the borders of Argentina, Paraguay, and Brazil intersect in central South America. The region is remote, with marginal government control, and much like the Beka'a Valley in its heyday, there exists a thriving underground economy. Supporters of Middle Eastern organizations have collaborated with Mexican drug traffickers, counterfeited knockoff goods, laundered money, raised revenue through extortion, and manufactured methamphetamines—using these proceeds to finance Hezbollah and other organizations (Treverton et al., 2009). The reason these enterprises exist in Latin America is that approximately 25,000 Middle Eastern residents form a thriving diaspora with close ties to compatriots in Lebanon and elsewhere:

> The region is known for its thriving illegal smuggling and financial criminal activities. Smugglers regularly cross international borders, and Hezbollah is quite adept at raising funds and laundering it to extremist causes. Narcotics trafficking alone generates billions of dollars in profit, and other contraband goods (including cash) add to the lucrative illicit economy. (Martin, 2013, p. 292)

In addition to significant financial support received in the Middle East from criminal activity in the Tri-Border Area, there exists a direct threat to security in the Western Hemisphere. Transnational criminals are as adept at smuggling human cargo as they are in smuggling weapons and drugs. Illicit networks move thousands of migrants into the United States through Central America and Mexico. It is quite plausible that terrorist groups are willing and able to associate themselves with transnational criminals specializing in transporting people into the United States. Using such networks, dedicated terrorists can easily travel through Mexico and cross the border, thus acquiring the capability to attack the American homeland.

Regional Considerations: Narco-Insurgencies in Latin America

Narco-terrorism in Latin America is a direct consequence of competition over illicit drug markets. Marijuana and cocaine make up most of the Latin American drug trade, but some opium and heroin are also trafficked. Both political insurgents and transnational organized crime groups receive enormous revenue from the drug trade. A large proportion of drugs produced in Latin America are controlled by competing drug cartels that directly challenge government authority. This poses a significant threat to hemispheric security because cartel operatives have been instrumental in destabilizing domestic security in Colombia, Mexico, and elsewhere.

To assess the distinctive aspects of narco-insurgencies in Latin America, it is instructive to differentiate the attributes of narco-terrorism carried out by political insurgents vis-à-vis criminal insurgents.

Political Insurgencies and Narco-Terrorism

The term *narco-guerrilla* has been used to describe autonomous political insurgencies that use profits from drug production and trafficking to sustain their revolutionary agendas. In Latin America, during the 1980s Peru's Maoist Shining Path (Sendero Luminoso) group financed its terrorist insurgency with money derived from controlling a sizable percentage of Peru's coca leaf and cocaine paste production, and from collaboration with Colombian cocaine cartels. Similarly, Colombia's leftist National Liberation Army (ELN) and Revolutionary Armed Forces of Colombia (FARC) and the rightist United Self-Defense Forces of Colombia (AUC) paramilitary used drug income to finance armed political insurgencies.

Shining Path in Peru: Peru's Shining Path group waged a decade-long terrorist insurgency that killed approximately 70,000 people during the 1980s and early 1990s. The movement strategically competed for a stake in Peru's then-lucrative coca trade. The Upper Huallaga Valley was the richest producer of coca leaf during this period, and both coca leaf and cocaine paste were exported to Colombian *narcotraficantes* who manufactured refined cocaine. Shining Path aggressively and violently entered the Upper Huallaga Valley, and its extreme interpretation of Maoist ideology was brought into play to justify these associations by announcing to drug farmers that its actions were in fact part of a strategy to liberate and safeguard growers from maltreatment by criminal drug traffickers. When this occurred,

> It is believed that Sendero garnered a minimum of $10 million a year (some estimates range as high as $100 million) between 1987 and 1992 from "taxes" on a large portion of the valley's 80,000 coca growers and from levies of up to $15,000 a flight on the mostly Colombian traffickers as they landed on the scores of clandestine runways in the valley to pick up their cargoes of cocaine paste. (Scott Palmer, 2001, quoted in Whittaker, p. 160)

Until its leader Abimail Guzmán was captured in 1992, Shining Path was a self-sustaining terrorist insurgency, having successfully established autonomous viability through participation in the drug trade. After 1992, Shining Path lost its ideological centrality, and most members surrendered or were captured during the 1990s.

Colombian Political Insurgencies: FARC and the ELN regularly employed terrorist and guerrilla tactics against Colombian civilians and government personnel, and as external patronage waned, they became self-sufficient through criminal activity. Both FARC and the ELN used criminal extortion and kidnapping for ransom to support themselves. However, although the ELN eschewed deep participation in the drug trade out of a sense of ideological purity, FARC participated heavily in drug trafficking. FARC has long produced drugs manufactured in "liberated" regions where government authority was weakened or eliminated. Since the inception of its Marxist war against the Colombian government, FARC allowed transnational criminals to ply their trade in FARC-controlled regions, as long as sufficient "tax" payments were made by the *narcotraficantes* to their FARC hosts—FARC also provided a measure of security to traffickers as they moved drugs through and from FARC-controlled areas. During the 1990s, FARC ceased relying on mid-level brokers and established direct relations with coca and marijuana growers, thus enabling them to deliver these illicit goods directly to Colombian drug lords. As in Peru during the Shining Path insurgency, it used Marxist liberation ideology to rationalize the takeover of coca production on behalf of poor farmers. This system was perceived by many to be a sensible and practical arrangement, from which all participants profited. The system became so embedded in FARC's operations, that

> some FARC units promote or manage coca cultivation, cocaine laboratories, trafficking, and bartering drugs-for-weapons arrangements with transnational organized crime groups. Other FARC units have been very active in the drug-producing southwestern province of Nariño, where ambushes of government troops are common. (Martin, 2013, p. 297)

At the height of their collaboration with transnational organized crime, FARC was believed to have received an annual income of $300 million to $1 billion from drugs. Interestingly, FARC established a valuable association with the Russian mafia following the dissolution of the large Cali and Medellín drug cartels (smaller drug gangs supplanted Colombia's cartels). The Russian mafia essentially bartered weapons and other supplies in exchange for FARC's cocaine. FARC also established lucrative associations with Mexican drug traffickers who became principals in the transnational trade as prominent Colombian cartels declined.

In reaction to the Marxist FARC and ELN insurgencies, rightist Colombians—including government officials and wealthy landholders—marshaled and trained regional right-wing paramilitary units. The AUC was the largest and foremost coalition of paramilitaries, comprising at its height 11,000 fighters. Using tactics similar to their Marxist adversaries, the AUC engaged in political terrorism, including death squad activity and massacres of civilians. AUC eventually splintered into five factions with members becoming complicit in, and dependent on, Colombia's drug trade. They became so involved in the trade that a June 2003 classified report stated that "it is impossible to differentiate between the self-defense groups and narco-trafficking organizations" (Wilson, 2003). The report estimated that the drug trade provided up to 80% of AUC's income.

Criminal Insurgencies and Narco-Terrorism

The foregoing discussion identified common associations between terrorist insurgents and transnational criminal organizations. This was discussed from the perspective of political insurgents and how this association was used by them to support their movements. However, the perspective of transnational criminal organizations—the other side of this collaboration—must also be investigated. Considered within this context, narco-insurgencies understandably occur as a reaction by criminal organizations to government suppression campaigns. Such reaction is distinguishable from routinely antisocial criminal behavior because it involves direct and violent resistance by criminal organizations against government officials and institutions. The cases of Colombia and Mexico epitomize this phenomenon in Latin America.

Colombian Drug Cartels: During the 1980s through the mid-1990s, Colombian *narcotraficantes* established the first large transnational drug cartels, through which they controlled global cocaine traffic from the cities of Cali and Medellín. Colombian cartels dominated other criminal groups during this period, in particular what were then mere smuggling gangs in Mexico. To protect their lucrative enterprises, Colombian cartels waged terrorist campaigns against all who opposed them, including government institutions and officials. Violence waged by cartel operatives was often extreme, and during the 1980s, *narcotraficante* organizations killed "3,000 soldiers and police officers, more than 1,000 public officials, 170 judicial employees, 50 lower judges, dozens of journalists, 12 Supreme Court judges, three presidential candidates, one attorney general, and one newspaper publisher" (Ehrenfeld, 1993, 86–87).

In addition to engaging in insurgent violence, cartels became quite expert at subverting government antidrug efforts via intimidation, corruption, and criminal extortion. However, this high-profile confrontational insurgent strategy ultimately led to the demise of Cali and Medellín. Colombian security forces disassembled the large cartels in collaboration with the United States, which delivered significant assets to aid the Colombian government. As a consequence, the large cartels were supplanted by a new *narcotraficante* paradigm in which Colombian criminal organizations reconfigured their organizational profiles as smaller (but still viable) drug gangs.

With the supplanting of the Cali and Medellín cartels, Colombian drug traffickers moderated their operational resistance to the government and they have not resumed narco-terrorism to the same degree as the large cartels. This has brought a measure of stability from the perspective of Colombian transnational organized crime, because drugs continue to flood the illicit market and Colombian gangs continue to prosper from the demand for drugs in Europe and the United States.

The Mexican Narco-Insurgency: Mexican criminals traditionally engaged in banditry, extortion, and prostitution. Some smuggling of locally produced opium, marijuana, and cocaine to the United States occurred, but this trade was controlled by gang-like enterprises. During the 1970s and 1980s, Colombian drug cartels retained Mexican gangs to smuggle cocaine across the border to the United States. The Mexican gangs served as junior partners to the Colombians, who paid them in cash. However, the Mexicans soon demanded quantities of drugs for their services, which were sold to new customers in new markets—this arrangement reportedly allowed Mexican criminals to retain 1 kilogram of cocaine for every 2 they smuggled to the United States.

Mexican gangs rapidly became autonomous and coequal associates of the Colombians, thereby experiencing their own transition from gangs to criminal cartel alliances. The most powerful alliances are the Gulf Cartel, Juarez Cartel, Tijuana Cartel, and Sonora Cartel. As occurred previously in Colombia, Mexican cartels began to resort to narco-terrorism when their drug enterprises were challenged by government officials and competitors. However, unlike the precedent of Colombian gangs and cartels, Mexican criminal enterprises do not usually collaborate and often violently compete for markets.

Extreme violence between drug-trafficking organizations is common, and the geographic scope of drug-related bloodshed is widespread. Mexican criminal insurgents not only assault each other over turf, they also launch attacks against government targets, members of the media, and civilian critics. When Mexican president Felipe Calderon declared an offensive against drug traffickers in December 2006, an outright narco-insurgency ensued. Fatalities during the insurgency have been extraordinarily high, exacerbated by heavily armed and well-trained paramilitary operatives such as the Los Zetas group employed by the Gulf Cartel. More than 50,000 Mexicans had been killed in the conflict, with the following statistics and incidents becoming common news during the narco-insurgency:

- Dozens of news reporters have disappeared or been killed by drug traffickers.
- Paramilitary Zetas have been implicated in many assassinations conducted independently and on behalf of the Gulf Cartel. Police commanders, newspaper reporters and editors, and rival drug traffickers have been killed or injured by Los Zetas.
- State police chiefs, federal officers, state police officers, and soldiers have been assassinated and kidnapped by drug traffickers. Alleged infiltration of local police forces by drug traffickers has led to the disarming of some police units after assassination attempts.
- Grisly mass graves have been found with dozens of bodies. Many victims have been beheaded. (U.S. Drug Enforcement Administration, 2012)

Regional Considerations: Asia

Drug production in Asia is primarily concentrated in two areas: Southeast Asia (the Golden Triangle) and Southwest Asia (the Golden Crescent). Because of their proximity to regions of political conflict, terrorists and insurgents have historically profited from drug trafficking in both regions. The countries of Afghanistan, Pakistan, and Iran make up the Golden Crescent, where opium poppies have been cultivated since antiquity, and modern traffickers refine much of the crop into pure opium and heroin. The countries of Laos, Thailand, and Myanmar (Burma) comprise the Golden Triangle, which also has an ancient tradition of cultivating opium poppies and a more recent reputation for manufacturing opium and heroin. Transshipment routes send large quantities of opium and heroin to Europe and the United States.

The Golden Triangle has a strong Cold War-era legacy of proxy wars fought by groups funded through drug trafficking. During the Cold War, the Chinese Kuomintang, Burmese Shan United Army, and the United Wa State Army all used the opium trade to fund their movements. However, these former Cold War proxies eventually ended their operations or became fully immersed in drug trafficking—absent old Cold War politics. The modern drug trade is largely an enterprise controlled by traditional

Asian crime groups. However, political insurgents in the Golden Crescent continue to be deeply involved in the regional drug industry, and the Golden Crescent serves as a major drug supplier to Europe through Central Asia. As a result of the collapse of the Soviet Union, Islamist extremists, transnational organized crime groups, and warlords in Central Asia profit from drugs traveling through these transshipment corridors (Latypov, 2009; Zhang, 2012).

Afghan Insurgencies and Transnational Organized Crime

Afghanistan has long been a prominent participant in the production of heroin, opium, and hashish, often functioning as the source of most of the world's illegal opiates. Present-day mujahideen, insurgents, and warlords prosper immensely from the drug trade. This has been especially true in the post-Soviet era. Beginning with the Taliban's regime (September 1996 to January 2002), opium poppy cultivation rose to unprecedented levels. An estimated 80% of the Taliban's income came from profits made in illicitly trafficked opium and heroin through transnational criminal networks. During this period, Afghanistan produced an estimated 70% of the global supply of opium. Interestingly, "The Taliban's radical interpretation of Islam allowed the cultivation of opium poppies but strictly forbade and severely punished the use of opium or heroin" (Martin, 2013, p. 299).

With the fall of the Taliban regime following the U.S.-led invasion, tribal Afghan warlords seized control of Afghanistan's opium-producing industry. The warlords expanded the cultivation of opium, increasing opium-producing acreage from 150,000 acres in 2003 to 510,000 acres in 2004 (Efron, 2005). Poppy production during the post-Taliban era hit record levels, and an estimated 90% of worldwide production of heroin came from Afghan poppies. Afghan warlords carefully stockpiled substantial amounts of opium, hoarding supplies that could reportedly service heroin laboratories for a long period of time. Thus, opium has become the largest cash crop for extremists in politically volatile Afghanistan with its warring factions, Islamist mujahideen, and terrorist sympathizers.

Other Asian Insurgencies and Transnational Organized Crime

Sri Lanka's Liberation Tigers of Tamil Eelam (LTTE) embedded themselves as middlemen in the Asian weapons- and drugs-smuggling markets. They financed their insurgency to a significant degree by receiving arms and drugs as mid-level brokers from transnational criminal enterprises in Myanmar (Burma) and India. The LTTE then sold the fronted drugs, purchased weapons with drug profits, and continued their association with criminal groups indefinitely in order to supply arms to their fighters. The LTTE were defeated in 2009 after waging a 30-year insurgency using this method.

In the Philippines, the Abu Sayyaf Group has sustained its Islamist terrorist insurgency largely through associations with traditional criminal enterprises. The Abu Sayyaf Group has been moderately involved in criminal revenue-generating endeavors such as drug trafficking, kidnapping, and extortion; these activities are rationalized as necessary tactics for its jihad. They have been known to exploit marijuana cultivation in the southern Philippines to support their insurgency (Berry, Curtis, Hudson, & Kollars, 2002, p. 105).

Regional Considerations: Europe

Europe has a long tradition of organized criminal activity. Criminal organizations have historically engaged in transnational criminal enterprise, and in the modern era, European criminal organizations are well established in the illicit global market. Perhaps the most traditional criminal enterprises exist in Italy. However, new aggressive criminal enterprises have arisen in Eastern Europe, especially in Russia. Sophisticated smuggling networks were also established in the Balkans after the dissolution of Yugoslavia and the civil wars that occurred in its aftermath.

Italian Organized Crime

The word *mafia* has come to symbolize criminal organizations around the world, with established codes of conduct and a sense of criminal (often violent) honor. However, the original mafia are criminal societies with deep cultural roots in Sicily and southern Italy. These societies possess qualities that are emulated internationally by other criminal organizations: "Secrecy under a code of silence (omerta); opposition to, and noncooperation with, security (and law enforcement) agencies and officials; a code of honor; absolute obedience and loyalty toward the respected heads of mafia groups" (Martin, 2013, p. 301).

Although Italian crime groups have not created a domestic terrorist environment approaching the levels of violence seen in Colombia or Mexico, they do engage in relatively low-intensity criminal terrorism. The Calabrian N'drangheta, Sicilian mafia, and Neapolitan Camorra have proved quite willing to use violence, extortion, and corruption to dissuade critics and opponents from airing public criticism and interfering in their illicit operations. Shootings, bombings, and other violence have been carried out against news outlets, government officials, judges, and others. Attacks are usually planned as "surgical" applications of intimidating force against specific officials. Despite the discriminating quality of violence, victimization is continual, and

> from 1971 to 1991, about 40 judges, law enforcement officers, politicians, and others were assassinated. The death toll has been higher among feuding organized crime groups and civilians. In Sicily alone, an average of 100 people are killed each year by Sicilian Mafia violence. (Martin, 2013, p. 302)

Italian criminal organizations are also heavily involved in international trafficking. For example, the N'drangheta established a specialization in weapons and drug smuggling, each year earning billions of dollars from the illicit trade.

The Russian Mafia

The Russian mafia is not a monolithic or centralized organization; it is a transnational network of criminal groups and a fluid association of gangs, some of them large with thousands of members. The Russian mafia network experienced enormous growth in the post-Soviet era, becoming one of the most extensive organized crime systems in the world. Its influence extends to regions of the former Soviet Union such as the Ukraine, Chechnya, and Georgia. In the 1990s, the Russian Ministry of Interior estimated that the Russian mafia at that time had 5,000 to 8,000 identifiable groups and possibly 100,000 members. Many private businesses and banks have been under Russian mafia influence since the 1990s.

The Russian mafia and its affiliates represent a modern model for transnational organized crime, both in the quality of its violence and in its associations with violent political extremists. Unlike its Italian counterparts, Russian mafia operatives are prone to kill politicians, journalists, and private businessmen who interfere with their enterprises. Approximately 600 murders occur annually, and during the 1990s and early 2000s, scores of bankers and businesspeople were assassinated. The Russian mafia profits from drug trafficking, weapons trafficking, extortion, and murder for hire. Affiliations with terrorists, insurgents, and other violent movements became established through trafficking of weapons in the developing world. Significantly, these ties were apparently strengthened through the efforts of former Soviet KGB intelligence officers. Threat scenarios posit that because of these and other connections within the military, weapons of mass destruction and other high-yield arms could be transferred to terrorists and other violent insurgents (Bowman, 2002).

Political Turmoil and the "Balkan Route"

The Balkans have long served as a smuggling route to Europe for illicit goods originating in the East. In the modern era, it became a profitable hub connecting Europe's illicit drug market with heroin historically trafficked from Turkey, Pakistan, and Afghanistan. Most heroin consumed in Europe moved through Yugoslavia prior to its disintegration, and thereafter passed through its splinter states and the Czech Republic, Bulgaria, Slovakia, and Hungary.

Albanian organized crime became the principal traffickers in heroin to Europe with the rise of Albanian nationalism and the need for revenue to fund insurgencies in Macedonia and Kosovo. Albanian insurgent groups such as the Kosovo Liberation Army in Serbia and the National Liberation Army in Macedonia were funded and armed via profits earned in the heroin trade. Collaboration between Albanian insurgents and transnational organized crime networks was quite cooperative, with heroin and arms exchanges becoming a lucrative arrangement. Chechen and Georgian criminal organizations delivered heroin and arms to Albanians, who paid for the weapons with the sale of heroin in Europe.

Plausible Danger: Transnational Organized Crime and the New Terrorism

A symbiotic relationship exists between transnational organized crime groups and terrorist movements. This relationship is the consequence of political realignment in the post–Cold War era and globalization of the illicit criminal market. It is highly likely this environment will continue to be deeply woven into the fabric of transnational criminal enterprise and violent political extremism. Because of the global scope of this environment, a plausible and ongoing threat is posed by the moral and organizational profile of the "new terrorism."

The modern terrorist environment is distinguished by organizational decentralization and moral ruthlessness. In comparison to previous generations of violent extremists, modern terrorists possess little compunction about inflicting mass casualties on civilian populations, or about employing highly destructive weapons against such soft targets. This represents an unprecedented mode of political violence, one characterized by complete acceptance of tactics specifically intending maximum destruction. Organizational decentralization has replaced organizational hierarchy, and operational command and control is devolved to cell-based configurations. Thus, an inspirational center such as Osama bin Laden may influence the overall direction of a movement, but there is little central control at the operational level. Cells are capable of operational autonomy, and can pre-position themselves as "sleepers" in foreign countries. Al-Qaeda and other similar extremists are in many respects stateless "because they have no particular home country that they seek to liberate, there is no homeland to use as a base, or their group has been uprooted from the land that they are fighting for." (Martin, 2013, p. 272).

With such operational fluidity, a significant global threat is highly conceivable should cell-based extremists establish associations with transnational criminal groups.

∭ CONCLUSION

Collaboration between transnational organized crime groups and terrorist movements poses a clear and present challenge to the world community. Mutual interests are driven by classic market forces whereby demand for certain commodities attracts criminal entrepreneurs who act as suppliers. Global security is also challenged by self-sustaining insurgencies involved in transnational criminal activities such as drug trafficking. In some regions, radical movements receive financial and other support from sympathizers, and these regions present plausible security challenges to the security of neighboring countries. Furthermore, modern narco-insurgencies threaten the domestic stability of drug-producing countries.

This chapter explicated the conceptual frameworks of illicit enterprise and political convergence, and illicit enterprise and asymmetrical insurgency. Three conceptual models were discussed within the framework of political convergence—profit-motivated traditional criminal enterprises, politically motivated criminal-political enterprises, and narco-insurgencies. An asymmetrical insurgency framework was discussed by examining terrorists' demand for requisite tools of the trade, and transnational organized crime's objective and ability to aid and abet the provision of arms and other materiel to insurgents and terrorists in the illicit global market. An examination was also made of the nexus between transnational organized crime and insurgencies within the context of regional terrorist environments. Idiosyncratic cultural and political considerations were examined within the context of associations between organized criminal groups and insurgencies in the Middle East, Latin America, Asia, and Europe. The plausible danger concerning the establishment of an association between transnational organized crime and adherents of the "new terrorism" was also examined.

⚜ REFERENCES

Apodaca, D. (2012, April 24). *RICO indictments for Sinoloa cartel leaders including "El Chapo" Guzman, "Mayo" Zambada, and 22 others.* Washington, DC: U.S. Drug Enforcement Administration.

Berry, L., Curtis, G., Hudson, R., & Kollars, N. (2002). *A global overview of narcotics-funded terrorist and other extremist groups.* Washington, DC: Library of Congress.

Bowden, M. (2002). *Killing Pablo: The hunt for the world's greatest outlaw.* New York, NY: Penguin Books.

Bowman, S. (2002). *Weapons of mass destruction: The terrorist threat.* Washington, DC: Library of Congress.

Dishman, C. (2001, January). Terrorism, crime, and transformation. *Studies in Conflict and Terrorism, 24,* 43–59.

Dishman, C. (2006). The leaderless nexus: When crime and terror converge. In R. Howard & R. Sawyer (Eds.), *Terrorism and counterterrorism: Understanding the new security environment, readings and interpretations* (2nd ed., pp. 367–382). Dubuque, IA: McGraw-Hill.

Efron, S. (2005, January 2). An Afghan quandary for the U.S. *Los Angeles Times.* Retrieved from http://articles.latimes.com/2005/jan/02/world/fg-afg handrugs2

Ehrenfeld, R. (1993). *Narco-terrorism.* New York, NY: Basic Books.

Grabosky, P., & Stohl, M. (2010). *Crime and terrorism.* Thousand Oaks, CA: Sage.

Grillo, I. (2011). *El Narco: Inside Mexico's criminal insurgency.* New York, NY: Bloomsbury Press.

Haselkorn, A. (2000, December 3). Martyrdom: The most powerful weapon. *Los Angeles Times.* Retrieved from http://pqasb.pqarchiver.com/latimes/access/64891041.html?FMT=ABS&FMTS=ABS:FT&type=current&date=Dec+3%2C+2000&author=AVIGDOR+HASELKORN&pub=Los+Angeles+Times&edition=&startpage=M.5&desc=Commentary%3B+Martyrdom%3A+The+Most+Powerful+Weapon

Latypov, A. (2009). Understanding post 9/11 drug control policy and politics in Central Asia. *International Journal of Drug Policy, 20,* 387–391.

Martin, G. (2007). Globalization and international terrorism. In G. Ritzer (Ed.), *The Blackwell companion to globalization* (pp. 644–661). Malden, MA: Blackwell.

Martin, G. (2013). *Understanding terrorism: Challenges, perspectives, and issues* (4th ed.). Thousand Oaks, CA: Sage.

Martin, J., & Romano, A. (1992). *Multinational crime: Terrorism, espionage, drug & arms smuggling.* Newbury Park, CA: Sage.

Rounds, D. (2000). *International criminal justice: Issues in a global perspective.* Boston, MA: Allyn & Bacon.

Siegel, D., & van de bunt, H. (Eds.). (2012). *Traditional organized crime in the modern world: Responses to socioeconomic change.* New York, NY: Springer.

Sommerville, Q. (2012, February 1). Pakistan dismisses NATO report on Afghan Taliban links. *BBC News.* Retrieved from http://www.bbc.co.uk/news/world-asia-16832359

Sullivan, C. (2011). Narcoterrorism. In G. Martin (ed.), *The SAGE encyclopedia of terrorism* (pp. 413–416). Thousand Oaks, CA: Sage.

Stern, J. (2000). The covenant, the sword, and the arm of the lord. In J. Tucker (Ed.), *Toxic terror: Assessing terrorist use of chemical and biological weapons* (pp. 139–158). Cambridge, MA: MIT Press.

Treverton, G., Matthies, C., Cunningham, K., Goulka, J., Ridgeway, G., & Wong, A. (2009). *Film piracy, organized crime, and terrorism.* Santa Monica: RAND.

U.S. Drug Enforcement Administration. (2012, June 21). Narcoterrorism press releases. Washington, DC: Author. Available from http://www.justice.gov/dea/pr/top-story/Narcoterrorism.shtml

Whittaker, D. J. (Ed.). (2001). *The terrorism reader.* New York, NY: Routledge.

Williams, P. (1995). Transnational criminal organizations: Strategic alliances, *Washington Quarterly, 18,* 57–69.

Wilson, S. (2003, June 26). Colombian fighters' drug trade is detailed. *Washington Post.* Retrieved from http://articles.chicagotribune.com/2003-06-26/news/ 0306260311_1_drug-trafficking-paramilitary-united-self-defense-forces

Zhang, Y. (2012). *Asia, international drug trafficking, and U.S.-China counter-narcotics cooperation.* Washington, DC: Brookings Institution Center for Northeast Asian Policy Studies.

Index

About the Editors

Jay Albanese is Professor and Criminologist in the Wilder School of Government and Public Affairs at Virginia Commonwealth University (VCU). He was the first PhD graduate from the School of Criminal Justice at Rutgers University. He served as Chief of the International Center at the National Institute of Justice (NIJ), the research arm of the U.S. Department of Justice for 4 years, while on loan from VCU. In this capacity, he was responsible for development of transnational crime and justice research projects and coordination with United Nations efforts in these areas. He has written and edited 15 books and 65 articles and book chapters and has made keynote and invited presentations in 15 countries. Recent books include *Transnational Crime and the 21st Century* (Oxford University Press, 2011), *Professional Ethics in Criminal Justice: Being Ethical When No One Is Looking* (Prentice Hall, 3rd ed., 2012), and *Organized Crime in Our Times* (Elsevier, 6th ed., 2011). He is recipient of the Elske Smith Distinguished Lecturer Award from VCU, the Scholar Award in Criminal Justice from the Virginia Social Science Association, and the Gerhard Mueller Award from the International Section of the Academy of Criminal Justice Sciences. He has served as Executive Director of the International Association for the Study of Organized Crime and president of the White Collar Crime Research Consortium. In addition, he is a past president and fellow of the Academy of Criminal Justice Sciences. He is currently Chair of the American Society of Criminology's Division of International Criminology.

Philip Reichel earned his PhD in sociology from Kansas State University and is currently Professor of Criminal Justice at the University of Northern Colorado. He is the author of *Comparative Criminal Justice Systems: A Topical Approach* (6th ed., 2013); coauthor of *Corrections* (2013), and coeditor of *Human Trafficking: Exploring the International Nature, Concerns, and Complexities* (2012). He has also authored or coauthored more than 30 articles, book chapters, and encyclopedia entries. He has lectured at universities in Austria, Germany, and Poland; has participated in a panel for the United Nations University; was a presenter for a United Nations crime prevention webinar; has presented papers at side events during the U.N. Congress on Crime Prevention and Criminal Justice (Brazil) and the U.N. Commission on Crime Prevention and Criminal Justice (Vienna); and was an invited speaker at Zhejiang Police College in Hangzhou, China. He was asked to provide a contribution for an anthology of 14 esteemed scholars who have made a significant contribution to the discipline of criminal justice within a comparative/international context (*Lessons From International Criminology/ Comparative Criminology/Criminal Justice,* 2004) and is an active member of the American Society of Criminology and the Academy of Criminal Justice Sciences, serving as a Trustee-at-large for the latter.

About the Contributors

Roderic Broadhurst is Chief Investigator, Australian Research Council Centre of Excellence in Policing and Security (CEPS), College of Asia and the Pacific, Australian National University. He has extensive experience in criminal justice, as a practitioner and researcher. His research has included studies of lethal violence, victimization, and cybercrime and has involved longitudinal research applying risk analysis methodologies to problems of recidivism, persistent offending, sex offending, and dangerous offending. His current research focuses on crime and modernization in Cambodia and China, monitoring serious crime in cyberspace and organized crime. He is Associate Fellow of the Australian Institute of Criminology and was formerly Associate Professor, the University of Hong Kong, and Head of the School of Justice, Queensland University of Technology. He was also the foundation editor of the *Asian Journal of Criminology* (2005). Recent publications include *Business and the Risk of Crime in China: The 2005–2006 International Crimes Against Business Survey 2005-2006* (ANU E-Press 2011).

James O. Finckenauer earned his PhD from New York University and is Professor Emeritus and Professorial Fellow, Rutgers University (New Jersey). His research and teaching interests include international and comparative criminal justice, transnational organized crime, and criminal and juvenile justice policy, planning, and evaluation. He has authored, coauthored, or coedited 10 books, as well as numerous articles, chapters, and reports. From 1998 to 2002, he was director of the International Center at the National Institute of Justice of the U.S. Department of Justice, and in 2007 he was a Fulbright Senior Specialist in Hong Kong. He continues to serve Rutgers as a member of the Core Faculty of the Division of Global Affairs and is currently a Visiting Lecturer at the University of Pennsylvania.

Mark Lauchs is Senior Lecturer at Queensland University of Technology in Australia. He is a former bureaucrat who moved to academia to research corruption and organized crime. His primary publications focus on the link between police corruption and organized crime.

Sally Lohrisch is a PhD Candidate at the Queensland University of Technology's School of Justice. Her doctoral thesis is an exploration of the Australian government's decision making in organized crime law and policy from 1975 until the present day. Prior to beginning her doctoral research, she worked as a lawyer in a commercial law firm and as a policy officer at the Queensland Department of the Premier and Cabinet. She is a member of the International Association for the Study of Organized Crime, and her research interests include Australasian organized crime activities, transnational crime, and organized crime law and policy.

Daniel J. Mabrey has his PhD in criminal justice from Sam Houston State University and currently serves as Executive Director of the Institute for the Study of Violent Groups and as an Assistant Dean in the Henry C. Lee College of Criminal Justice and Forensic Sciences at the University of New Haven. He is a coauthor of numerous articles and a book on homeland security. He also serves as an adviser and consultant to numerous private and government organizations.

Mary Fran T. Malone received her PhD from the University of Pittsburgh and currently serves as Associate Professor in the department of political science at the University of New Hampshire. Her research focuses on the rule of law, examining the impact of the current crime epidemic on citizens' evaluations of their justice systems and support for the rule of law. Her most recent book, *The Rule of Law in Central America* (2012), examines how Central American countries abandoned civil war and dictatorship in favor of democracy in the 1990s and whether this step is threatened by the current crime crisis. She is currently working on a second monograph, *Fighting Crime Without Undermining Democracy: Lessons From Latin America*, which examines how some Latin American countries have successfully reformed their police and justice systems.

Christine B. Malone-Rowe received an MS in criminal justice at St. Joseph's University in Philadelphia in 2003. For more than a decade, she has used her expertise to work in various parts of the justice system in Philadelphia, ranging from pretrial detention to supervised release.

Gus Martin is Professor of Criminal Justice Administration at California State University, Dominguez Hills, where he has also served as Associate Vice President for Faculty Affairs and as chair of the Department of Public Administration and Public Policy. He began his academic career as a member of the faculty of the Graduate School of Public and International Affairs, University of Pittsburgh, where he was an Administration of Justice professor. His current research and professional interests are terrorism and extremism, administration of justice, and juvenile justice. He is author and editor of several books on the subject of terrorism, including *The SAGE Encyclopedia of Terrorism* (2012); *Terrorism and Homeland Security* (Sage, 2011); *Essentials of Terrorism: Concepts and Controversies* (Sage, 2013); *Understanding Terrorism: Challenges, Perspectives, and Issues* (Sage, 2013); and *The New Era of Terrorism: Selected Readings* (Sage, 2004).

Mark Shaw holds a PhD from the University of Witwatersrand, Johannesburg, and currently is Director, Communities, Crime and Conflicts at STATT Consulting, Hong Kong. He previously worked at the U.N. Office on Drugs and Crime, including as Inter-regional Advisor, Chief of the Criminal Justice Reform Unit and with the Global Programme against Transnational Organised Crime, with extensive field work in fragile and postconflict states. He has held a number of other positions in government and civil society, including Director of Monitoring and Analysis in the South African Ministry for Safety and Security; Head of the Crime and Police Programme at Institute for Security Studies, Pretoria; Ford Foundation Senior Fellow on Justice in Transition at the South African Institute of International Affairs; U.S. Institute of Peace Researcher on local conflicts at the Centre for Policy Studies, Johannesburg; and as a violence monitor for the South African National Peace Secretariat during the transition to democracy.

Toine Spapens is Full Professor of criminology in the Department of Criminal Law at Tilburg University and Professor of environmental crime at the Police Academy of the Netherlands. He received his PhD in criminology in 2006. Since the early 1990s, Spapens has done extensive empirical research on (organized) crime and its containment and on international law enforcement cooperation. His studies include illegal firearms trafficking, ecstasy production, large-scale cannabis cultivation, illegal gambling, and environmental crime. More recently, his research also focuses on network theories in relation to organized crime and on the regulation of illegal markets.

Jan van Dijk has a degree in law from Leiden University (1970) and a PhD in criminology from the University of Nijmegen (1977). He currently holds the Pieter van Vollenhoven Chair in Victimology and Human Security at the International Victimology Institute Tilburg (INTERVICT). He is a member of the Group of Experts on Action against Trafficking in Human Beings (GRETA) of the Council of Europe. In 1998, he joined the United Nations as officer in charge of the U.N. Centre for International Crime Prevention in Vienna. His latest monograph in English is *The World of Crime: Breaking the Silence on Issues of Security, Justice and Development* (Sage, 2008). In 2009, he received the Sellin-Glueck Award of the American Society of Criminology and in 2012 the Stockholm prize in criminology.

Klaus von Lampe is Associate Professor at John Jay College of Criminal Justice in New York. He has previously been a researcher at Free University Berlin, Germany. He holds graduate degrees in law and political science from Free University Berlin and a doctoral degree in law/criminology from Goethe University in Frankfurt/Main, Germany. He teaches courses at the graduate and undergraduate levels in international criminal justice and criminology. He has studied various manifestations of organized crime, including cigarette smuggling, drug trafficking, and underworld power structures, as well as strategic crime analysis. He is the editor in chief of the journal *Trends in Organized Crime* and a member of the editorial boards of the journal *Crime, Law and Social Change* and of the Cross-border Crime Colloquium book series. He is also the President of the International Association for the Study of Organized Crime (IASOC) for 2012–2013.

Richard H. Ward is currently Associate Vice President for Research at the University of New Haven where he also served as Dean of the Henry C. Lee College of Criminal Justice and Forensic Sciences. He holds his doctorate in criminology from the University of California at Berkeley and has held senior administrative positions at John Jay College of Criminal Justice, the University of Illinois at Chicago, and Sam Houston State University. His primary areas of academic specialization focus on international crime and criminal investigation, and he has served as a lecturer or consultant in more than 50 countries in a career spanning more than 40 years.

ⓈSAGE research**methods**

The essential online tool for researchers from the world's leading methods publisher

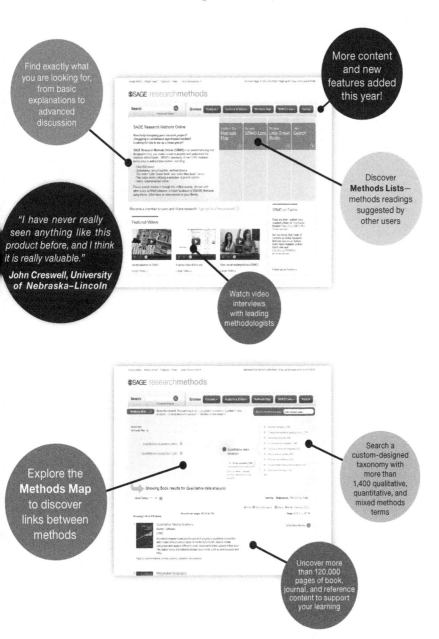

Find exactly what you are looking for, from basic explanations to advanced discussion

More content and new features added this year!

Discover **Methods Lists**— methods readings suggested by other users

"I have never really seen anything like this product before, and I think it is really valuable."
John Creswell, University of Nebraska–Lincoln

Watch video interviews with leading methodologists

Explore the **Methods Map** to discover links between methods

Search a custom-designed taxonomy with more than 1,400 qualitative, quantitative, and mixed methods terms

Uncover more than 120,000 pages of book, journal, and reference content to support your learning

Find out more at
www.sageresearchmethods.com